# *Broadcast Fairness*
## DOCTRINE, PRACTICE, PROSPECTS

# LONGMAN SERIES IN PUBLIC COMMUNICATION

SERIES EDITOR: RAY ELDON HIEBERT

# *Broadcast Fairness*

## DOCTRINE, PRACTICE, PROSPECTS

FORD ROWAN

*A Reappraisal of the Fairness Doctrine
and Equal Time Rule*

## Longman

New York & London

625 388

Longman Inc., 1560 Broadway, New York, N.Y. 10036
Associated companies, branches, and representatives
throughout the world.

Copyright © 1984 The Media Institute

DEVELOPMENTAL EDITOR: Gordon T. R. Anderson
EDITORIAL AND DESIGN SUPERVISORS: Joan Matthews and Russell Till
PRODUCTION SUPERVISOR: Ferne Y. Kawahara

KF
2812
.R68
1984

Library of Congress Cataloging in Publication Data

Rowan, Ford.
   Broadcast fairness.
   (Longman series in public communication)
   Includes index.
   1. Fairness doctrine (Broadcasting)—United States.
2. Equal time rule (Broadcasting)—United States.
I. Title.   II.   Series.
KF2812.R68     1984      343.73'09945       83-19998
ISBN 0-582-28434-1      347.3039945

MANUFACTURED IN THE UNITED STATES OF AMERICA
9  8  7  6  5  4  3  2  1      92  91  90  89  88  87  86  85  84

*To the memory of*
*Leonard J. Theberge*

# Contents

# *Preface*

It has been said that Bismarck, while chancellor of Germany, once remarked that there were two things no citizen should ever have to witness. No one should ever see how laws are made and no one should have to see how sausage is made.

The quotation may be apocryphal, but it reflects reality. One who has witnessed the mixtrue of ingredients into sausage may find his appetite dulled; Bismarck found his government barraged with demands that it regulate meat processing to prevent health hazards.

This book is about the regulation of communications, and, forgive me, the American equivalent of sausage, broadcasting. It does bring out the ham in its stars. It is a staple of our daily diet. Viewers are sometimes addicted to it and sometimes repelled by what they see.

This book is about more than just regulation or just broadcasting. It is about politics, the partisan side that influences—and is itself shaped—by broadcasting. It's also about the broader political system that resolves questions of fairness, equal time, and the like.

This book is about the public interest, a worthy but amorphous ideal. It is about citizen groups that purport to speak for the public; special interest groups that advocate causes; industry groups that seek to protect exclusive licensees, maximize profits, and avoid trouble with the regulations.

It is about public policy, which appears to have evolved in an ad hoc way. And it is about that institution that covers and interacts with government, the news profession.

And it is about change, the major changes sweeping the telecommunications industry and its regulatory environment.

Consider the following item:

The publisher of *Hustler* magazine, Larry Flynt, states that he will run for the Republican nomination for President of the United States. Ronald Reagan does not tremble, of course, but broadcasters begin wondering about the implications. After all, Flynt, who recently shouted obscenities during a Supreme Court session, threatened to use X-rated film clips in his campaign commercials on TV.

This raised an interesting possibility. Under current law, broadcasters must provide reasonable access to candidates for federal office; that is, they must sell time for campaign commercials. Moreover, broadcasters cannot censor what the candidate wants to say during these commercials. However federal law also prohibits the broadcast of obscene material.

In light of the potential Flynt candidacy, what's a broadcaster to do?

Whether Flynt ultimately runs or not, it set a lot of folks to thinking about the ramifications of forcing stations to air whatever federal candidates can afford to say.

The reexamination of broadcast regulation reached a high intensity as this book neared completion. The rules are in a state of flux. For example, at the Federal Communications Commission, these changes and proposed changes were underway as 1984 began:

- The FCC moved to "deregulate" television along the lines of earlier rule changes for radio stations, with the aim of eliminating requirements that licensees formally ascertain community needs, keep detailed logs, broadcast minimum amounts of news and public affairs, and not run too many commercials.
- The FCC moved toward eliminating the Personal Attack and Political Editorializing rules, which require stations to permit some of those criticized or editorialized against to respond on the air.
- The FCC was poised to liberalize the multiple ownership rule, which has restricted broadcasters to the ownership of no more than seven television stations, seven AM, and seven FM radio stations.
- The FCC was ready to change the financial interest and syndication rules, thus letting networks profit from reruns of entertainment programs, but objections from Ronald Reagan put this plan on hold.
- The FCC altered the equal time rule to allow broadcasters who air

debates between candidates to exclude some candidates from such programs.
- The FCC has asked Congress to eliminate the Fairness Doctrine and equal time rule.

Meanwhile Congress was considering a whole host of bills to change various parts of the Communications Act. Some of the pending items in Congress included,

- Proposals to eliminate the Fairness Doctrine, equal time, and reasonable access provisions.
- Proposals to prohibit the FCC from changing the Personal Attack and Political Editorializing rules.
- Proposals to block X-rated political commercials.
- Proposals to prohibit changes in the financial interest and syndication rules.
- Proposals to deregulate cable television.
- Proposals to change the license renewal procedures for broadcasters by eliminating comparative renewal hearings for competing applicants.
- Proposals to beef up procedures whereby citizens can file petitions to deny license renewals for stations.
- Proposals to require stations to air minimum quantities of news and programming on public affairs issues, children's fare, and minority-oriented shows.

This nonexhaustive list gives some idea of the potential for legislative change.

Meanwhile, the U.S. Court of Appeals in Washington was considering various challenges to a number of the deregulatory moves initiated by the FCC.

In short, the regulatory future is uncertain.

Consider one rule change initiated by the FCC in late 1983, after this book was completed. The FCC exempted debates among candidates from the equal time provisions. Under the previous application of the rule, if a station staged the debate, it had to afford equal time for all the candiates in the race; but coverage of debates staged by others, like the League of Women Voters, did not mandate equal time for candidates excluded form the forum.

Under the change, broadcasters will now be able to stage debates on the air and exclude third party and minor candidates from the program.

This could have at least four major consequences:

First, it frees broadcasters to practice good journalism. Fringe candidates and kooks with money to pay a campaign filing fee can be excluded so the focus can be on those seriously contesting for the office.

Second, it enhances the electoral advantage of Democrats and Republicans and further weakens the chances of independents and third party challengers.

Third, it increases the potential political power of the broadcast industry to frame the public debate by excluding some candidates from the airwaves.

Fourth, by excluding those deemed to be fringe, nonserious, or kook candidates, mainstream viewpoints may be reinforced, and radical or reactionary views expunged from public consideration.

These are the types of public policy considerations that this book attempts to examine.

I have tried to bring my varied experiences to bear on these subjects. I've been a news reporter, an attorney specializing in communications, and a journalism professor. I've tried to avoid letting where I sit determine how I stand on the issues. That's not always easy, but I'm less interested in persuading than describing. Gibbon once wrote of another subject that "it is easier to deplore than to describe." How right that is about this topic: I've tried to write a balanced book, of use to all those interested in this subject. In sum, I've tried to present contrasting points of view.

It is hoped that this volume will be of use to broadcasters, journalists, public officials, business leaders, scholars, and citizens interested in television and radio, news, and public policy, communications, and law.

The goal is to provide an examination of regulation of the content of what is broadcast, to explore what was intended, how fairness and equal time rules evolved, how they work, how they could be changed. The first two chapters explore questions regarding the purposes of regulation, the constitutional issues, and the politics that characterizes the process.

Chapters Three and Four examine how the regulations actually are implemented on a regular basis. They explore a seeming contradiction: how formal FCC procedures rarely result in adverse Fairness Doctrine rulings against stations, yet the effect of the regulation is to force stations to capitulate to demands by interest groups for access to the airwaves. An examination of the usually overlooked informal impact of the regulations sheds new light on how government controls affect the presentation of issues.

Chapters Five and Six look at the impact of regulation on news coverage, judging whether the Fairness Doctrine has assured fair coverage or inhibited diversity in the public discussion of issues. Is the news more "fair"? Have broadcasters been "chilled"?

Chapter Seven discusses special areas of regulation: personal attacks, political editorials, and controversial commercials. Here the rules pose more rigorous requirements yet are often inconsistently applied.

Chapters Eight and Nine examine how politicians and politically active individuals and groups obtain access to state their views on radio and television. It examines how politics and communications interact. Have the equal time and fairness regulations invited manipulation by politicians? How has the system of regulation altered American political life?

Chapter Ten evaluates various proposals for changing the current system of regulation, by abolishing the Fairness Doctrine and equal time rule, mandating access, or letting market forces prevail.

The reader is encouraged to consider whether the Fairness Doctrine is fair to the public, fair to the broadcasters and journalists it regulates, or fair to those who seek to express their views on television and radio. Does enforcement of the equal time rule result in equal access to the airwaves? This volume does not provide definitive answers to the difficult questions of policy and law. Rather, it explores the arguments, issues, and competing interests involved to facilitate the reader's evaluation of various proposals for change.

This study draws heavily upon three other books which have helped illuminate the fairness issue. The serious student of regulation is urged to read them. Steven J. Simmons's 1978 study, *The Fairness Doctrine and the Media* (Berkeley, University of California Press) is a wide-ranging examination of the doctrine. Henry Geller's *The Fairness Doctrine in Broadcasting* (Santa Monica, Calif., Rand, 1973) is a major study of the problems and alternatives. Fred W. Friendly's *The Good Guys, the Bad Guys, and the First Amendment* (New York, Vintage, 1975) is a lively look at the dispute, a book that proves constitutional law can be exciting. These studies, taken together, provide a look at fairness from the vantage points of a scholar, a government official and a journalist.

Three other books on related subjects are well worth close examination. Daniel L. Brenner and William L. Rivers have assembled an excellent collection of essays on various First Amendment issues entitled *Free But Regulated* (Ames, Iowa State University Press, 1982). Erwin G. Krasnow, Lawrence D. Longley, and Herbert A. Terry have published a third edition of *The Politics of Broadcast Regulation* (New York, St. Martin's Press, 1982), which includes five case studies on other non-fairness issues. Andrew O. Shapiro's *Media Access* (Boston, Little, Brown, 1976) describes the rules and how citizens can use them to obtain airtime.

This volume was funded by The Media Institute, a nonprofit organization that has served as a watchdog, issuing critical reports on television news and promoting better understanding between journalists and those in the private sector. While many who are involved with The Media Institute deplore instances of news reporting they consider unfair, they have not wavered in their defense of freedom for the electronic press.

I wish to express my appreciation to Leonard J. Theberge, president of The Media Institute, who conceived this project and whose own energy was a key to its success. His vision and friendship was instrumental every step of the way. While he had strong views on the Fairness Doctrine, he gave me complete freedom to pursue the topic. Len died as the project was nearing completion. This volume is dedicated to his memory.

Much credit should go to Timothy G. Brown, who conducted many of the interviews and much research on how the Fairness Doctrine actually works. His efforts produced the illuminating information about the daily workings of the FCC and about the informal impact of the regulation. My thanks to Richard T. Kaplar and James W. Quiggle, who helped edit the text. Diane Hubbard's help was instrumental in organizing the subject matter. Also many of my students at Northwestern University's Medill School of Journalism assisted in this project, especially Nancy Winkley, who helped proof the manuscript.

I would like to thank the people at Longman who helped with the book, Gordon T. R. Anderson, Joan Matthews, and Russell Till.

I appreciate the support of the law firm Sanford, Adams, McCullough & Beard, where I have been of counsel; I especially am thankful for the clerical assistance of Janice Gernhart.

*Ford Rowan*

# ONE

# The Quest for Fairness and Equality

THIS WOULD BE A BETTER SOCIETY if all people behaved well, were charitable and just. Suppose the government, in an effort to promote this ideal, enacted a Goodness Doctrine requiring that citizens be good. Such a regulation could not be faulted for its purpose. What minor inconvenience it might impose upon citizens could be justified by reminding one and all that our advanced society confers many benefits upon individuals, and that we must all be trustees of our society and act in the public interest.

There would be immediate practical problems, however, in implementing the Goodness Doctrine. Aside from those who are downright evil, most people fail to be good all the time. Few would measure up to a Goodness Standard. Moreover, honest people can disagree about what's good in a particular situation. The vagueness inherent in legislating goodness would, of necessity, leave a lot of discretion to the individual. Many people might act reasonably, in good faith, only to find that the government regulator's idea of goodness did not correspond to their own. On the other hand, some would take advantage of the flexibility built into such a doctrine to try to rationalize heinous behavior.

The resulting disparity in conduct would cry out for government action. People would not know what was expected of them; abuses would be highlighted. Before long it would become clear that government policy is inadequate and inconsistent when it requires adherence to a vague standard of right conduct. Vigorous regulation would risk unacceptable infringements upon individual freedom.

On the other hand, government law enforcement is most effective when its boundaries are clearly marked and the government states, with great specificity, what it is that citizens *cannot* do. In short, the lawmakers would find that it is far easier to decree "Thou shalt not's" than to attempt to mandate goodness.

In a perfect world, goodness, justice, and love would motivate all. But in our imperfect society the best that government can require of citizens is that they refrain from committing proscribed acts. This is the foundation of the rule of law.

The same problems that would make a Goodness Doctrine unworkable plague the federal government's efforts to mandate fairness in the broadcasting of controversial issues and equality in the treatment of candidates. It's hard to quarrel with fairness and equality as ideals, as goals. In fact, fairness is enshrined in the ethical code which most journalists observe.[1]

Fairness is difficult to measure, nearly impossible to quantify. Recognition of these difficulties has led the Federal Communications Commission (FCC) to assert that it is not trying to force broadcasters to conform to some notion of what constitutes the ideal in journalism. The FCC sees its role as just issuing general guidelines for minimal standards of fairness.[2] But implementation of the Fairness Doctrine has been troublesome because of the problem of specifying exactly what is unfair.

While it may be possible to articulate clear rules of conduct, some broadcasters complain that FCC enforcement of the Fairness Doctrine amounts to second-guessing under uncertain standards. This may threaten broadcasters who depend upon the FCC for permission to continue in business.

Some advocates of regulation emphasize that it is the public which is threatened by broadcasters eager to make as much money as possible in a business where making money is sometimes easy. Regulation is a reaction to unseemly business practices, according to Les Brown, editor of *Channels* magazine. In a recent article, Brown wrote,

> Left to their own devices, broadcasters have been known to practice deception in news programs, game shows, and made-for-television sporting events; to discriminate against women and minorities in their broadcasts as well as in their hiring practices; to exploit the gullibility of children with violent cartoon programming and highly manipulative commercials; and to keep people off the air whose views don't agree with their own.[3]

Certainly there are problems in broadcasting. Some licensees fail to be fair or good. But it must be asked: Can government make them behave? Do the costs of regulation outweigh the benefits? Ought government try to make stations adhere to standards? Are there dangers to society in zealous efforts to protect the public interest?

As we shall see, the answers are not simple. And they go beyond the current system as applied to radio and television. New forms of communicating are coming on line—posing opportunities and risks. Technologies ranging from cable to satellite transmission, from low-power to high-resolution television, are becoming available. What is the future of regulation?

The Fairness Doctrine now applies to cable television systems that originate their own programming. Some municipalities require cable systems to provide channels for public access. Should cable systems be required to function partly as a common carrier leasing channels to individuals and groups? The long-range future of regulation of the newer forms of telecommunications, including videotext and teletext, is uncertain, although the FCC decided in 1983 that teletext is only an ancilliary service and need not comply with fairness and equal time regulations.[4]

The FCC in the early 1980s moved to deregulate some aspects of broadcasting and urged Congress to abolish the Fairness Doctrine and the equal time rule. While the mood had shifted away from vigorous enforcement of the rules, it appeared that Congress was not ready to eliminate these regulations.

Proposals considered most likely to pass called for changing license renewal processes—making it easier for broadcasters to keep their licenses—in return for requirements that they air sufficient quantities of news and public affairs programming. The outlook—as of this writing—is for relaxation of some rules while preserving the Fairness Doctrine and equal time rule.

Similarly, the Federal Appeals Court in Washington emphasized in September 1983 that the Fairness Doctrine has "continuing vitality" despite efforts at the FCC to abolish the rule.[5]

It should be noted how quickly the attitude had shifted toward deregulation and away from a penchant for regulation in the 1960s and 70s, suggesting a pendulum effect. If that's the case, deregulation may fall short only to be replaced by more regulation.

Examination of the effect of regulation clarifies options and might free us from any pendulum. This chapter is designed to introduce the rule, to establish the regulatory context, to examine the rationale underlying the Fairness Doctrine, and to assess the rule's role in the light of the First Amendment to the Constitution.

## The Fairness Doctrine

In its famous *Red Lion* decision, which upheld the Fairness Doctrine, the U.S. Supreme Court stated that the law requires that "discussion of public issues be presented on broadcast stations, and that each side of those issues . . . be given fair coverage."[6]

Broadcasters have a two-fold duty under current FCC application of the Fairness Doctrine: (1) to devote a reasonable percentage of time to the presentation of public issues, and (2) to provide a reasonable opportunity for presenting contrasting views on controversial issues of public importance.[7] The obligation to cover major issues and present contrasting viewpoints includes the duty to seek out opposing views and air them without charge to the spokespersons, if necessary to assure overall balance.

The first duty has been largely overlooked because the FCC has not vigorously enforced the rule. The commission has asserted that broadcasters have a responsibility to air public issues but only in one case has it insisted that a station cover a specific issue. That case involved a major debate over strip mining, an issue of particular significance to the audience of the station located in a mining state.[8] The case raised questions about the FCC's potential role in the editorial process, which shall be explored as part of the assessment of the rule's impact on news coverage in Chapter 5.

Despite pronouncements from the FCC about the duty of stations to devote time for the presentation of issues, the commission has done little to make sure broadcasters do not feed the public a diet composed mostly of music, game shows, situation comedies, police dramas, soap operas and the like. As Bill F. Chamberlin has stated,

> The FCC has misled the public and the broadcast licensee by maintaining that the most important aspect of a licensee's service in the public interest is the responsibility to provide a reasonable amount of public issues programming, while making no effort to enforce compliance with this duty, and, indeed, providing no appropriate regulatory mechanism.[9]

The general practice has been that some stations present very little discussion of public issues. That's usually a safe course because while the first part of the rule is rarely enforced, the second part of the Fairness Doctrine sometimes is. So once a station does air a public issue of controversy it may find itself confronted with a demand for airtime for the expression of an opposing viewpoint. Although the duty to air issues is listed first, it has taken a backseat to litigation over the second half of the rule.

Despite the general obligation to cover significant issues, the broadcaster has discretion in choosing which issues to present. But when a controversial issue of public importance is covered, the broadcaster may not restrict coverage to the viewpoint with which he agrees; he is required to afford a reasonable opportunity for discussion of contrasting viewpoints. Generally, the broadcaster has wide leeway in deciding how other viewpoints will be presented, and by whom.

As long as he makes his judgments in a reasonable, good-faith way, the Federal Communications Commission is reluctant to reverse a broadcaster's decision.[10]

It should be stressed, however, that this is an affirmative obligation. In theory, the broadcaster must take steps to air major issues, and—in practice—must seek out contrasting views. It is not enough for the broadcaster simply to wait for someone to seek access to present the other side.

If in the course of presenting a controversial issue, the broadcaster airs an attack on the honesty, character, integrity, or like personal qualities of an individual or group, the Personal Attack Rule becomes applicable. The station has a duty to notify the person or group attacked, provide a transcript or summary of the program, and offer an opportunity to respond.

Although the Personal Attack Rule is part of the Fairness Doctrine, it differs from the doctrine in that it does not apply to statements made during newscasts. Also exempt from the Personal Attack Rule are attacks upon candidates for office, or against foreign groups or foreign public figures. The FCC has failed to define *personal attack* precisely, and so some of its rulings appear inconsistent.

If a station editorializes on controversial issues of public importance, it must make time available for contrasting points of view. If a station airs political editorials endorsing or opposing a candidate, the Fairness Doctrine requires the station to notify all other candidates for the office who are not endorsed and offer them airtime to respond before the election.[11] If the broadcaster airs an editorial on a subject that a candidate is closely identified with, even if the candidate is not mentioned, the candidate may be entitled to response time.

If a broadcaster sells time for advertising that takes a stand on a controversial issue of public importance, the broadcaster must make certain that contrasting views are presented as part of the station's overall programming. This often means that if a station accepts issue advertisements, it will have to give away free time to impecunious opposing groups. This is part of the Cullman Principle, which requires that when a broadcaster airs one side of an issue, he must broadcast other viewpoints at his own expense if sponsorship is not available.[12] The prospect of airing free announcements to counter paid commercials has discouraged some broadcasters from accepting advertisements that advocate stands on issues.

Accusations that a station has deliberately slanted or staged news do not fall under the Fairness Doctrine, but if extrinsic evidence shows that the owners or top managers of the station ordered the slanting of news (for instance, testimony by an employee that he was instructed to stage the news), then regulatory procedures similar to those of the Fairness Doctrine are triggered.[13]

The Personal Attack Rule, the Political Editorializing regulations, and the Cullman Principle complicate the Fairness Doctrine by imposing obligations on a broadcaster beyond the basic requirement of covering major issues and presenting contrasting views. As more detailed discussion in later chapters will show, what started as a praiseworthy effort to assure the fair presentation of important issues has become a complicated but crude tool for obtaining access to the airwaves, one that invites use by spokespersons for various interest groups, by those who believe they have been criticized on the air, by those pushing political causes, and by those running for office. Some proponents of the Fairness Doctrine concede that it falls short of providing the kind of access they desire. Opponents of the doctrine assert that it does not assure fairness, may actually chill broadcasters' interest in airing controversies, and moreover, that the intrusion of the government into the editorial process undermines the integrity of the journalistic process in covering public issues.

Proponents of the rule assert that it is the only means now available to assure that diverse and divergent views are broadcast. Without the rule, the business motivations of broadcasters might overwhelm the public interest in the airing of public issues. Supporters of the Fairness Doctrine also worry that broadcasters might only air views with which they agree if they were freed from complying with the rule. Because they are privileged to use the public's airwaves, broadcasters must serve the public interest, including, proponents say, the providing of balanced, fair programming. Since good journalists would do this in the absense of government decree anyway, the regulation poses no burden to the conscientious broadcaster, in the view of its supporters. The rule is seen as a way to protect the public. The change that is needed, some proponents assert, is that the FCC ought to *strengthen* enforcement of the rule.

## The Equal Opportunities Rule

Because there is a great deal of confusion about the Fairness Doctrine, it is important to point out what it is not. It is not an equal-time rule. In fact, *equal time* applies only to political candidates and is properly referred to as the Equal Opportunities Rule.[14] This rule is less flexible than the

Fairness Doctrine, requiring as it does *equal* treatment of candidates for public office who are sold or given air time (outside of regular news programming). Thus, if a candidate for Congress is permitted a free half-hour of prime time by a station, the station must afford identical access to each of his or her opponents.

Section 315 of the Communications Act requires a licensee that permits a legally qualified candidate for any public office to use a station's facilities to provide the same opportunity to all of the candidate's opponents. "Use" of a station includes both paid commercial time and free appearances (except on exempt news programs). Equal time does not just mean that candidates can obtain identical amounts of airtime; they have the right to obtain time in a period likely to attract about the same size audience as the opposing candidate obtained. In other words, if one candidate buys 5 minutes in prime time, the station must be willing to sell the opponent 5 minutes in prime time—not at 8 o'clock Sunday morning.

Section 315 also sets the maximum rates a station may charge a candidate. A station is never allowed to charge a candidate more for time than it would charge a regular commercial advertiser, and during some periods it must give candidates the benefit of volume discounts the advertiser might not receive. The candidate cannot be charged more than the lowest unit charge the station charges for the same class and amount of time for the same period.

Section 315 also prohibits the station from censoring candidates who appear on the air in paid commercials or free appearances. The rule against censorship does not apply to exempt news programs, where a candidate's remarks may be edited.

The idea behind the equal time rule is simple: to prevent broadcasters from discriminating between competing candidates. It also should be noted that the rule affects cable systems as well. If they sell time to political candidates for appearances on a cable channel, they must provide equal opportunities to opponents.

While regular newscasts, news interviews, on-the-spot news coverage, and most news documentaries are not covered by the equal time rule, it used to apply to debates organized by the station (or cable system) and still applies to documentaries about a campaign or a candidate. Only a documentary in which the appearance of the candidate is "incidental to the presentation of the subject" is exempt from the rule.

The Equal Opportunities Rule does not affect most news programs; a news director may select which candidates he wishes to cover, ignoring those he thinks are minor and not newsworthy. The Fairness Doctrine, however, does affect news programs, and issues covered in newscasts are subject to the rule requiring expression of contrasting views in the overall programming. Unlike the Equal Opportunities Rule, the Fairness Doctrine does not require equal treatment, only *overall balance* in the presentation of controversial public issues.

While the Fairness Doctrine permits flexibility, the Equal Opportunities Rule requires *equivalent* access for opposing candidates. Under the Fairness Doctrine the broadcaster not only chooses the issues, but has discretion to select views to be presented, the spokesperson to be featured, and the format of the program.

The confusion over application of the Fairness Doctrine and Equal Opportunities Rule is not surprising; the dividing line between coverage of campaign issues and use of a station by candidates is not always clear. As we shall see in the discussion of the political impact of these regulations in Chapter 9, even the commission has blurred the line with its Zapple Doctrine requiring stations to provide equal opportunities to *spokespersons* of candidates.[15] It should be noted, however, that the concept of Equal Opportunities was made explicit in the law as early as the Radio Act of 1927, while the Fairness Doctrine evolved more slowly and was not codified by Congress until 1959.

The two rules are intertwined in the law. When the Fairness Doctrine was inserted into the Communications Act in 1959, it was made a subsection of the Equal Opportunities requirement. 47 U.S.C.A. §315(A) states:

> Nothing in the foregoing sentence shall be construed as relieving broadcasters, in connection with the presentation of newscasts, news interviews, news documentaries, and on-the-spot coverage of news events, from the obligation imposed upon them under this chapter to operate in the public interest *and to afford reasonable opportunity for the discussion of conflicting views on issues of public importance.* (Emphasis added.)

Champions of abolishing the Fairness Doctrine often urge abolition of the Equal Opportunities Rule as well, but it would be possible to alter one without undoing the provisions of the other.

As currently constituted, these rules overlap with some of the requirements that stations program news and public affairs programs, ascertain what community leaders and the public view as significant problems, provide access to political candidates, limit time devoted to advertising, label sponsored material as such, and refrain from airing deceptive ads, lotteries, or obscene material.

Since 1960 the commission has expected stations, in general, to include the following types of programming: local self-expression, shows with local talent, children's programs, religious programs, educational programs, public affairs programs, editorials, political broadcasts, agricultural programs, news, weather and market reports, sports, service to minority groups, and entertainment programs. In 1981 the commission moved to ease the regulations as they affect AM and FM radio. Radio was "deregulated" with the elimination of formal ascertainment, advertising guidelines, requirements for broadcasting news and public affairs, and the like. Radio deregulation did not free AM and FM stations from all regulation. Statutory requirements enacted by Congress, such as the fairness and equal time rules, continue to apply to radio, as well as television and programming originated by cable systems.

## The Rationale for Fairness and Equal Treatment

On one hand, it is possible to justify government regulation by the ends it would achieve: provision of public issue programming, fairness in news, equal treatment of political contenders, and such things as quality children's programming, locally originated shows, avoidance of over-commercialization, and the like. But using such worthwhile social goals as the *sole* justification for government intervention would make little sense if applied *only* to broadcasting. After all, why not insist that similar goals be incorporated into the production of newspapers, magazines, motion pictures, sports, computer software, town meetings, and books? Why not require that other forms of information distribution and artistic endeavor meet certain socially useful standards?

Just stating the question that way implies an answer: it is an elitist view of the role of the arts and information with which many Americans are uncomfortable. We have been willing to accept it for broadcasting, however, because the social ends have not been the sole reason—or even the main justification—for regulating the airwaves.

It is possible to discern several distinct reasons why society has chosen to impose special rules over radio and TV:

1.  The airwaves are considered a public resource, subject to public control and government ownership.
2.  The airwaves are considered a scarce resource; there are not enough frequencies for everyone to broadcast.
3.  Since government must allocate this resource, it should require broadcasters to serve the public interest.
4.  The public's need for vigorous, wide-ranging debate on public issues outweighs the rights of broadcasters to select programming.
5.  Offensive material ought not to be aired, especially when children are watching and listening.
6.  The grant of a license is a grant of power, political and economic power, which ought to be subject to checks and balances.

7. The exercise of power by broadcasters has become so pervasive in society that the peculiar characteristics of the medium require special rules.

While it is possible to evaluate each of these separately, they are so bound together that it is more useful to consider them as interwoven. This section focuses on the first three concepts of public ownership, scarcity, and government allocation. The next section evaluates the constitutional issues, including arguments about the public's right to know. Chapter 2 elaborates on the role of the idea of power in shaping regulation.

From the invention of radio it was realized that the number of frequencies available for broadcasting is finite. Rather than permit private ownership of any frequency, the federal government asserted public control over the airwaves and gave stations licenses to broadcast for short terms, renewable if the station served the public interest. The scarce resource, the airwaves, was to be allocated in such a way that the public interest was dominant over the private interests of broadcasters. The scarcity and public ownership concepts required that broadcast stations be licensed by a government commission, unlike newspapers, magazines, or pamphlets, which can be published by anyone without government permission.

Proponents of regulation recognize that it is an imperfect attempt to balance the rights of broadcasters and the public interest. Michael Pollan has stated,

> Since broadcasters enjoy a government-granted monopoly to use a scarce public resource—the airwaves—they have certain responsibilities to the public, and should be prevented from exploiting their monopolies.[16]

While it does not appear that the authors of the federal statutes regulating broadcasting wanted to *nationalize* the airwaves by asserting federal ownership, it is clear they intended to prevent private ownership of frequencies by instituting *public control* over the spectrum. But it is important to note that even when government chose to assert public control over a finite resource it need not have imposed public interest standards over the use of the resource. The Federal Communications Commission could more simply function as a traffic director, parceling out frequencies among applicants, without obliging them to program their stations in any particular way. But government licensing did not evolve that way. Stations are considered to be public trustees, an approach affirmed as constitutional by the U.S. Supreme Court.[17] The public interest, it was argued, required that broadcasters treat candidates for public office equally and present various viewpoints on controversies, not just their own points of view.

Scarcity was the rationale for government intervention in programming decisions, an approach endorsed in the 1943 case *National Broadcasting Co. v. United States.*[18] Justice Frankfurter noted the "confusion and chaos" that had prevailed before regulation because "the radio spectrum simply is not large enough to accommodate everybody."[19]

FCC intrusion into what aired has been justified because the commission's role is not restricted "merely to supervision of the traffic" on the airwaves. The Court ruled it also includes "the burden of determining the composition of that traffic."[20]

Since the advent of radio, however, the number of stations has grown dramatically. There are more than 9,000 radio stations and 1,000 television stations. The number of radio outlets has grown 38 percent since 1969 when the Supreme Court upheld the Fairness Doctrine in the *Red Lion* case. The number of TV stations increased 21 percent in the same time span. The number of daily newspapers has remained fairly constant, with less than 2,000 now publishing. Less than 40 American cities are served by two or more competing daily papers.

The scarcity rationale is questioned by those who assert that broadcast stations and cable channels are less scarce than newspapers, and that marketplace forces ought to be permitted to prevail in television, cable, and radio. After all, the argument goes, there are more than five broadcast stations for each daily newspaper. Cable is rapidly bringing new channels to households across the country. At this writing, about one-third of the nation's households are wired, many with more than 50 channels.

According to the National Association of Broadcasters, 97 percent of the 80 million TV households can receive 4 or more broadcast stations, 67 percent can receive 7 or more, and 38 percent can receive 10 or more stations. A 1981 study by the staff of the House Subcommittee on Telecommunications, Consumer Protection and Finance paints a similar picture. It found that in the largest market, New York City, there were four daily newspapers, 14 television stations, and 54 radio stations. In the smallest market surveyed, Miles City, Montana (with 10,800 households), there was one daily newspaper, two television stations, and one radio station. In between, in the other 209 communities examined, there were always more broadcast stations than newspapers.[21]

Broadcasting hardly seems scarce when compared to the skimpy availability of newspapers in most areas. But there's an important difference. Proponents of regulation argue that while the number of newspapers is limited by the economics of publishing, no one, however wealthy, can begin broadcasting without a license, and in most cases, there are more would-be broadcasters than frequencies available.

Because there is a surplus of would-be broadcasters and a deficit of available frequencies, the government decides who can and, hence, who *cannot* utilize part of the spectrum. Since the government's licensing scheme excludes some from broadcasting, those who are blessed with licenses are required to act as trustees—airing views they might not endorse and programming they might not prefer. It is the governmental policy of excluding some from broadcasting that differentiates ownership of radio and television stations from newspapers and magazines.

It may seem paradoxical that there is a relative abundance of that which the government allocates because of scarcity while that which is unregulated in an open market is characterized by relative scarcity. This should not obscure the fact that the government is the gatekeeper for one and not the other.

If one looks strictly at the numbers, it makes little sense to regulate broadcasting but not print. If one disregards the numbers, assumes every resource is scarce, and focuses on the method of allocating the resource, the different treatment seems more reasonable.

Advocates of regulation state that the scarcity question cannot be resolved by comparing the number of broadcast stations with newspapers, but by noting the number who desire to broadcast. According to the Supreme Court, there are "substantially more individuals who want to broadcast than there are frequencies to allocate."[22]

However, a number of channels are still available for broadcasting, but go begging. There are no more full-power VHF channels available in the largest markets, but under the current allocation setup, available radio and TV channels lack takers in smaller communities. This is especially the case with UHF channels, where some have been unclaimed for decades.

Beyond that, if the FCC chooses, additional radio and television stations could be added if the band width were narrowed for FM, AM, and UHF. In other words, technical adjustments could permit existing stations to use less of the spectrum, creating room for more licensees.[23] Interference would be avoided, but broadcasters and listeners would have to purchase new equipment, a cost that might not be worth bearing. Beyond such considerations, it should be noted that the government itself is the biggest single user of the spectrum, with little incentive to use its large share efficiently.

The notion that the airwaves are a scarce resource may misstate the technical reality and obscure the debate over how to allocate the spectrum. Milton Mueller argues that the spectrum is not a resource, just a man-made classification scheme for identifying the frequencies on which transmitters and receivers can make connections.[24] Broadcasting does not use up the spectrum; the number of transmitters is only limited by economics. The problem comes when one transmission overlaps or interferes with the reception of another transmission. This is a technical problem and Mueller states that FCC policy has retarded technical solutions and efficient use of frequencies. Our assumptions about scarcity may have been off base, but the idea that a scarce natural resource was at stake has dominated policy considerations.

Whatever the scarcity of traditional broadcast outlets, it is clear that there is a growing number of alternate forms of transmission: cable, low-power television, multipoint distribution systems, direct-broadcast satellite, satellite master antenna systems. The most pressing question is no longer the one posed by scarcity, but the one mandated by abundance: How will this multitude of voices be economically supported?

Some advocates of the Fairness Doctrine assert that no matter how abundant the number of broadcast, cable, and other electronic services, scarcity is a fact of life on *each and every* channel. "Each part of the spectrum is scarce because it can be used for only one purpose and at one time and place," according to Samuel A. Simon, director of the Telecommunications Research Action Center. "The receivers of the information have been denied access to all information other than that actually transmitted at that time and place," he stated.[25] Simon believes that we should treat the spectrum as a natural resource, common property for all. Just as it would be unfair to let only a few use the nation's navigable waterways, so, Simon argues, would it be unfair to let only licensees use the spectrum.

The broadcast industry rejects this notion. Erwin G. Krasnow, general counsel of the National Association of Broadcasters, stated that the spectrum has value to the public only when broadcasters use it. "Without a signal supplied by the broadcaster, the spectrum is just so much empty space." "Like air, sunlight, or wind, [the airwaves] cannot be owned by anyone," Krasnow contends. "Does a person who uses a windmill to grind grain or pump water owe the 'public' for the use of the wind?"[26]

Conceding, however, that the spectrum is finite and will accommodate only a limited number of "windmills," one must next consider if this poses a predicament unique to broadcasting. In an economic sense virtually every resource is scarce, including, as we have discovered in this environmentally conscious age, clean air and water. For example, land is also a scarce resource. There are more individuals who want to use it than there is land to allocate. Fortunately for those who prefer private ownership of real property, a system of law has evolved that respects property rights. Even socialists who advocate government ownership of the means of production justify their policy goals by the social ends they purportedly would achieve, rather than the notion that there is a surplus of demand over supply.

The scarcity of the spectrum no more dictates a policy of public ownership of the airwaves than does the scarcity of asparagus dictate the necessity of government allocation of the vegetable. Consider the hypothetical example concocted by Bruce M. Owen, a former telecommunications advisor in the Nixon Administration.[27] Imagine that the papermaking industry was nationalized because timber was scarce, it had a big effect on the environment, and there was sentiment that "trees belong to the people." As a public resource, paper would be allocated by license granted by a Federal Paper Commission. Because this allocation should reflect the public interest and not the market, paper would be assigned a zero price. This would have two consequences in Owen's model: Demand would exceed supply, and the government would have to devise some rational system for allocation, probably by limiting licenses to those who served the public interest.

To ascertain which paper users were serving the public interest, the Federal Paper Commission would have to inquire into the content of what was being printed on the paper. Socially worthy publications would be favored over those deemed only to promote the viewpoints of their publishers. Owen's scenario only seems farfetched because traditionally we have had a system of property rights in trees and paper, there exists a constitutional reluctance to regulate what is printed, and society has lost most of its fear of the technology of publishing.

Radio arrived on the scene very rapidly, lacked a developed system of property rights, and invited government allocation to prevent overlapping use and interference. The federal government asserted public ownership and the power to allocate the spectrum. When it makes its choice as to who shall be permitted to broadcast on a specific channel, the government must do so on some basis: by lottery, bid, rental, outright sale, or the public trustee approach. As long as the choice is by the trustee model, the government may attach obligations for the broadcaster to operate in the public interest.[28]

But how would the public interest be defined? What is the interest most likely to be protected and enhanced by government intervention in communications? Is it unreasonable to assume that it would be oriented toward the status quo? Toward preserving the media advantage of newsworthy incumbents of federal office? Toward assuring that broadcasters must be responsive to political appointees on the FCC? Toward guaranteeing that activities of the two main political parties could dominate news coverage? Toward forcing licensees to cater to those controlling the White House and Congress? Such outcomes are not axiomatic, just more likely than not. As we shall see in subsequent chapters, some policies of Congress and the FCC have favored such results. They flow not from some conscious policy of imposing government controls over the content of what is aired, but are a logical consequence of the initial requirement that allocation be based on the public interest. But even a limited rule has unanticipated consequences and raises difficult questions of freedom of speech and press.

## The Constitutional Issue

The requirement that a broadcaster provide contrasting viewpoints on controversial issues is a limitation on the broadcaster's First Amendment right to select what he wants to present on his station. The editorial content of newspapers is not constrained by government regulation, and the Supreme Court has ruled that newspapers cannot be required to furnish access to political candidates in the way television must.[29]

The First Amendment was devised so that those who wished to write and speak about political affairs would be shielded from government harassment and punishment for their views. The freedom to express views not only protects the speaker or writer; society as a whole benefits from open discussion of issues. "Speech concerning public affairs is more than self-expression; it is the essence of self-government," according to the Supreme Court.[30] The First Amendment "rests on the assumption that the widest possible dissemination of information from diverse and antagonistic sources is essential to the welfare of the public. . . ."[31] Permitting every speaker to state his or her ideas will help the public adopt those which are correct and worthy.

To facilitate the public interest in free discourse, the Constitution expressly exempts the press from government control. Although the press is the only business selected for such special protection, the amendment was designed for the individual writer, such as Thomas Paine, and the small publishing outfits of his time. Although it has come to be applied to big publishers, such as the *New York Times,* the First Amendment rights of the individual who takes to the stump, sits at a typewriter, or draws on a placard are equivalent to the rights of the *New York Times,* at least in theory. If any of us chooses to publish, the government may not restrain us.

But what happens if instead of typewriter, printing press, placard, or loud voice, the tools chosen to express ideas are a microphone, camera, and transmitter? Have First Amendment rights changed? If government licensing is accepted (as it now must be if one wishes to broadcast), must some degree of First Amendment protection be surrendered?

Both the Radio Act of 1927 and the Communications Act of 1934, in Section 326, specifically prohibit the FCC from censoring what is broadcast. Censorship would clearly infringe on the broadcaster's freedom of speech. But the authors of the 1927 Act clearly did not have a broad view of what constitutes censorship. The same law prohibiting censorship also banned profanity, indecency, and obscenity from the airwaves. On one hand it opposed censorship; on the other it mandated censorship of some phrases.

Content regulations, unlike censorship, require more speech, not less. Regulations like the Equal Opportunities Rule and Fairness Doctrine, while less intrusive than censorship, require that the broadcaster comply with government orders to air material he might otherwise choose not to carry on his station. The rules affect the editorial and programming choices a broadcaster makes in the operating of his station. While he is relieved of concern that the government might order him *not* to carry some viewpoint, he realizes he must carry points of view that he may oppose. Instead of having to face a prospect of censorship and therefore adjust the expression of views to meet the anticipated demands of a censor, the broadcaster must guess what the regulator would require and then adjust the expression of views he broadcasts to meet what is expected of him by the government. In sum, the broadcast output changes, whether under overt censorship or more flexible content regulation. Under either form of government oversight, the broadcaster faces the very real prospect of having to espouse viewpoints with which he does not agree.

It happens all the time in radio and television; stations carry editorial replies, free replies to commercial messages about issues, and paid political announcements from candidates for federal office,[32] as well as interviews with various persons on news programs. Newspapers and magazines may choose to report conflicting viewpoints, but the government will not require them to do so. The print medium's right to ignore someone or something was made clear when the Supreme Court struck down a Florida law that ordered newspapers to devote space to candidates for replies to personal attacks. In the case of *Miami Herald Publishing Co.* v. *Tornillo,* 418 U.S. 241 (1974), the Court held that a responsible press is not mandated by the Constitution and cannot be legislated. But the same right of reply declared unconstitutional in the *Miami Herald* case had been approved when the Court evaluated broadcasting regulation in the *Red Lion* case.[33] In *Red Lion* the Court upheld the Personal Attack Rule and the Fairness Doctrine, saying that access to the airwaves would enhance public debate.[34] The Court said that the listener's right to be informed outweighed the broadcaster's right to choose what he would broadcast:

> Because of the scarcity of radio frequencies, the Government is permitted to put restraints on licensees in favor of others whose views should be expressed on this unique medium. But the people as a whole retain their interest in free speech by radio and their collective right to have the medium function con-

sistently with the ends and purposes of the First Amendment. It is the right of the viewers and listeners, not the right of the broadcasters, which is paramount.[35]

The final sentence of that quotation from *Red Lion* merits close attention. The First Amendment protection of individual speech has evolved into a protection for society as a whole, permitting the speech of one group of persons (broadcasters) to be regulated for the good of all. It should be compared with the very different First Amendment rationale in the *Miami Herald* case, where the Court held:

> A newspaper is more than a passive receptacle or conduit for news, comment, and advertising. The choice of material to go into a newspaper, and the decisions made as to limitations on the size and content of the paper, and treatment of public issues and public officials—whether fair or unfair—constitute the exercise of editorial control and judgment. It has yet to be demonstrated how governmental regulation of this crucial process can be exercised consistent with First Amendment guarantees of a free press as they have evolved to this time.[36]

This is not to say that publishers are enjoying freedom while broadcasters are saddled with all-pervasive controls. The Federal Communications Commission has limited its involvement in editorial decision making, as we shall see in examining the formal and informal workings of the Fairness Doctrine. Most news programs have been exempted from the equal time rule. And the Supreme Court has noted that requiring access to the airwaves is like walking a constitutional tightrope:

> This role of the Government as an "overseer" and ultimate arbiter and guardian of the public interest and the role of the licensee as a journalistic "free agent" call for a delicate balancing of competing interests. The maintenance of this balance for more than 40 years has called on both the regulators and the licensees to walk a "tightrope" to preserve the First Amendment values written into the Radio Act and its successor, the Communications Act.[37]

Traversing the First Amendment "tightrope" is no simple task. Friend and foe of the Fairness Doctrine cite the First Amendment as the basis for their differing stands on the issue. Henry Geller, a former FCC General Counsel, has stated that a broadcaster can cover controversial issues without fear of governmental reprisal, has wide discretion to present vigorous programming, and even if he's found to have acted unreasonably in some instance, he is simply required to present some additional speech. "The Fairness Doctrine thus never prevents any speech, however robust, but only adds more voices or representative views to the debate," Geller said, echoing the argument that the doctrine furthers the purpose of the First Amendment.[38]

Even some journalists have moved away from emphasizing the First Amendment's explicit prohibition on government control of speech and press, and instead have stressed the concept of the public's right to know. Such a right, of course, is implicit in the amendment. The right to free speech would be meaningless if such speech could not be heard. But the public's right to know is an inferred right, more amorphous than the command that the government "shall make no law."

In some cases journalists have invoked the public's right to know as a shield for conduct that has drawn criticism upon the press. Confidential sources have been kept anonymous, stolen documents printed, intrusive techniques employed, and deceitful news-gathering practices condoned, all in the name of furthering the public's right to know. It certainly is a catchy slogan. It seems much less self-interested than declaring press immunity. But reliance on the *public's right* is precisely the main justification for the Fairness Doctrine.

In decisions affecting the press, the Supreme Court has asserted that the constitutional goal is "uninhibited, robust, and wide open debate." [39] Accordingly, the right to receive information and ideas is constitutionally protected. [40] The Court has struck down laws designed to restrict the right of persons to receive "communist political propaganda," for example. [41] As Justice Brennan noted in that case, the dissemination of ideas can accomplish nothing if people cannot receive them and "it would be a barren marketplace of ideas that had only sellers and no buyers." [42]

What is at stake is access, the public's access to information and, on the other hand, an individual or group's access to the airwaves to present views to the public. Although obviously related, it is important to distinguish between these two types of access. The first asserts that the public has a right to hear. The second declares that citizens have a right to have their voices amplified. For the purpose of the following discussion the term *access* will refer to the latter type, access to the means of communication to present viewpoints. The distinction is important, and not always clarified in judicial decisions on freedom of expression.

The Supreme Court has held that First Amendment guarantees "are not for the benefit of the press so much as for the benefit of all of us." [43] In the *Red Lion* case the court focused on the right of the public to hear and largely ignored the right of ordinary citizens to use radio and television to speak.

In the preelectronic age, the flourishing of diverse viewpoints was best assured by keeping the government out of the business of regulating speech and press. But protecting the speaker's right to say whatever he wants may not lead to the expression of diverse views in an electronic environment where the licensee can exclude others from his station. As

Judge David Bazelon of the U.S. Appeals Court has stated, "Protecting the speaker's right may tend to suppress viewpoints—the viewpoints of those who do not have a broadcast license."[44]

The Supreme Court, however, has been ambivalent about endorsing a right of access for those who wish to express views on radio and television, but lack FCC licenses. It upheld the right of someone who was personally attacked to respond on the air in *Red Lion,* but later refused to extend access rights to those seeking to buy airtime to express views on the Vietnam war.[45] The Court rejected a claim that the First Amendment and the public interest standard in the Communications Act required stations to sell airtime for editorial advertisements.[46] Special access rights have been carved out, however, for candidates for federal office.[47]

Thus if one were to try to list competing rights, the various First Amendment values include:

1. The public's right to hear a robust, wide-ranging debate.
2. The right of candidates for federal office to obtain access to the airwaves.
3. The right of broadcasters to select what they shall air.
4. The right of individuals and groups to obtain access to the airwaves.

Of course, different factual situations affect how conflicting rights would be resolved in specific cases. While somewhat oversimplified, the above list reflects the priorities as set by the courts. The public's right to hear a robust debate predominated over the broadcasters' right to select what he airs in the *Red Lion* case. The right of candidates to obtain access to the airwaves predominated over broadcaster discretion in a 1981 case.[48] But the right of broadcasters to pick and choose what they aired won out against an asserted right to buy time for issue advertisements in 1973.[49] This synthesis of leading cases suggests that although the courts have not clearly enunciated which values shall prevail it is possible to discern priorities.

While such a priority list is not useful in predicting how a court or agency might rule in a particular case in the future, it has utility in evaluating what kind of public policy has emerged from our rather ad hoc system of adjudicating communications questions.

It seems inconsistent that the paramount goal of assuring a diverse debate ranks on the list above the goal of providing access for individuals and groups, which, one would assume, is the way the debate is made more diverse. It seems that the current ordering of values extols the ends, but shortchanges the means to assure the desired result. It's a topsy-turvy way of solving a problem. If one wishes to assure a broad airing of divergent views it makes more sense to mandate access than proclaim the need for fairness.

Imagine, if you will, how a different system of regulation might work if the list of rights were inverted. Broadcasters would still complain that they would not have full First Amendment rights if they had to provide a set amount or percentage of time for public access to their frequencies. But once that access was provided, the broadcaster would retain full control over the remainder of his airtime. Such an alternative, and others, shall be explored in detail at the conclusion of this book; but the point is worth pondering. Has the system of regulating broadcasting stood the First Amendment on its head, giving individuals too little access, giving broadcasters too little protection?

The Supreme Court has stated baldly that broadcasting "has received the most limited First Amendment protection." [50] Need this be the case? Are we better served by government regulation that assures some form of access to the airwaves, or by removing government interference entirely from the marketplace of ideas? Or in this "high tech" age is there a freely accessible marketplace of ideas?

These are difficult questions. As Judge Skelly Wright of the U.S. Court of Appeals in the District of Columbia has stated,

> The problems of figuring out the right thing to do in this area—the system that will best serve the public's First Amendment interest—are enormous. In some areas of the law, constitutional values are clearly discernible, as where one is required to balance some right protected by the Constitution against an asserted countervailing government interest. . . . [I]n some areas of the law it is easy to tell the good guys from the bad guys. In the current debate over the broadcast media and the First Amendment, however, each debater claims to be the real protector of the First Amendment, and the analytical problems are much more difficult than in ordinary constitutional adjudication. [51]

Because all sides in the debate over the Fairness Doctrine invoke the First Amendment, it is essential to consider *whose* First Amendment rights are advanced or threatened by the particular form of regulation that has evolved. Ideally, the goal should be to devise a system that fulfills the public's right to know while not trampling on anyone's right to free speech and press. The worst outcome would be one where the public's right to hear a diverse, wide-ranging debate goes unfulfilled while the government intrudes into day-to-day journalistic decisions. Perhaps the conflicting rights cannot be completely reconciled, but the underlying tensions should be recognized and clear-cut policy choices made on questions so fundamental to our democracy.

It has been said that the "peculiar characteristics" of broadcasting make it necessary to apply constitutional standards that are different from those applied to print.[52] Government power has been used to shape the content of broadcast programming toward various social goals in the name of the public interest, including, in addition to fairness and equal time, encouraging locally oriented fare, childrens' programs, material of relevance to minorities, diverse radio formats and discouraging violence and indecency on the airwaves.[53] Some readers of this volume who may support these goals are encouraged to examine the *means* employed in government regulation. It is worth noting the comments made by a 1974 cabinet level committee, and the question it posed:

> It is only in the broadcast media that the First Amendment has been interpreted to permit governmental efforts to foster the expression of certain ideas or information by intruding upon the creation, selection, and editing functions of the private media owners. Why this difference?[54]

## *References*

1. Sigma Delta Chi, *Code of Ethics* (1973).
2. FCC, *Fairness Doctrine and Public Interest Standards, Fairness Report Regarding Handling of Public Issues,* 39 Fed. Reg. 26375 (1974). Technically, Fairness is not an FCC "rule," but it has the force of regulation.
3. "Fear of Fowler," *Channels of Communication* (December 1981/January 1982), p. 21.
4. FCC, Report No. 17427, April 1, 1983. See Richard M. Neustadt, Gregg Skall, and Michael Hammer, *The Regulation of Electronic Publishing,* 33 *Federal Communications Law Journal* 331 (1981).
5. *Democratic National Committee v. FCC,* slip opinion, Case No. 82–1872 (D.C. Cir. 1983).
6. *Red Lion Broadcasting Co.* v. *FCC,* 395 U.S. 367, 369 (1969).
7. 1974 *Fairness Report, op. cit.,* p. 23674.
8. *Patsy Mink,* 59 FCC 2d 987 (1976).
9. "The FCC and the First Principle of the Fairness Doctrine: A History of Neglect and Distortion," 31 *Federal Communications Law Journal,* 361, 407–408 (1979).
10. *Democratic National Committee* v. *FCC,* 460 F.2d 891 (D.C. Cir. 1971), *cert denied,* 409 U.S. 843 (1972).
11. 47 C.F.R. Secs 73.123, 73.300, 73.679.
12. *Cullman Broadcasting Co.,* 40 FCC 576 (1963).
13. Henry Geller, *The Fairness Doctrine in Broadcasting* (Santa Monica, Calif., Rand, 1973), pp. viii, 4.
14. 47 U.S.C. §315 (1970).

15. *Nicholas Zapple,* 23 FCC 2d 707 (1970).
16. "Keeping Television Regulated," *New York Times,* December 22, 1981, op-ed page.
17. *National Broadcasting Co.* v. *United States,* 319 U.S. 219 (1943). *Red Lion Broadcasting Co.* v. *FCC,* 395 U.S. 367 (1969).
18. 319 U.S. 190 (1943).
19. Id. at 213.
20. Id. at 215–216.
21. *Telecommunications in Transition: The Status of Competition in the Telecommunications Industry,* 310–325.
22. *Red Lion Broadcasting Co.* v. *FCC,* 395 U.S. 367, 388 (1969).
23. See Mark S. Fowler and Daniel L. Brenner, "A Marketplace Approach to Broadcast Regulation," 60 *Texas Law Review* 1, 15–20 (1982).
24. Milton Mueller, "Property Rights in Radio Communication: The Key to the Reform of Telecommunications Regulation," (Washington, D.C., The Cato Institute, 1982, pp. 6–13).
25. "Does the Public Own the Airwaves?" *Channels* (October 1982) 66, 67.
26. Id. at 66.
27. *Economics and Freedom of Expression, Media Structure and the First Amendment* (Cambridge, Mass., Ballinger, 1975). Reprinted in Daniel L. Brenner and William L. Rivers (Eds.), *Free but Regulated* (Ames, Iowa State University Press, 1982), pp. 37–38.
28. Geller, op. cit., pp. 5–9.
29. *Miami Herald Publishing Co.* v. *Tornillo,* 418 U.S. 241 (1974).
30. *Garrison* v. *Louisiana,* 379 U.S. 64, 74–75 (1964).
31. *Associated Press* v. *United States,* 326 U.S. 1, 20 (1945).
32. Stations are required to afford reasonable access to candidates for federal office by Section 312(a) (7) of the Communications Act of 1934.
33. 395 U.S. 367.
34. Id. at 392.
35. Id. at 390.
36. 418 U.S. at 258.
37. *CBS* v. *Democratic National Committee,* 412 U.S. 94, 117 (1973).
38. Geller, op. cit., p. 5.
39. *New York Times* v. *Sullivan,* 376 U.S. 254, 270 (1964).
40. *Stanley* v. *Georgia,* 394 U.S. 557 (1969).
41. *Lamont* v. *Postmaster General,* 381 U.S. 301 (1965).
42. Id. at 308 (Brennan concurring).
43. *Time, Inc.* v. *Hill,* 385 U.S. 374, 389 (1966).
44. "The First Amendment and the "New Media"—New Directions in Regulating Telecommunications," 31 *Federal Communications Law Journal* 201 (1979).
45. *CBS* v. *Democratic National Committee,* 412 U.S. 94 (1973).
46. Id.
47. *CBS* v. *FCC,* 453 US. 367 (1981).
48. Id.
49. *CBS* v. *DNC,* 412 U.S. 94 (1973).

50. *FCC* v. *Pacifica Foundation,* 438 U.S. 726, 748 (1978).
51. Commencement Address, George Washington University's National Law Center, Washington, D.C., June 3, 1973.
52. *National Association of Independent Television Producers and Distributors* v. *FCC,* 516 F.2d 526, 531 (2d Cir. 1975).
53. Henry Goldberg and Michael Couzens, "Peculiar Characteristics: An Analysis of the First Amendment Implications of Broadcast Regulation," 31 *Federal Communications Law Journal,* 1, 3 (1978).
54. *Report to the President of the Cabinet Committee on Cable Communications* (1974), p. 23.

| | TWO |
|---|---|

# *Power and the Public Interest*

EVERY NEW TECHNOLOGY is potentially destabilizing to society. The impact of the automobile on America, its economy, its cities, and its mores was hardly perceived when Henry Ford started turning out cars. Economic progress, as it used to be called, usually brought some good, some bad, and a lot of the unintended. By boosting the fortunes of some and competing with others, technology threatened the status quo. Every major threat to the status quo invites government intervention.

This is especially the case with communications, a force that can motivate, inform, entertain, inflame. When Gutenberg developed his printing press, kings and bishops rushed to license printers and their product. Before the rapid development of printing, the written word was much less of a threat to the authorities. Technological progress in the sixteenth century spurred censorship and the index expurgatorius. Concern for the impact of mass communications was well founded; the Bibles rolling off the new presses fueled the Reformation across Europe.

This century has seen a communications revolution that surely will accelerate in the future. Even today, the implications of technological change are not understood. The marriage of computer and telecommunications technologies has opened new frontiers. The status quo is threatened; regulation often seems a safe way to cope with so complex a force.

One need not look into a crystal ball to see how communications can help shape events. National Socialism in Germany and Marxism in the developing world are recent and current manifestations of the power of the printed and broadcast word.

While less dramatic in political impact, the use of radio and television has not been without result in the United States. Franklin Roosevelt, John Kennedy, and Ronald Reagan stand out as American leaders who skillfully used the media. The modern use of television and radio has changed the political system, contributing to the decline of the two-party system and old-time political machines, and assisting the rise of single-issue campaigns and mediagenic candidates.

Early in the development of radio as a mass medium, politicians realized its potential to alter the way politics is conducted in this country. At the First National Radio Conference, in 1922, Herbert Hoover warned that it was necessary to establish a "public right" over the airwaves to prevent them from falling into "uncontrolled hands." At the Third Radio Conference in 1924, President Calvin Coolidge stressed "the benefits of increased governmental regulation" to ensure "against the danger of a few organizations gaining control of the airwaves." While Coolidge warned against government controlling the flow of information, he said the greater risk was that it "should come under the arbitrary power of any person or group of persons."

During early congressional debate over regulating broadcasting, it was urged that private broadcasters should not have unfettered power to determine what the public would or would not hear. According to Steven J. Simmons, during the 1920s there was widespread fear that broadcasting could shape public opinion in an unprecedented manner. As one congressman put it, "If the strong arm of the law does not prevent monopoly ownership and make discrimination by such stations illegal, American thought and politics will be largely at the mercy of those who operate these stations."[1]

To assure that congressional candidates were not at the mercy of broadcasters, the Radio Act of 1927 required stations to afford equal broadcast opportunities to candidates for federal office. While politicians pondered the effect radio might have on their careers, the medium was growing rapidly. And the explosive growth caused pressures that made government regulation an attractive alternative to the cacophony caused by the free market in radio in the early 1920s.

This chapter traces the history of the regulation of broadcasting with special attention to how the idea of *power* shaped and was shaped by regulation.

Before examining the power of the media today, it is necessary to look at the genesis of broadcast regulation, the turbulent use of the spectrum in the 1920s, and the ironic desire of broadcasters themselves for government action.

The federal government began regulating broadcasting at the broadcasters' request. The Radio Act of 1927 was enacted because of the pressing need to allocate frequencies among stations and stop the electronic chaos of interference that was thwarting clear reception of stations' signals. But the government's role grew beyond what the broadcasters had envisioned—simply a traffic director to keep transmissions from overlapping.

In return for protecting broadcasters from interference with their signals, Congress imposed the requirement that they act as trustees of the public interest. Those who were chosen for protection from harmful competition were required to comply with certain standards. The Radio Act of 1927 created a system of licensing, with relatively short-term licenses granted on the condition that broadcasters operate in the public interest. Alternative methods of allocation, by public bid or by renting channels to private companies or individuals, were rejected.

The public trustee idea evolved into several related requirements centering on public service programming. Rather than just pursue profitable programming, licensees were expected to devote a reasonable amount of time to programs that focus on public issues and cover such issues fairly. This two-fold duty prohibits a broadcaster from ignoring major issues or presenting only the viewpoint he himself espouses. To understand the evolution of this dual requirement it is necessary to step back into the early days of radio.

## The Roaring Twenties

In its dawn, radio was as roaring as the decade in which it was introduced. With no system for allocating frequencies, the sudden, explosive growth of radio led to instances of signals being so overlapped and garbled that clear reception of radio stations was impossible. In 1920 there were only three radio stations with regular programming; five years later the number was nearly 600. There were two networks linking stations across the continent in 1930.

The Radio Act of 1912 had been designed for such things as ship-to-shore communications. It proved inadequate for anything other than two-way message transmission. The 1912 act required all radio stations to acquire licenses from the Secretary of Commerce and it also specified wavelengths for different types of stations. But in the early 1920s the courts undercut the Secretary's regulatory authority by holding that he had no discretion to refuse a license to an applicant within the classifications or penalize a broadcaster for transmitting on an unauthorized frequency.[2] An Attorney General's opinion also held that the Secretary lacked the authority to assign wavelengths or to limit the transmitting power of stations.[3]

New stations began transmitting on any frequency they desired. Established stations shifted wavelengths, wattage, and operating times at will. The garble and static were so intense that one account of the period stated that "chaos rode the airwaves, pandemonium filled every loudspeaker and the 20th century Tower of Babel was made in the image of the antenna towers of some thousand broadcasters who, like the Kilkenny cats, were about to eat each other up."[4]

Those who now consider the airwaves a scarce resource would, if transported to the 1920s, see why it was in the public interest, as well as the broadcasters' interest, to devise a way of allocating the resource and restricting its use. In retrospect it is clear that without government action radio would have been rendered useless by "the cacophony of competing voices, none of which could be clearly and predictably heard."[5]

In the mid 1920s Secretary of Commerce Hoover urged legislation to remedy the problem. He justified government regulation not only on the grounds that interference had to be eliminated, but that "a public right" over broadcasting must be established to prevent a "great national asset" from falling into "uncontrolled hands."[6]

Government allocation of the airwaves was seen as a way to provide the public with transmissions free of interference, provide broadcasters with protection from competition and provide politicians protection from broadcasters.

In his excellent description of the Fairness Doctrine, Simmons traces the development of the idea that the airwaves were a public resource, not private property, and notes that the need for government intervention to assure fairness was argued nearly from the beginning of commercial radio.[7]

From the inception of broadcasting there was fear it would be used by powerful interests to dominate debate and influence elections.[8] One senator warned in 1926 that the interests controlling stations should not use their power "to disseminate the kind of publicity only of which they approve and leave no opportunity for the other side of public questions. . . ."[9] One group contended that "radio is a power, and the question is not of clearing the air but of power control for the future."[10]

Simmons quotes Secretary Hoover, in 1925: "We hear a great deal about freedom of the air, but there are *two* parties to freedom of the air, and to freedom of speech for that matter. Certainly in radio I believe in *freedom for the listener. . . .*"[11] This idea of a shared First Amendment right between broadcaster and listener would reappear in the Supreme Court decision upholding the Fairness Doctrine.[12] But the Third and Fourth Radio Conferences during the 1920s included recommendations that censorship be prohibited—a recognition that government's role must be limited.

The Radio Act of 1927 created a Federal Radio Commission to license broadcasters and decide which frequencies and wattage power they could use. The airwaves were recognized as a public resource that private corporations and individuals could use as licensees, not owners. While censorship was prohibited in the act, the new commission was empowered to grant licenses so the "public convenience, interest or necessity" would be served. An Equal Opportunities provision mandating equal time for political candidates was incorporated into the law. Congress debated whether to enact a specific provision requiring that broadcasters provide balanced treatment of public issues but such a provision was not included.[13]

In reviewing the legislative history of the 1927 act, a House of Representatives study in 1968 concluded that the earlier deliberations "would appear to cast serious doubt" that the Fairness Doctrine is "a necessary corollary of the 'public interest' standard" in the law.[14]

In 1932, however, Congress passed amendments to the Radio Act, including a provision stating, "it shall be deemed in the public interest for a licensee, so far as possible, to permit equal opportunity for the presentation of both sides of public questions."[15] The provision never became law because of a pocket veto by Herbert Hoover, who had moved from the Commerce Department to the White House.

## Regulation Consolidated

The Communications Act of 1934 consolidated regulation of radio broadcasting and common carrier (telephone and telegraph) activities under one Federal Communications Commission. The 1934 act continues to be the foundation for the regulation of broadcasting, despite the advent of television, cable, and other new communications technologies. Congress passed the act "under the spur of a widespread fear that in the absence of governmental control the public interest might be subordinated to monopolistic domination in the broadcast field."[16]

While debating passage of the act, Congress once again considered whether to insert Fairness Doctrine language into the act, including a provision requiring "equal opportunities . . . in the presentation of views on a public question to be voted upon at an election," and a provision stating that it was "in the public interest for a licensee, so far as possible, to permit equal opportunity for the presentation of both sides of the public question."[17] But these provisions were deleted before passage of the 1934 act, another instance during the early years of broadcasting when explicit Fairness-Doctrine-type language was unsuccessfully proposed for incorporation into law.

It was not until 1959, when Congress amended the 1934 act, that the Fairness Doctrine was explicitly added to the law. It is relevant that the Fairness Doctrine evolved through regulatory action and court rulings. It was not mandated by the 1934 statute, but was justified over the years as necessitated by the broad public interest standard incorporated in the 1934 act. Congress was concerned about balanced coverage of public issues, but left it to the FCC to develop regulations as problems arose.[18]

The development of the Fairness Doctrine stems from the idea that stations are public trustees and must act in the public interest. The public interest requires that they give a fair break to all responsible positions on major controversial issues. When early attempts to legislate this goal as an "equal opportunity" standard were rejected, a system evolved whereby broadcasters have wide discretion in what they program and who they permit on their air. But a failure to provide overall balance in such programming could result in revocation of their licenses or FCC action denying renewal of such licenses. Concern about broadcast fairness was evident from radio's early days.[19] Several cases from that period show how.

In 1928 the Federal Radio Commission ruled that station WEVD in New York could keep its license, even though it broadcast the propaganda of the Socialist Party. But the commission warned that, "Such a station must, of course . . . be conducted with due regard for the opinions of others."[20] Thus the owner's viewpoint could be aired, but other views had to be treated fairly.

In 1929 the commission denied a request by a station owned by the Chicago Federation of Labor that it increase its power and hours of operation. The federation wanted "a frequency to be used for the exclusive benefit of organized labor," but the commission ruled that since only a limited number of stations could broadcast, "all stations should cater to the general public and serve public interest as against group or class interest."[21]

In 1931 the commission denied a license renewal to the owner of KFBK in Kansas, a doctor who dispensed medical advice and promoted certain drugs and his own goat-gland rejuvenation operations. The commission concluded that rights of the listeners were paramount and denied a license renewal.[22] KFBK complained that this was government censorship, but an appeals court said that since the number of frequencies is limited there was not room "for every business or school of thought."[23]

The court ruled that the commission could apply the public interest standard against KFBK.

In 1931 the commission also denied a license renewal to the owner of KTNT, in Muscatine, Iowa, who had used his station to promote a cancer cure.[24]

In 1932 the Federal Radio Commission denied a license renewal to the owner of KGEF in Los Angeles because of programming that consisted of unsubstantiated accusations against organized labor, local judges, and the Board of Health, and nasty remarks about Jews and Catholics. An appeals court upheld the commission's scrutiny of the use of the station under the public interest standard and rejected the First Amendment claims of KGEF. The First Amendment prohibits prior restraint, but the court held that subsequent punishment, including license denial, was not unconstitutional.[25]

While these cases do not invoke the specific provisions of the Fairness Doctrine, they do show early use of the public interest standard to assure that the public is served by broadcasters. And they demonstrate that the commission could take the drastic action of denying a license to a broadcaster who aired material the commissioners felt was unfair.

## The Mayflower Doctrine

In the late 1930s and early 1940s the FCC became more restrictive about what causes broadcasters could espouse. The major case that led to formulation of the Fairness Doctrine did not come until 1941, when the commission announced its decision in *Mayflower*.[26] Mayflower Broadcasting was an unsuccessful applicant for a frequency already used by WAAB, owned by Yankee Network, Inc. Mayflower's application was rejected on other grounds, but the renewal of WAAB's license was conditioned on WAAB's promise that it would not broadcast editorials. In the late 1930s the station had broadcast editorials favoring political candidates and supporting and opposing public issues. The FCC found that "no pretense was made at objective, impartial reporting."[27]

The FCC denounced the partisan use of the station. It said that "truly free radio cannot be used to advocate the causes of the licensee. It cannot be used to support the candidacies of his friends. It cannot be devoted to the support of principles he happens to regard most favorably." The forceful holding stated flatly, "the broadcaster cannot be an advocate."[28]

The Mayflower Doctrine was the most repressive policy against broadcasters' freedom of speech asserted by the FCC. But the commission used a free speech rationale to justify its action:

> Freedom of speech on the radio must be broad enough to provide full and equal opportunity for the presentation to the public of all sides of public issues. Indeed, as one licensed to operate in a public domain the licensee has assumed the obligation of presenting all sides of important public questions, fairly, objectively and without bias. The public interest—not the private—is paramount.[29]

The *Mayflower* case made clear that had WAAB not promised to abandon editorializing it would have lost its license. The Mayflower Doctrine created enormous controversy within the broadcasting industry, which opposed the ban on editorializing as interfering with the broadcaster's First Amendment rights (seemingly meager rights at that moment). Recognizing the confusion its decision had created, the FCC held hearings in 1948 on an editorializing policy. The hearings led to the 1949 FCC *Report on Editorializing by Broadcast Licensees.*

The 1949 *Editorializing Report* made clear that broadcasters could editorialize, but imposed Fairness Doctrine obligations to present contrasting views. The report stated that the "paramount right" is for the "public in a free society to be informed and to have presented to it for acceptance or rejection the different attitudes and viewpoints concerning these vital and often controversial issues which are held by the various groups which make up the community."[30] The 1949 *Editorializing Report* relied on the public interest standard in the Communications Act and on the First Amendment principle of the public's right to know as justification for the imposition of a two-fold obligation on broadcasters:

> This requires that licensees devote a reasonable percentage of their broadcasting time to the discussion of public issues of interest in the community served by their stations and that such programs be designed so that the public has a reasonable opportunity to hear different opposing positions on the public issues of interest and importance in the community.[31]

In his additional views in the 1949 *Editorializing Report,* Commissioner Webster stated that a licensee might be left in a "state of confusion" after reading the report. The instructions were vague, and while a great deal of discretion was purposely left to the broadcaster, he exercised it at his peril.

### Fairness Codified and Expanded

In 1959 Congress amended the Communications Act to incorporate the Commission's Fairness Doctrine into the statute. The reason for this action was not any burning controversy over broadcast fairness; the debate was rather one-sided and assumed fairness was a worthy goal that should be incorporated into the amendment. Congress did not fully consider the implications of ratifying the Fairness Doctrine, but there was overwhelming support for the policy.

The amendment was generated by an unusual equal-time case that arose in Chicago. A perennial candidate for mayor, Lar Daly, had filed for the campaign and was a legally qualified candidate for the office. Daly demanded equal time on a Chicago television station after it ran a news item about Mayor Richard Daley, who was the frontrunner for the post. The FCC ruled in the *Lar Daly* case that a news story about Mayor Daley greeting the president of Argentina required the station to offer equal time to Lar Daly.[32]

Congress moved quickly, realizing that if stations were required to give equal time to minor candidates every time a major candidate appeared on the air, stations would probably stop covering political campaigns on their newscasts, and the congressmen and senators themselves might vanish from the tube during the very period when they most sought exposure. Congress speedily considered amendments to exempt news programming from the equal opportunities requirement of Section 315.

Within days of the *Lar Daly* ruling, legislative committees were fashioning language to make it clear that equal time would not be required when a station carried an appearance by a candidate in a bona fide newscast, interview show, on-the-spot coverage of an event, or in a news documentary. If the documentary was about the candidate or the campaign, however, it would not be exempt from the Equal Opportunities Rule. If the candidate's appearance in the news documentary was incidental to the subject presented, only then would the exemption from the rule apply.

Congress, in its haste to amend the law, adopted a suggestion to make clear that the exemption for news from the Equal Opportunities Rule was not an exemption from the Fairness Doctrine. Accordingly, the following language was tacked on to the Equal Opportunities section: "Nothing in the foregoing sentence shall be construed as relieving broadcasters, in connection with the presentation of newscasts, news interviews, news documentaries, and on-the-spot coverage of news events, from the obligation imposed upon them under this Act to operate in the public interest and to afford reasonable opportunity for discussion of conflicting views on issues of public importance." The Conference Report stated that this was a "restatement of the basic policy" that the commission had imposed on broadcasters in its "standard of fairness." It is clear from the legislative history that the members voted to write the Fairness Doctrine into the statute, even though there was no extensive debate about the doctrine and its implications.[33]

The speed with which Congress moved to assure that news coverage of its members would continue in campaign times is testimony to the awareness of the political force of televised news, even in 1959. In what could have been a simple reversal of agency action, Congress went beyond the equal time problem to assert the need for broadcasters to play fair with issues. This underscores the concern of many that without such assurance broadcasters could exercise even greater power over the political agenda.

But the amendment had another impact, as well. It reinforced the power of the two major parties, the Democratic and Republican parties, and handicapped those outside the mainstream of American politics. One exemption to the equal time provision had the effect of permitting stations to exclude minor, third-party candidates from regular news interview programs, thereby strengthening the position of newsworthy incumbents. Another provision exempted coverage of national political conventions from the Equal Opportunities Rule, assuring that the networks could cover the Democratic and GOP conventions and ignore the meetings of the Citizens Party, Libertarians, Socialist Workers, et al.

Congress has moved in other ways to assure that broadcasters provide airtime for candidates during campaigns. In 1972 it passed federal campaign reforms which obliged stations to "allow reasonable access to or to permit purchase of reasonable amounts of time" for legally qualified candidates for federal office.[34] Because stations face equal time obligations as well, they avoid giving *free* time to members of Congress during campaigns because they would have to give time to all opponents. Instead the Reasonable Access Provision has come to apply principally to *sale* of commercial time for political messages. The law has been interpreted to strip broadcasters of much discretion in handling requests by federal candidates for commercial time.[35] The Supreme Court has held that the statute created an affirmative right for candidates for federal office to purchase airtime, that the FCC can determine when the campaign begins, and that the candidates' needs predominate over the broadcaster's desires.[36] Candidates must be allowed reasonable time for use of station facilities: in other words, so they can present an uncensored presentation in contrast to an edited appearance on a news program.[37]

Moreover, just before elections stations must sell time to candidates at the station's "lowest unit charge," assuring that broadcasters do not raise rates for campaign advertisements.[38] This provision helps fix prices for campaign spots. Former FCC Chairman Charles Ferris and Commissioner Joseph Fogarty, who were Senate aides at the time of the bill's passage, have called the law "a selfish piece of legislation."[39]

Taken together, Congress has fashioned the Equal Opportunities Rule, the Reasonable Access Provision, and the lowest unit charge provision to protect the members of Congress themselves. Under the statutory framework, they enjoy access rights greater than any other category of citizens. One need only compare the 1981 case upholding reasonable access for candidates, *CBS* v. *FCC*,[40] with the Supreme Court's 1973 decision in *CBS* v. *Democratic National Committee*[41] where a right of access for individuals and groups to purchase airtime for issue advertisements was rejected. The judiciary has endorsed the system the legislative branch fashioned for its own purposes.

In short, Congress protects its own.

## Whose Interest?

When Congress created the Federal Communications Commission, it empowered it to regulate broadcasting in the public interest, convenience, and necessity, yet that is an ill-defined mandate. "Few independent regulatory commissions have had to operate under such a broad grant of power with so few substantive guidelines," according to one study.[42] "Rather than encouraging greater freedom of action, vagueness in delegated power may serve to limit an agency's independence and freedom to act as it sees fit."[43]

Defining the interest of the public in general is much more difficult than accepting the notion that the public interest is a much more flexible set of expectations that do not offend or contradict the goals and values of powerful special interests. Avery Leiserson has indicated that "a satisfactory criterion of the public interest is the preponderant acceptance of administrative action by politically influential groups."[44]

We have seen how Congressional concern about broadcaster power has shaped regulation. It has also been shaped by the way the broadcast industry and other interest groups have utilized the regulatory system. Powerful interests interact, often clashing, sometimes cooperating.

When federal regulation of industry began in the nineteenth century, the public interest was thought to require curbs on the abuses resulting from concentrated economic power. Beginning in the 1920s and accelerating in the 30s, coincidental with the advent of broadcasting, a new ethic emerged. The notion took hold that the public interest is also served by preserving and promoting the regulated industry itself.

In agency after agency, the regulatory thrust swung away from pro-competitive, antitrust policies designed to cure the ills of monopolistic behavior. More and more as the Depression deepened, administrative action tended to protect the cartel. This was the trend at the FCC until recently when "deregulation" was promoted by Chairman Ferris during the Carter Administration and "unregulation" was pressed by Chairman

Mark Fowler under the Reagan Administration. But it remains to be seen how far the opponents of regulation will be able to press their program, how sweeping the changes endorsed by Congress will prove to be, and whether new policies will promote competition or permit monopolistic concentrations of power in new technologies. It is important to differentiate between the regulation of content (what must be aired) and the regulation of the structure of the industry (who controls the airwaves).

Regulation has been described as a "two-way process" where the agency and the industry "attempt to control each other."[45] Commissioners often come from the industry, having been owners, executives, or attorneys for broadcast or telecommunications businesses. Very often they plan to return to the industry or to law practices representing broadcasters, cable companies, or common carriers. This hardly makes it difficult for them to comprehend and sympathize with industry points of view on issues before the FCC. Perhaps commissioners have been "controlled" and the agency "captured" by the interests they are supposed to regulate, but there is no doubt that any administrative agency must "come to terms" with significant power centers it deals with, and at least the FCC has a number of competing industries attempting to influence its output.[46]

Technological improvements have caused radio to be replaced by television as the dominant mass medium, have forced AM stations to share an increasing part of the audience with FM stations, have encouraged UHF stations to compete with VHF outlets, have brought cable systems—with the signals of distant "superstations"—into the homes of millions of people. Moreover, looming on the horizon is low-power television offering the possibility of minority programming, Direct Broadcast Satellite offering hope for technically improved national programming and more of it, Multipoint Distribution Systems with pay-TV programs, and electronic publishing—teletext and videotext.

Two points need to be made when discussing this technological bounty. First, the dominant broadcasters have attempted to use the FCC to restrict entry of the new competitors. Second, when entry could no longer be prevented, the dominant communications companies have moved to invest in and—if possible—control the new entrants.

The FCC has been ambivalent about the new technologies. For example, the decision in 1952 not to move all TV into the UHF band but to intermix UHF and VHF significantly impeded the growth of UHF stations and killed chances for a fourth network. Economically secure VHF stations quickly crippled UHF competitors.[47] Later the FCC obtained legislation from Congress to assist the struggling UHF industry by requiring manufacturers of television sets to include tuners that could receive UHF stations.

Additionally, the FCC's policies have protected the power of the three dominant broadcasters—CBS, NBC, and ABC. The commission approved an allocation formula which has permitted only three VHF commercial stations in most communities and which had the effect of killing the struggling Dumont network, which had access to VHF stations in only seven of the biggest 50 cities in the 1950s.[48] As the FCC itself has conceded, the "three to a market" approach has guaranteed the dominant positions of the three commercial networks.[49] Because of prior grants of licenses to CBS, NBC, and ABC to own and operate TV, AM and FM stations in seven of the largest markets, the networks have been assured a strong economic base. As Judge Bazelon has stated:

> Under this regime, the networks have flourished. To a large extent the triumph of telecommunications as the preeminent medium of our time is the victory of the networks. Every index—ratings, revenues, public opinion surveys—confirms our impression that the networks are the dominant source of entertainment, news and information. Our national political life has been moved from the meeting hall to the living room by the pervasiveness of the network camera.[50]

New networks have started to emerge only with the growth of cable and the late blooming success of independent television stations willing to cooperate with each other to acquire programming. But the FCC's long-standing hostility to the speedy expansion of cable protected the television networks and their affiliates for nearly two decades. As one FCC commissioner stated:

> In future years, when students of law or government wish to study the decisionmaking process at its worst, when they look for examples of industry domination of government, when they look at Presidential interference in the operation of an agency responsible to Congress, they will look to the FCC handling of the never-ending saga of cable television as a classic case study.[51]

FCC policies tended to stunt development of alternate programming sources such as cable and pay TV.[52] Barriers to entry were erected to protect existing broadcast licensees from competition. The barriers were dropped only in 1979 and 1980.[53]

For years broadcasters were able to retard competition by cable, arguing that it must not be allowed to destroy broadcasting's ability to perform public service duties. To protect the status quo the FCC extended regulation over electronics manufacturers, communication satellites, and cable. In each case the extension of regulation was justified as protecting the regulatory framework, and hence, the public interest. But in practice, as Bruce M. Owen has noted, the extensions were promoted by "vested interests seeking to protect monopoly profits, and sometimes by unregulated firms seeking federal protection from local regulation or relief from 'excessive' competition."[54]

The system has aided not only the networks, but the other major communications conglomerates as well—Westinghouse, Cox, Gannett, Tribune Company, Metromedia, RKO General, and the like. FCC regulations may limit any single company from owning more than seven TV stations, but it has not stopped corporations like Metromedia from selling stations in smaller markets in order to purchase stations in markets like Chicago and Boston.

The dominance of major communications companies is felt in cable and newspaper publishing as well. Many publishers have moved into cable as they simultaneously buy up smaller papers. The Washington Post predicted in 1977 that within 20 years almost all daily newspapers in the country will be owned by perhaps fewer than two dozen major conglomerates.[55] Thirty percent of newspapers were owned by chains in 1960; the figure grew to sixty percent by the late 1970s.[56]

Given the potential political power of the media, these trends toward concentration of economic power are particularly troublesome to those who believe that pluralism is an important safeguard to democracy. Max Kampelman has warned about the dangers to our democratic system posed by an "ever growing institution with huge financial resources to supplement the power it wields in its control over the dissemination of news, but with fewer and fewer restraints on that power."[57]

People both inside and outside the press have recognized the power inherent in choosing what is news. "The power to determine each day what shall seem important and what shall be neglected is a power unlike any that has been exercised since the Pope lost his hold on the secular mind," according to Walter Lippmann.[58] As Kevin Phillips has noted, a 1974 survey of national leaders ranked television ahead of the White House as the number one power in America.[59]

This impression, of course, could be erroneous. Television may not be as powerful as many believe. The point is that those who care about power think television is powerful. The perception is often overwhelming.

No wonder there have been efforts to curb the media. Television in particular is a socializing force which "comes into the living room, the very core of the household where the family gathers," as FCC Commissioner Abbott Washburn once put it. He added, "If it's *there,* it must be okay."[60] Washburn calls it an "awesome power." When broadcasters demand First Amendment rights comparable with publishers', Washburn points to the impact of TV:

It's like an orange wanting to be a banana. This medium enters the home on a massive scale. The airwave spectrum space it rides on is a limited public resource, a public trust. But there are considerable advantages to being an orange: the broad scope of coverage, the exclusive right-to-use of the signal, and the profitability.[61]

The Supreme Court has opined that "the broadcast media have established a uniquely pervasive presence in the lives of all Americans."[62] Because of broadcasting's impact the Court has upheld FCC efforts to prohibit use of indecent language on the air, especially during times when children might be listening.[63] While the Court may have overstated this impact, it was only echoing the widely held view that radio and TV have clout.

When one examines the impact of broadcasting and the conventional wisdom that it is pervasive and powerful, the rationale for regulating it becomes clearer. It's not so much that the airwaves are scarce, but that they have become enormously valuable and the allocation of frequency is a grant of power—something that directly affects politicians no matter where they stand on the political spectrum.

Perhaps that's why the debate over regulation of broadcasting cuts across partisan and ideological lines—and causes learned individuals to have mixed feelings about the media. For example, Judge Bazelon once led the appeals court in approving extensions of the FCC's power over what was aired, but in late 1972 he was dissenting from such views, claiming that the First Amendment prohibited content regulation. Senator William Proxmire, who proposed the amendment in 1959 which codified the Fairness Doctrine into law, has since criticized it as unconstitutional.

Henry Goldberg and Erwin G. Krasnow have pointed out that most liberals and most conservatives believe in regulating broadcasting to some degree, but they disagree why.[64] Many liberals want regulation to make broadcasting do wonderful things; many conservatives want regulation to restrain broadcasting from doing terrible damage. Goldberg and Krasnow state that "both liberals and conservatives have been comfortable with regulation of broadcast program content, either as a form of censorship, usually urged by conservatives, or as a form of propaganda, usually urged by liberals."[65] That may be an oversimplification that obscures the uneasiness many feel toward government exercise of power. In either case, the media are viewed as instruments of power which could affect social change and undermine the status quo.

If that is so, it is fair to ask if the mass media have been a force for political, including partisan, change. The answer seems to be both yes and no. Certainly the way we elect candidates and perform governmental tasks has been altered by electronics—but it does not seem to be a tool that's been of exclusive use by any one group. Despite the clear potential of television and radio, the media seems more to reflect the attitudes of the electorate than shape them. As a creator of the public agenda, the media could not be matched; yet a conservative like Ronald Reagan with excellent broadcast skills and a liberal like Lyndon Johnson—whose talents were anything but televisual—could catapult their programs to the forefront. In sum, the media power is as much a tool for others to use as it is an instrument for its owners to wield. This is not to say, however, that the media's power might not increase dramatically as regulatory fetters fall.

When Nicholas Johnson was an FCC Commissioner he warned of the danger of "abuse by conglomerate corporate licensees generally."[66] He suggested that because the three networks and many broadcast stations are owned by large corporations it might affect the news reporting aired on television and radio. It would be subtle, Johnson intimated, but the business interest of a conglomerate could dictate its news judgment:

> How would one "prove" that RCA/NBC gives more coverage to space shots and NASA news (or the Vietnam war) than it would if it were not a major space and defense contractor? (Defense business was 18 percent of RCA's total sales in 1967.) How does one investigate any possible relationship between NBC's coverage of foreign governments and RCA's corporate relations with those governments? (In 1967 alone, RCA established major new investments in Australia, Canada, Italy, Mexico, Puerto Rico [sic], Taiwan, and the United Kingdom.)[67]

Johnson lamented that the Commission would find it difficult to penetrate beyond the "camouflage" of network assertions that it exercised reasonable, good-faith news judgment.

Johnson's concerns that conglomerate interests might dictate what is aired cannot be easily dismissed. But the author's experience as an NBC News correspondent is diametrically opposed to Johnson's insinuation; at no time was there any indication that the corporation had ordered slanted news coverage to advance its private interests. The journalists responsible for NBC News programming would never have tolerated such "front office" interference; resignations—and attendant publicity—would have been immediate. But such individual experience is no guarantee that at some future time, especially if the broadcasting business becomes more monopolistic, that top management could not dictate the story line and employees, with no alternate employment opportunities in the industry, might capitulate. Depending on how it's formulated, deregulation could remove the meager government protections against slanting.

There are several protections against corporate dominance of news that do not require government regulation of the content of material broadcast. The first is news professionalism, the encouragement of the independent streak long present in reporting in this country. The second is prohibition of the automatic dominance of just three networks over national news. The third is the encouragement—by public policy—of a multiplicity of voices. If there are many sources of information, the public will be able to choose those that seem most accurate, honest, and objective. Diversity can be encouraged by restricting multiple ownership of stations, prohibiting cross ownership of different media (for example, newspaper ownership of TV stations), requiring separation of cable ownership from cable programming, and assuring ownership opportunities for minorities and nonprofit groups.

The marketplace of ideas, if it flourishes, would permit the public to select the voices it cares to hear, the ideas it wishes to ponder, and ultimately, the policies it chooses to endorse. In the past, government policy has unduly limited the number of those given exclusive licenses to use the airwaves while interfering with licensee's rights to espouse views on the air. Might not a reversal of these policies work better to assure freedom? This will be explored in the final chapter. Diversity in ownership of the media does not assure diversity of viewpoints aired on the media; the question is whether the long-standing policy of protecting existing licensees from competition while interfering with their choice of which views to present on the air has, indeed, done more to serve the public's interest.

## The Club over Broadcasters

No licensee operates without a realization that his enterprise would come to naught if his license were yanked. It permeates the conduct of broadcasters, even if such a sanction is so rarely invoked.

Broadcasters take the regulations seriously. The FCC has power to issue cease-and-desist orders, to renew licenses for shorter periods than usual, to fine a station, and, the ultimate power, to deny renewal of a license or revoke an existing one. But the commission rarely exercises such powers, instead relying almost exclusively on the warning force of its ruling on fairness complaints. The FCC has declined to impose fines for general Fairness Doctrine violations, but it may fine stations for transgressions of the Personal Attack Rule.

In no case has the FCC revoked a license for violations of the Fairness Doctrine. The commission was ordered by the U.S. Court of Appeals in Washington in the late 1960s to vacate its renewal of Lamar Life Broadcasting Company's license for WLBT in Jackson, Mississippi.[68] The United Church of Christ had objected to renewal of the license on grounds that WLBT's news and public affairs programming was marred by racial and religious discrimination, but the FCC went ahead and renewed WLBT's license. The appeals court reversed, criticizing the FCC for "a profound hostility" to the intervention of the listeners who challenged WLBT.[69]

The only other instance of nonrenewal of a license involved Brandywine Main Line Radio, Inc., and its station, WXUR, on grounds of both Fairness Doctrine violations and the owners' misrepresentations of their intent to abide by the rules.[70] The nonrenewal was upheld by a divided appeals court, but the court's judgment relied on the misrepresentation grounds.

Both WLBT and WXUR were notorious offenders. One practiced segregation, the other broadcast right-wing evangelism. Both blatantly excluded opposing views. It is important to understand the political context. WLBT propounded the racist views of the white Citizens Council during the time of civil rights turmoil in the South. It refused to air views favoring integration and sometimes cut off network programming when civil rights stories were reported on the evening news.

WXUR was owned by a religious group led by the Rev. Carl McIntyre, a conservative preacher. The transfer of the station to McIntyre's group came only after it pledged to comply with the Fairness Doctrine; loss of the license followed a failure by the group to live up to its assurances.

In both cases it was the Circuit Court of Appeals in the District of Columbia that pulled the plug. The appeals court is noted for its activist, liberal decisions. It overruled the FCC in the WLBT case, depriving Jackson of a segregationist voice, and upheld the FCC in the WXUR case, silencing Media, Pennsylvania's right-wing voice.

This is not to imply that fairness regulation is a tool exclusively for the left, or for that matter for the courts. Before the Watergate scandal upset the designs of the Nixon Administration, the White House decided to try to wrest away some of the Washington Post's television licenses. After his reelection President Nixon pushed for challenges to renewal of the broadcast licenses held by the Post. Presidential assistants leaned on Dean Burch, Nixon's appointee as Chairman of the FCC, demanding transcripts of network commentaries following a presidential news conference. The White House Office of Telecommunications Policy helped put the squeeze on stations; its director reminded licensees that they could be held responsible by the FCC for any network programming they aired. The White House also moved to discourage public television from carrying national broadcasts on subjects Nixon didn't want aired.[71]

Licensing is not the only way, or even the most common way, political pressure is brought to bear on broadcasters. Chapter 9 explores the efforts by the Democratic Party to use the Fairness Doctrine to silence right-wing broadcasts. Congressional leaders are not without clout over broadcasters.

An instance of congressional pressure occurred after CBS aired the news documentary "Selling of the Pentagon," which criticized military public relations. As will be discussed in the next chapter, the documentary utilized editing techniques that were criticized as having distorted the statements of Pentagon officials. The deletion of parts of the answers made little difference to the thrust of the program, but the question of the misquotes was seized upon by proponents of increased military activity. Pentagon officers and hawkish congressmen attacked the network, persuading Rep. Harley Staggers, Chairman of the House Commerce Committee, to order a subpoena served on CBS requiring tape or film "out takes" from interviews, the parts that were not shown on the air. CBS President Frank Stanton refused, arguing that Congress could not constitutionally demand such journalistic work product from a newspaper, and to require it of a network was to assert that the First Amendment did not protect broadcasters. Stanton faced the prospect of a jail sentence after Stagger's committee voted to hold him in contempt. CBS still refused to comply and only the intervention of Speaker Carl Albert prevented the House from approving the contempt resolution.[72] It was a close call for CBS, and while the network's journalistic fervor might not be dampened by such an episode, it was a reminder to less committed and less well-heeled broadcasters that such conflicts are best avoided.

The issue transcends right-wing or left-wing use of the system of regulation. The government entities that affect broadcast regulation, the FCC, the courts, and the Congress, are filled with political appointees. Their partisan neutrality is never guaranteed. Content regulations in particular are always susceptible to political manipulation and abuse.

There is an ever-present danger that when a regulator has power over content, the power will be invoked in ways that are unfair. Fortunately the record of broadcast regulation has been neither as heavy-handed nor as overtly partisan as it could be.

## Ad Hoc Policymaking

Political manipulation of the media is often covert, with basic value choices obscured by the rhetoric of the public interest. Moreover, fundamental choices are made more difficult in a system of regulation that is an ongoing process, that moves from case to case, that only occasionally attempts to codify what has been created piecemeal or correct inadvertent missteps. The case approach to lawmaking has the advantage of relating rules to real experience, to concrete facts, and to interested—usually outspoken—parties. It has the defects of missing the big picture, failing to anticipate technological developments, overlooking the interests of those not represented in adjudicatory proceedings.

The Communications Act of 1934, itself largely based on the Radio Act of 1927, continues as the basic framework for regulation, despite the advent of television, cable, satellite broadcasting, microwave transmission, videotext, teletext, and computer technologies. It should be noted that "the statutory scheme, although little changed by Congress since its inception, is not the product of a clear, full-blown theory of how to handle the special problem of broadcasting, but is a curiously ad hoc effort. . . ."[73]

Broadcast regulation has been characterized by the absence of a well-reasoned telecommunications policy. What passes for policy emerged from the deliberations of key congressional committees, particularly subcommittees of the Commerce Committees, actions of the FCC, its bureaucracy, and political appointees, and review by the courts, particularly the U.S. Circuit Court of Appeals for the District of Columbia. Content regulations like the Fairness Doctrine evolved as a result of administrative activism and congressional ambiguity.[74]

As in all political activities, the key question is "who gets what, when, and how."[75] But systematic consideration of such fundamentals is rare.[76] The key participants in allocating values in this field, aside from Congress, the FCC, and the Courts, have been the Executive Branch, particularly the White House, the industry groups long dominated by major broadcasting chains and networks, and citizens groups clamoring for a voice in what is aired.[77] "There is just no insulating the FCC from politics," according to Erwin G. Kransnow, Lawrence D. Longley, and Herbert A. Terry.[78]

According to a report prepared for President-elect John Kennedy in 1960, the FCC "has drifted, vacillated, and stalled in almost every major area. It seems incapable of policy planning, of disposing within a reasonable period of time the business before it, of fashioning procedures that are effective to deal with its problems."[79] More recently a congressional committee evaluated FCC performance and pointed to several defects:

(1) insufficient public representation to offset the assiduous attention paid by commercial interests,
(2) failure to anticipate or keep pace with technical and commercial developments in communications,
(3) a deficiency of technical expertise for analysis of complex issues resulting in failure to develop facts basic to regulation of the broadcasting and telephone industries, and
(4) inertial acceptance of prevailing patterns.[80]

Although opponents of the regulation of the content of material aired on radio and television often portray the issue as a zero sum conflict, where broadcasters lose if regulators win, and vice versa, the reality is neither as simplistic nor as bipolar. Broadcasters and regulators often share mutual goals. For example, case-by-case adjudication of complaints about broadcasters' compliance with fairness and equal time rules is very intrusive. On the other hand, overall evaluation of station performance in general at license renewal time interferes less in the daily operation of stations. Yet many broadcasters prefer the FCC to resolve cases as they arise because this permits stations to correct misdeeds and avoid a devastating result in a license renewal hearing. In effect, by playing it safe, the broadcast industry has endorsed more vigorous government oversight. Broadcasters fight the rules in principle while accepting methods of enforcement which aggravate First Amendment problems.

Many broadcasters do not even fight on the principle. After all, the rules are not particularly onerous for a licensee who carefully stays away from controversial topics, keeps a docile news department, rejects issue advertisements, and offers a steady diet of bland programming. That is a comfortable course of conduct, and while the public may not hear a robust debate, the station may reap huge profits.

By keeping within the letter, if not the spirit, of the Fairness Doctrine, a broadcaster protects himself from challenges to his license. The former chairman of the House subcommittee concerned with broadcast regulation, Lionel Van Deerlin, once remarked on how stations at license renewal time prepare extensive explanations of how they've met all the FCC's requirements, including provision of the Fairness Doctrine. This "documented litany" of compliance helps stations win license renewals, Van Deerlin said.

> "I don't understand all this criticism of the Fairness Doctrine," the manager of a prosperous TV property told me once at a public meeting. "We operate very well under its provisions. We like it."
> You bet he does. Like so much of present law, the Fairness Doctrine provides one more defensive weapon against license poachers.[81]

If the conflict over regulation isn't always a battle, and it rarely is a zero sum contest between two parties, it still sparks a lively debate. Perhaps that's because no situation arises in which only the regulators and the regulated have an interest. There are many more participants in this "subgovernment," as Nicholas Johnson once characterized it.[82] It includes broadcast lobbyists, communications lawyers, citizen activists, consultants, engineers, public relations experts, and the trade press, in addition to the bureaucrats and broadcasters.

But how has a regulatory system functioned that is characterized by pressure groups, piecemeal decisionmaking, and intense politicking? How has the public interest fared? Who gets what, when and how?

## Conclusion

The history of broadcast regulation reflects the struggle over a new form of power—the power to inform, inflame, persuade—*electronically*. The course of regulation has been shaped by America's uneasiness with unrestrained power. It has manifested itself in policies designed to prevent broadcasters from using their frequencies for partisan purposes.

The system of regulation reflects a tug of war between two powerful elites—the elected politicians in Congress and the broadcasters themselves. While broadcasters have been successful in utilizing the system to protect their economic interests and maximize profits, the politicians have been triumphant in assuring that the power of radio and television is not turned against them, that they have access to the airwaves, that stations must be neutral in selling or giving time to candidates.

In sum, the regulatory system has permitted established broadcasters to reap great profits and establishment politicians to preserve political power. Of course, it's not always so neat, as the frequent battles suggest. But when the power struggle is played out in Congress, the courts and the Federal Communications Commission, this overtly political process is masked by concepts such as "the public interest."

Broadcasters recognize the FCC's power. That licenses are seldom revoked does not mean that licensees are not cognizant of the commission's power to silence stations. This can affect broadcasters' behavior. After all, nuclear deterrence does not require occasional nuclear warfare. In the cold war over broadcast regulation, the feds have all the nukes.

## References

1. Steven J. Simmons, *The Fairness Doctrine and the Media* (Berkeley, University of California Press, 1978), p. 24, quoting views of Rep. Johnson. The Simmons material is useful for an understanding of the evolution of the Fairness Doctrine, and was helpful in the compilation of this survey.
2. *Hoover* v. *City Intercity Radio Co.,* 52 App. D.C. 339, 286 F. 1003 (D.C. Cir. 1923); *United States* v. *Zenith Radio Corp.,* 12 F.2d 614 (N.D. Ill. 1926).
3. 35 Op. Att'y Gen. 126 (1926).
4. Francis Chase, Jr., *Sound and Fury,* p. 21 (1942).
5. *Red Lion Broadcasting Co.* v. *FCC,* 995 U.S. 367 (1969).

6. First National Radio Conference, minutes, pp. 4–5 (1922).

7. Simmons, op. cit., pp. 19–22.

8. Id. at 58, note 67, quoting views of Rep. Davis.

9. Id. at 59, note 79, quoting views of Sen. Howell.

10. Tibor R. Machan, "One Sided Fairness," *Barrons,* April 22, 1968, p. 9, quoting the Radio League of America.

11. Id. at 21; *Fourth National Radio Conference, Proceedings and Recommendations for Regulation of Radio,* p. 6.

12. 395 U.S. 367.

13. Simmons, op. cit., pp. 22–26.

14. *Staff Study of the House Committee on Interstate and Foreign Commerce, Legislative History of the Fairness Doctrine,* 90th Cong. 2d Sess. at p. 197 (1968).

15. *H.R. Rep. No.* 2106, 72nd Cong. 2d Sess. at p. 4 (1933).

16. *FCC* v. *Pottsville Broadcasting Co.,* 309 U.S. 134, 137 (1940).

17. S.3285, Sec 315(a), 73d Cong., 2d Sess. (1934), discussed in Simmons, op. cit., pp. 28–30.

18. Simmons, op. cit., pp. 28–31.

19. *Applicability of Fairness Doctrine in the Handling of Controversial Issues of Public Importance,* App. B. 29 Fed. Reg. 10416, at p. 10425 (1969).

20. 2 F.R.C. *Annual Report* at p. 155 (1928).

21. 3 F.R.C. 36 (1929). The action was affirmed on other grounds, *Chicago Federation of Labor* v. *FCC,* 41, F.2d 422 (D.C. Cir. 1930).

22. *KEKB Broadcasting Assn.* v. *FRC,* 47 F.2d 670 (D.C. Cir. 1931).

23. Id. at 672.

24. Erik Barnouw, *The Golden Web: A History of Broadcasting in the United States,* Vol. II, p. 29 (1968).

25. *Trinity Methodist Church, S.* v. *FRC,* 62 F.2d 850 (D.C. Cir.), *cert. denied,* 284 U.S. 685 (1932).

26. *Mayflower Broadcasting Corp.,* 8 F.C.C. 333 (1941).

27. Id. at 339.

28. Id. at 340.

29. Id.

30. *Report on Editorializing by Broadcast Licensees,* 13 F.C.C. 1246, 1249 (1949).

31. Id. at 1246, 1249.

32. *Columbia Broadcasting System, Inc.* 26 F.C.C. 715 (1959).

33. Simmons, op. cit., pp. 46–51.

34. 47 U.S.C. Section 312 (a) (7).

35. *CBS* v. *FCC,* 453 U.S. 367 (1981).

36. Id. at 377–382, 388, 413.

37. See Henry Geller and Jane H. Yurow, "The Reasonable Access Provision (312) (a) (7) of the Communications Act: Once More Down the Slippery Slope," 34 *Federal Communications Law Journal,* 389, 414 (1982).

38. 47 U.S.C. Section 315 (b) (1).

39. *Broadcasting,* July 17, 1978, p. 28.

40. 453 U.S. 367 (1981).

41. 412 U.S. 94 (1973).

42. Erwin G. Krasnow, Lawrence D. Longley, and Herbert A. Terry, *Politics of Broadcast Regulation,* 3rd Edition (New York, St. Martin's Press, 1982), p. 18.

43. Id.

44. *Administrative Regulation: A Study in Representation of Interests* (University of Chicago Press, 1942), p. 16.

45. Marver Bernstein, *Regulating Business by Independent Commission* (Princeton University Press, 1955), p. 279.

46. Krasnow, Longley, and Terry, op. cit., p. 49.

47. Id., pp. 176–187.

48. See Television Assignment Amendment of Section 3.606 of the Commission Rules and Regulations (Sixth Report & Order), 41 FCC 148 (1952); Mark S. Fowler & Daniel L. Brenner, *A Marketplace Approach to Broadcast Regulation,* 60 Texas Law Review 1, 17–18 (1982).

49. Office of Network Study, FCC, Second Interim Report, Television Network Program Procurement 27–30 (1965).

50. David L. Bazelon, 31 *Federal Communications Law Journal* 201 (1979), reprinted in Daniel L. Brenner and William L. Rivers, (Eds.), *Free but Regulated* (Ames, Iowa State University Press, 1982), p. 55.

51. Krasnow, Longley, and Terry, op. cit., p. 26, citing views of Commissioner Johnson.

52. House Subcommittee on Communications of the Committee on Interstate & Foreign Commerce, 94th Cong. 2d Sess., *Cable Television: Promise Versus Regulatory Performance* (1976).

53. Cable Television Syndicated Program Exclusivity Rules, 71 FCC 2d 951 (1979); Inquiry into the Economic Relationship between Television Broadcasting and Cable Television, 71 FCC 2d 632 (1979); Cable Television Syndicated Program Exclusivity Rules, 79 FCC 2d 652 (1980), affirmed *sub nom, Malrite TV* v. *FCC,* 652 F.2d 1140 (D.C. Cir. 1981).

54. Bruce M. Owen, *Economics and Freedom of Expression: Media Structure and the First Amendment* (Cambridge, Mass., Ballinger, 1975), excerpted in Brenner and Rivers, op. cit., pp. 47–48.

55. *Washington Post,* July 24, 1977, p. G1.

56. Ben H. Bagdikian, "Newspaper Mergers—The Final Phase," *Columbia Journalism Review,* March/April 1977, p. 18.

57. Max Kampelman, "The Power of the Press: A Problem for Our Democracy," 6 *Policy Review,* p. 7 (1978).

58. Quoted in Irving Kristol, "The Underdeveloped Profession," *The Public Interest* (Winter 1967), pp. 47–50.

59. Kevin Phillips, *Mediacracy* (Doubleday, 1975), p. 25.

60. Abbott Washburn, "Regulating the Airwaves Is Not the Same as Censoring Them," excerpted in Brenner and Rivers, op. cit., p. 181.

61. Id. at 186.

62. *FCC* v. *Pacifica Foundation,* 438 U.S. 726, 748 (1978).

63. Id. at 731–741.

64. "Dirty Words and the Airwaves—A Political Tower of Babel," p. 25.

65. Id. at 26.

66. *National Broadcasting Co.,* 14 FCC 2d 713, 720 (1968), (Johnson, dissenting).
67. Id. at 721.
68. *Office of Communication of United Church of Christ* v. *FCC,* 359 F.2d 994 (D.C. Cir. 1966).
69. Id.
70. *Brandywine-Main Line Radio, Inc.,* 27 FCC 2d 565 (1971), aff'd 473 F.2d 16 (D.C. Cir. 1972), *cert. denied* 412 U.S. 922 (1973).
71. Lionel Van Deerlin, "The Regulators and Broadcast News," in Marvin Barrett (Ed.), *Broadcast Journalism* (New York, Everett House, 1982), p. 209.
72. Id. at 207–208.
73. Kalven, *Broadcasting, Public Policy, and the First Amendment,* 10 *Journal of Law and Economics* 15, 26 (1967).
74. See Note, *"The Fairness Doctrine: Fair to Whom?,"* 30 *Cleveland State Law Review* 485, 490 (1981).
75. Harold D. Lasswell, *The Political Writings of Harold D. Lasswell* (New York, Free Press, 1951) 295, 309.
76. For an exception, see the excellent treatment in Erwin G. Krasnow, Lawrence D. Longley, and Herbert A. Terry, *The Politics of Broadcast Regulation,* 3rd Ed. (New York, St. Martin's Press, 1982).
77. Id., pp. 33–86.
78. Id., p. 34.
79. James M. Landis, *Report on Regulatory Agencies to the President-Elect,* published by Subcommittee on Administrative Practice and Procedure of the Senate Committee on the Judiciary, 86th Cong. 2d Sess. (1960), p. 53.
80. Subcommittee on Oversight and Investigations of the House Committee on Interstate and Foreign Commerce, *Federal Regulation and Regulatory Reform,* 94th Cong., 2d Sess. (1976), p. 2.
81. "The Regulators and Broadcast News," in Marvin Barrett (Ed.), *Broadcast Journalism* (New York, Everett House, 1982), p. 213.
82. "A New Fidelity to the Regulatory Ideal," 59 *Georgetown Law Journal* 883–884 (1971).

# THREE

# The Day-by-Day Operation of the Fairness Doctrine

IN FISCAL YEAR 1980, citizens brought 21,563 Fairness Doctrine and political broadcasting matters to the FCC. Many of these complaints came during the election campaign, for candidates and their supporters, interest groups, and advocates of various propositions contacted the FCC by letter and telephone to complain of unfairness and unequal treatment.

Of those inquiries, 11,262 dealt with Equal Opportunities and Reasonable Access Questions regarding campaigns by candidates for public office. The remaining 10,301 were Fairness Doctrine matters. The FCC found cause in only 28 of these cases to even ask the broadcaster to respond to the complaint. Only six cases were decided against the stations, and admonitions were issued.

Thus, out of more than 20,000 complaints, broadcasters "lost" only six.

The regulations affecting broadcasting are badly misunderstood by most of the people affected by them. Confusion abounds, even though no other FCC policies have attracted as much attention as the fairness and equal-time rules.

Those who misunderstand the Fairness Doctrine include people who watch TV and become upset when they think a program is unfair; organized interest groups wanting to use the Doctrine to get their viewpoint on the air; politicians seeking publicity, and the broadcasters who are supposed to abide by the rules in their daily programming. Only specialists in communications law, broadcasters who have been involved in extensive litigation, and representatives of groups that routinely use the doctrine seem to grasp the complexities and difficulties inherent in Fairness Doctrine cases.

For those who feel a station has failed to live up to its obligation, the route to Washington is open. The FCC itself does not police the fairness of radio and television stations; a complaint must be initiated by an individual or a group. As we shall see, the complainant has a heavy burden, and only the most determined and well-documented complaints stand much chance of success on the Eastern Front of the regulatory wars. What follows is an attempt to describe and demystify the complaint process as it works in practice. The information is drawn from interviews with representatives of the FCC, broadcasters, complainants, and advocates of the Fairness Doctrine.

The FCC expects to receive about 10,000 Fairness Doctrine complaints in an election year, and about 6,000 in a nonelection year. Such figures are often cited by organizations such as the National Association of Broadcasters (NAB) and by Fairness Doctrine writers as evidence of the number of complaints "handled" each year by the FCC. The figures are a bit misleading, however, because telephone calls are included in the complaint statistics. This problem is compounded by the fact that the FCC figures make no distinction between the telephone inquiries and actual complaints. FCC documents indicate that 80 to 90 percent of Fairness Doctrine "complaints" are in fact telephone calls, and such calls do not result in any FCC action against a station unless buttressed by extensive documentation.

Of the 10,000 fairness complaints the FCC receives in an election year, only 1,000 to 2,000 are letters.

What happens to a complaint letter at the FCC? When it arrives at the FCC, it is opened and read in the Control Section and assigned a correspondence number. The call letters of the station or network involved are put on a control slip stapled to the letter. The letter is then sent to the appropriate section of the commission.

A sheaf of letters is delivered daily to the Fairness/Political Broadcasting Branch of the Complaints and Compliance Division of the commission's Broadcast Bureau. Each letter is logged in again, this time by the control number, the date it was received by the Control Section, the date it was received by the Fairness Branch, the date on the letter, the writer's name, and the station's call letters. A broadcast analyst or a legal technician reads the letters and makes initial dispositions.

About half of all complaint letters never get past this point. Copies of letters addressed to stations and sent to the FCC for information are put into NRN files (No Response Necessary), where they are filed under the writer's name. Other letters that make general complaints not addressed to particular stations or networks often go into the NRN files as well. And the usual quota of "crank" letters meet this fate.

About half the remaining letters are answered by sending out a Form 8330-FD. This is a five-page document telling the complainant that there is a lot more to making a Fairness Doctrine complaint than just writing to the FCC. The form makes it clear that anyone who tries to make a complaint stick faces a very rough ride.[1] Most people who receive this form are never heard from again.

That's because the commission's rules require a complainant to specify with precision what he or she objects to and why. To relieve broadcasters of the burden of disproving vague complaints, the FCC requires that complaints provide specific information about the following:

(1) the name of the station or network involved;
(2) the controversial issue of public importance on which a view was presented;
(3) the date and time of its broadcast;
(4) the basis for [the] claim that the issue is controversial and of public importance;
(5) an accurate summary of the view [or] views broadcast;
(6) the basis for [the] claim that the station or network has not broadcast contrasting views on the issue or issues in its overall programming; and
(7) whether the station or network has afforded or has expressed the intention to afford, a reasonable opportunity for the presentation of contrasting viewpoints on that issue.[2]

If a letter appears to raise a question that the analyst or legal technician cannot or should not deal with, the letter is passed on to the Branch Chief for assignment to one of four staff lawyers. The lawyer assigned may simply send out a Form 8330-FD, in which case the complainant usually joins the ranks of those who don't write back.

Occasionally more information will be requested from the complainant, but more often a letter is sent out informing the complainant that he or she has not made a *prima facie* case and that therefore the FCC is not going to proceed with the matter. The complainant could provide more information and try again, but this seldom happens.

The complainant also has the right to appeal any decision by the staff to the full Federal Communications Commission membership for a review. In more formal cases, which the staff designates as "rulings," this right of appeal is pointed out in the final paragraph of the staff letter rejecting the complaint. As Milton O. Gross, Branch Chief, noted, technically every letter is a ruling in that it disposes of a case, but that designation is reserved for more important or involved cases. A review of the FCC files indicates that letters are called rulings when a station has been asked to respond to a complaint, when a staff decision has been appealed to the full FCC, or when an attorney has represented the complainant.

The letters of complaint and the FCC staff responses are filed in public files under the station or network call letters. In most cases the station has not been asked to respond to the complaint or even been sent copies of the correspondence.

This accounts for about 99.5 percent of all Fairness Doctrine complaints the FCC receives.

If a complainant builds a strong enough case, and complies with all the requirements discussed elsewhere in this book, then the FCC will ask the station or network involved to reply. The complainant may file a response to the station's reply, but the station gets the last word. The FCC will then decide whether or not a Fairness Doctrine violation has occurred, based solely on the record before it. The initial decision is made at the staff level and a right of appeal lies to the commissioners.

The effectiveness of this right of appeal is questionable, given that the staff decision was upheld in all 18 Fairness cases appealed to the full commission from 1979 to 1981.

If the losing party is still unhappy with the result, he can file an appeal with the federal courts.

Henry Geller noted that in 1973 the time between airing the program in question and final resolution of complaints to the FCC was approximately eight months.[3] A review of recent FCC rulings indicates the average time for resolution is now more than a year.


## Sanctions

If all procedural matters are complied with, and the FCC concludes that a violation of the Fairness Doctrine has occurred, the commission typically does one of two things: (1) It admonishes the station in a letter that is placed in the station's file and theoretically considered at license renewal time. However, such letters are meaningless unless some other major offense jeopardizes a license.[4] (2) The FCC writes to the station or network, asking the violator how it intends to comply with the Fairness Doctrine regarding that particular issue.

One case concerned a ballot proposition to repeal an existing rent control law in California. Between mid-March and mid-May 1980, KKHI (AM) in San Francisco had aired 135 spots in favor of Proposition 10. The vote was scheduled for June 30, and apparently nothing advocating defeat of Proposition 10 had been aired. On behalf of Californians Against

Initiative Fraud (CAIF), Robert DeVries filed a Fairness Doctrine complaint, stating that KKHI had ignored a letter of April 22 requesting free airtime for spots against Proposition 10, and that the operations manager of the station had been abusive in a May 5 telephone conversation, hanging up on the CAIF representative.

On May 9, the FCC asked KKHI to reply to the complaint, giving the station four days to answer. KKHI replied, stating that (1) the station had not received the CAIF letter, (2) the CAIF representative was the one who had been abusive on the telephone, (3) CAIF had been offered time to oppose the ballot initiative with one spot for every five paid ads, running in comparable time periods, (4) CAIF had not yet sent over the spot tapes so it wasn't the station's fault nothing had been aired, and (5) the opposition to Proposition 10 would get coverage on KKHI news.

On May 23, the FCC wrote KKHI, saying that its answer wasn't good enough, noting that the amount of news coverage was unspecified, and it was unclear whether the offered five-to-one ratio included the 135 spots aired before the complaint or just the spots scheduled between the time of the complaint and the June 30 vote. The station was also upbraided for not living up to its responsibility to seek out opposing views. The FCC said the fact that the group hadn't yet provided a spot tape was no excuse for unbalanced programming on Proposition 10. KKHI was asked what it intended to do to live up to its responsibilities under the Fairness Doctrine.

On May 28, one month before the scheduled vote, KKHI informed the FCC that it had given CAIF 42 free spots. The station said it had provided the free spots even though it "had requested CAIF to demonstrate to KKHI that it could not pay for them. KKHI's request for the financial data was prompted by the fact that CAIF had paid for considerable advertising in the print media." The result was a ratio of pro-con ads of almost 1.4 to 1 during the last month of the campaign. As well, KKHI said it was airing a 30-second comment against Proposition 10 made by a local newspaper editor, and the station planned to air a 55-second statement by a local minister whose parish included many older, minority parishoners who would be adversely affected by Proposition 10. The minister's statement was to be aired 18 times. The FCC acknowledged that KKHI's programming satisfied both CAIF and the FCC.

Even if the FCC finds a broadcaster in violation, it is apparent that negotiations between the complainant and the station are critical to resolving the issue. In some cases things don't work out as well as they did with KKHI.

Two affiliated Texas stations, KLRN and KNRU, became embroiled in controversy over the management of the stations themselves. What started out as a dispute over KLRN's refusal to air a program on natural childbirth turned into an 8-month investigation of the station's management, including allegations of fraud, and an FCC inquiry. Six employees had testified before the FCC under a promise of no reprisals from the station. But according to local newspaper reports, three were fired, one resigned, and another was disciplined and ordered not to associate with critics of the management. On October 5, 1979, KLRN management aired a half-hour show called "KLRN Under Fire," during which station personnel took questions from reporters and call-in listeners. No statements from those opposing management were allowed.

A long-time critic of the station complained to the FCC under the Fairness Doctrine. On May 1, 1980, the FCC affirmed a violation of the doctrine. To meet its responsibilities, KLRN negotiated a deal with the complainant. At first KLRN offered a half-hour for statements opposing station management. A half-hour question and answer period was later added, but KLRN management adamantly refused to go on the show. The complainant accepted the terms, but the planned show fell apart because station critics and reporters refused to participate unless the station management could be questioned on the air.

The station itself tried to get eight spokespersons for the show, under the same conditions, but no one would agree to participate. The complainant wrote to the FCC, asking it to assist him. On January 29, 1981, the FCC wrote the complainant, telling him that he had agreed to the original terms and was stuck with them. If he refused to accept the station's reasonable offer within 30 days, the FCC considered the case closed.

The FCC is not powerless in such situations. It simply chooses to let the parties work things out themselves as much as possible.

The FCC can deny renewal of a license, issue a short-term renewal (keeping the station on tenterhooks), temporarily suspend a license or even revoke a license outright—all for a violation of the Fairness Doctrine. Milton Gross, chief of the Fairness/Political Broadcasting Branch, surmises that forfeitures or fines might even be imposed, but this has never been done (except in cases involving a personal attack).

In no instance has the FCC revoked a station's license solely because of Fairness Doctrine violations. As mentioned previously, the FCC did revoke the license of WXUR, Media, Pennsylvania, in 1970. The courts upheld the revocation, but only partly on Fairness Doctrine grounds. WXUR was a conservative religious station that aired such telephone calls as the following exchange:

> HOST: And who do you think is behind all this obscenity that daily floods our mails, my dear?
> CALLER: Well, frankly, Tom, I think it is the Jewish people.
> HOST: You bet your life it is.[5]

The license of WLBT-TV, Jackson, Mississippi, was denied a renewal because of racist programming. As noted earlier, it was a federal court that ordered the license renewal denied, not the FCC.

WLBT's license renewal was challenged in 1964 by the United Church of Christ, among others, on the basis that the licensee had not acted in the public interest—discriminating against blacks in both entertainment and public affairs programs. Interruptions of the Huntley-Brinkley Nightly News' civil rights coverage were cited, as was WLBT's refusal to carry local programs dealing with the integration issue. When James Meredith tried to enroll as the first black student at the University of Mississippi, WLBT's general manager (a prominent member of the all-white Jackson Citizens Council) went on TV, exhorting whites to rally at the campus and "stand shoulder to shoulder with Governor Barnett and keep the nigra out of Ole Miss."

Fred Friendly wrote, "There is no record that during the civil rights struggle any black was ever invited to appear in a discussion on a controversial issue," and that both children's programming and religious programming were blatantly segregationist.[6]

The FCC decided to extend the WLBT license for a year, but the Court of Appeals said the FCC was wrong to grant the extension, and sent the case back. The FCC still didn't revoke the license. And when the case came before the Court of Appeals again, the court ordered WLBT's license revoked—five years after the original renewal hearing.[7]

The sanctions available to the FCC are powerful, but clearly the FCC applies only the most modest reprimands in Fairness Doctrine cases. As Geller notes, "Even if the broadcaster is found to have acted in good faith but unreasonably in some particular instance, he is neither fined nor has his license put in jeopardy—he is simply required to present some additional 'speech.'"[8] Yet, as one NAB attorney put it, "The broadcaster's perception is that his license is at risk" whenever a fairness issue arises, and stations, particularly in small markets, want to avoid any FCC involvement in a fairness complaint.[9]

The next section traces a typical Fairness Doctrine complaint through the FCC process.

## A Typical Case at the FCC

This case is typical in several respects: An organized group's representative has discussions and correspondence with the broadcaster; a complaint is filed; some kind of access offer is made; lawyers get involved; the FCC asks the station to respond to the complaint; each side has another chance to make its case; then the FCC decides.

Ed Armstrong, a professional engineer and an officer of Abate, a national organization for motorcycling, brought a Fairness Doctrine complaint against CBS over an episode of "30 Minutes," titled "Motorcycle Safety." The episode was about 10 minutes long, reported by Christopher Glenn and Betsy Aaron. Abate argued that the issue of mandatory helmet wearing was unfairly covered. Following are highlights of the negotiations and complaint process:

September 22, 1979:

"Motorcycle Safety" airs. The reporter introduces the episode with "The motorcycle is macho—a two-wheeled fury that roars with power and speed, as long as nothing gets in the way of the bike and rider."

Part of the show's transcript is reproduced below:

GLENN: Michael Bethke, also a quadriplegic because of a motorcycle accident, has had seven major operations, faces seven more, and is trying to regain his ability to speak.

DANASE MALKMUS: Okay, let's try "mother" and "father." (Michael Bethke making an effort to speak) Okay . . .

GLENN: Therapist Danase Malkmus is a specialist in disorders caused by brain damage.

MALKMUS: Think about it and try again.

(To Glenn): This is my 10th year of working with head injury, and in many, many of our cases, maybe half, motorcycles are the cause. I wish they could be banned. And I'm really tired of seeing young people come in so broken and so injured. This shouldn't have happened to him—to any of these young people.

(Sound of motorcycle engines)

GLENN: 1976—a massive protest was staged in Washington pressuring Congress to repeal regulations requiring the states to have compulsory helmet laws. As a result of this and local pressures, 26 states dropped their helmet laws. In 1977, 4,067 people died on motorcycles—a 24 percent increase in deaths over 1976, against only a 4 percent increase in registrations. Yet, despite these facts, many, many cyclists simply don't believe in helmets.

MOTORCYCLIST: What you do when you put that on, it's like going in the downtown driving, put blinders on and earmuffs. You know, you're—you're helping yourself, maybe, if you get hit, but you're increasing your odds of getting hit by wearing it.

GLENN: Were you wearing a helmet at the time that you had the accident? (Head gesture) No?

When you had the accident, Mike, were you wearing a protective helmet?

MIKE CORSINI: No. No, I wasn't.

JON McKIBBON: The data regarding helmets is—is just overpowering. In my opinion, anybody that rides a motorcycle out of their garage without a helmet on is a fool. And I . . .

GLENN: Jon McKibbon held the world's speed record for motorcycles from 1971 through 1977. He is a respected engineer, and is a member of the University of Southern California's accident research team.

McKIBBON: Helmets cause no problems. They do not cause injuries. They do not cause people to have more crashes. And they do afford an enormous degree of protection to the head. Generally speaking, whatever you hit with the motorcycle you will hit with your body. It's kind of like out there playing football with a bunch of automobiles.

GLENN: Using dummies, UCLA photographed in detail what happens when motorcycles collide with cars. The rider absorbs the full impact of the crash with his body. Typically, the rider is launched over the handle bars and becomes a human missile. In this test, at 40 miles per hour, the helmet failed and both the rider and the driver were destroyed.

September 26, 1979:

On behalf of Abate, Armstrong writes to J. Heller, executive producer of "30 Minutes," stating that the show was unfair because "The program used the Ch. McCarthy-E. Bergen approach . . . a dummy took the side of the opposition to the helmet law, a city slicker took the government point of view of forcing helmets on everyone who rides."

Armstrong also alleged the show chose to "ignore the causes of accidents, not the least of which is the lack of training for the many new riders." Armstrong noted that New York State had the highest motorcycle accident rate in spite of its mandatory helmet law. Other facts contradicting information in the show were also offered.

Armstrong said the subject was a major controversy and that he had testified "before six different state legislative bodies and twice before committees in Washington.

Armstrong requested a copy of the script and "the procedure to arrange for" a rebuttal "using informed persons."

November 28, 1979:

Marjorie Holyoak, CBS Director of Audience Services, writes to Abate stating that the report was "an accurate and objective look at motorcycle safety and included interviews" with those opposing helmets.

December 6, 1979:

"30 Minutes" executive producer Joel Heller writes to Abate, stating that the letter of complaint had been sent to the program "Your Turn—Letters to CBS"—"This is a program which allows viewers time on the air to express their dissatisfaction or appreciation for CBS News broadcasts. I'm sure they will give your comments careful consideration with an eye to having you on the program as a guest. But that's up to them."

January 31, 1980:

Abate complaint submitted to the FCC.

February, 1980:

Abate submits magazine articles, newspaper clips, and copies of testimony before legislative committees concerning motorcycle safety and compulsory helmets. Abate also marshals support in letters to the FCC from the American Motorcycle Association, United Sidecar Association, Inc., the Motorcycle Safety Foundation, individual cyclists, and medical evidence from doctors and a hospital.

April 28, 1980:

Abate writes followup letter to FCC asking what is happening to the complaint.

May 8, 1980:

Abate forwards transcript of the program to FCC, along with other correspondence with CBS.

July 10, 1980:

Abate refuses an offer from CBS to tape a 45-second response that might or might not be used on "Letters to 30 Minutes." Armstrong says 90 seconds to two minutes would be necessary to make his points, in any event.

September 17, 1980:

Almost one year to the day after the original broadcast, the FCC writes to CBS asking for a response to the complaint.

October, 1980:

CBS replies to the complaint through its attorneys, arguing that the complaint should be rejected because: (1) The issue of helmet wearing was a sub-issue of motorcycle safety generally, and does not qualify for Fairness Doctrine treatment; (2) The issue of motorcycle safety and helmets is not a controversial issue of public importance that is the subject of vigorous debate; (3) Abate failed to prove lack of balance in CBS's overall programming relating to the issue; and (4) CBS aired 30 seconds in the segment showing an interview with someone pro-helmets and 15 seconds showing an interview with someone anti-helmets, so the show gave a reasonable opportunity for contrasting views.

Citing articles in the Chicago papers, Abate argues that the issue is controversial, and suggests more programming.

April 13, 1981:

Approximately one year and seven months after the program aired, the FCC decides the case, noting that there were 30 seconds pro-helmet and 15 seconds anti-helmet, and "From the information presently before us we cannot determine that CBS acted unreasonably in its determination that both sides of the issue had been presented on the broadcast 'Motorcycle Safety.' Accordingly, no further action is warranted on this aspect of your complaint."

In its decision, the FCC did not address the major complaint in this case; i.e., did the televised discussion of mandatory safety helmets provide balanced coverage of the issue? Instead, the FCC totaled the amount of time devoted to each side of the issue and decided that the 2:1 ratio provided a reasonable opportunity for presenting contrasting views. Using the "stopwatch" approach to fairness has led to accusations that the FCC hides behind procedural devices and dodges the real issue of whether a controversial topic has received balanced coverage.

For its part, the FCC declines to look at the quality of presentation, arguing that this would intrude on the editing function and infringe on the broadcaster's discretion. Hence, the use of the stopwatch to figure out how much time each side got, regardless of how the time was used.

However, as Geller points out,[10] even figuring out times with a stopwatch involves the FCC in editorial judgments, deciding whether a piece of programming is pro, con, or neutral on a topic. This is a very thorny issue when "image" ads are involved. The stopwatch method becomes even more difficult to implement when many presentations are involved and when there are more than two "sides" to an issue. Questions of balance are especially troubling when time of day, frequency of broadcast, and audience composition and size come into play. For example, how is a 5-minute midmorning interview to balance against five spot ads in prime time? In a 1971 case, the Wilderness Society complained that Esso commercials on the Alaska pipeline were unbalanced.[11] Esso ads were countered in a total *time* ratio of 2:1 on NBC, but the Esso ads were broadcast on that network with a *frequency* of almost 5:1. The FCC rejected the complaint, but even the commissioners disagreed about how to calculate balance in this case.

The next section will review some of the complaints that were successful at the FCC.

## Successful Complaints

The Telecommunications Research and Action Center recently compared the low number of succesful complaints with the total number of radio and TV stations. It estimated that the likelihood is about one-tenth of one percent that a broadcaster would be found in violation of the fairness and political broadcasting rules in a given year.

Steven Simmons notes that "the average complainant truly had only about a one in a thousand chance" of success.[12] The Simmons study covered fiscal years 1973 to 1976, in which there were 49,801 Fairness Doctrine complaints.[13] For each thousand, there were four station inquiries and only one ruling adverse to a station.

Since 1976 even these odds have been reduced. The odds of success are about one in 2,000, according to recent figures. If a complaint comes from an individual and not an organized group with legal counsel, the chance of success is virtually nil.

As noted above, in 1980 approximately 10,000 complaints produced only six adverse rulings. In 1981 (a nonelection year) there were 5,932 fairness complaints.[14] Only 30 rulings were issued; 27 were in favor of the broadcasters.

The three rulings against broadcasters all concerned inadequate identification of sponsors of issue advertising. No rulings against broadcasters in 1981 were based solely on programming imbalance.

One station admonished was KERO-TV in Bakersfield, California. The station aired the show "Energy Options for Tomorrow" three times, as a "special report." The program was provided free to the station by DWJ Associates, a New York advertising firm. The KERO public affairs director had screened the tape and decided to use it. KERO management said it was unaware that Mobil Oil Corporation had paid for the program, or even that it was a pronuclear piece, until the complainant brought it to the station's attention. KERO promptly scheduled an hour-and-a-half program of antinuclear opinion, invited the complainant to appear on the air, and acknowledged its error. The FCC admonished KERO for not listing Mobil as the sponsor on the air and in its public files, but took no further action.[15]

WTAX-AM in Illinois was admonished for identifying an ad sponsor as the Concerned Taxpayers of Illinois' 21st Congressional District. The

FCC said "such identification does not inform the public by whom it is being persuaded."[16] The ads had called attention to three public housing construction contracts that apparently were handed out to firms that were not the lowest bidders. The ads began, "What do you think of spending $175,917 of government money and getting approximately nothing in return?" The advertisements were placed by an agency that identified the sponsor as an Illinois taxpayers group, but the ads apparently were paid for by a disgruntled businessman from Missouri.[17]

The third station slapped on the wrist in 1981 was KCOS-TV in El Paso. The main thrust of the complaint was "staging" of a news documentary that wasn't adequately identified as a political advertisement. County employees posed as jail prisoners in a minidocumentary produced by a group in favor of a bond issue to improve the jail. The television audience was not told that the "prisoners" were county jail employees. The group that sponsored the production was inadequately identified.

Even though KCOS equipment was used to make the show, the FCC staff decided, "We do not believe it would be an efficient use of the Commission's resources to pursue this matter further."[18]

On appeal to the full commission, the staff decision was upheld. But the FCC did admonish the station for not identifying the sponsor both before and after the piece aired.

### Why Complaints Fail

Almost all fairness complaints to the FCC come from individual viewers—not groups, companies, or politicians. But the success rate for individuals is virtually zero. In 1981, only three individuals pushed their complaints to the ruling stage. All three individuals were attorneys themselves.

The major reason for the high failure rate is the FCC policy of discouraging complaints. The FCC has intentionally erected barriers of policy, procedure, and substance. Only those with a great deal of legal expertise, time, and resolve can negotiate those barriers. The FCC official in charge of enforcing the Fairness Doctrine, Milton O. Gross, says, "Of course we make it tough."[19]

The FCC sends Form 8330-FD to some of those who complain. It states in part:

> By placing high procedural burdens on complainants, station inquiries are made only when we receive thorough, well-documented complaints. We would place a heavy burden on broadcasters if we asked them to demonstrate compliance with the Fairness Doctrine based on every complaint. Broad-

casters might tend to avoid controversies and present only bland programming rather than subject themselves to that burden. Such a result would
clearly be contrary to the public interest, particularly because we seek to encourage vigorous coverage of the controversial issues of public importance
that face us every day.

Because the Fairness Doctrine applies to the overall programming of
a broadcaster, the complainant must state that he or she is a regular
listener or viewer, a person who consistently or as a matter of routine
listens to the news, public affairs, and other nonentertainment programs
carried by the station involved.[20]

If the complainant meets the substantial burden of making a prima
facie case, the commission staff asks the licensee to respond. The rules
provide that the broadcaster should state whether the issue specified in the
complaint "is a controversial issue of public importance, whether the program in question addressed that issue, and whether other programming
has been or will be presented on that issue."[21] The commission then determines whether the broadcaster's response is reasonable. The FCC's policy
is to grant broad discretion to licensees regarding these determinations.
The commission is not supposed to substitute its judgment for the broadcaster's; only to assure that the broadcaster made a reasonable, good-
faith judgment.[22] The commission and courts have stressed "ad infinitum
ad nauseum, that the key to the doctrine is no mystical formula but rather
the exercise of reasonable standards by the licensee."[23]

The FCC wears two hats: (1) as an arbiter of broadcasters' reasonableness and good-faith compliance with the Fairness Doctrine, and (2) as
gatekeeper to protect broadcasters from an intruding public and governmental interference so stations will not shy from controversial issues.
Both roles, however contradictory, are justified as advancing the public
interest. In balancing these roles, it seems clear that the FCC has chosen to
err on the side of its gatekeeper role, protecting broadcasters rather than
imposing notions of fairness, except in the most outrageous cases. Critics
have charged that the agency has come to exist for the benefit of the industry it was originally supposed to police; that the FCC now protects the
industry from the public instead of the other way around.

Another reason for the rejection of individuals' complaints is the
public's misunderstanding of the FCC's role in enforcing the Fairness
Doctrine, and of just what is covered by the Doctrine.

One major public misconception is that the FCC *investigates* complaints about unfair broadcasting and will *punish* broadcasters for one-
sided, inaccurate, or unfair programming.

Many letters in the FCC files begin with, "I want you to investigate
station . . . " What such writers do not understand is that the FCC does
not "investigate" in the usual sense of that word.

Unlike their counterparts at the Environmental Protection Agency, for example, FCC regulators do not build the case against a station for violation of rules, at least not of the Fairness Doctrine. The complaining viewer must build the case. Then the FCC decides if the case is strong enough to even bother the broadcaster for a reply.

The FCC applies a rather simple test, deciding if the broadcaster is (1) being unreasonable or (2) acting in bad faith. Only then will the FCC uphold a complaint. In effect, the FCC simply decides whether the station's position is so "off the wall" that no reasonable person could accept it. Unless unreasonableness or bad faith is proven, the FCC will not substitute its opinion for that of the broadcaster.

As will be explored in greater detail in Chapter 5, a broadcaster can avoid Fairness Doctrine problems if he can reasonably assert that the issue aired was not an important public controversy. The FCC often obliges; it has upheld decisions by broadcasters that husband beating is not a controversial issue of public importance,[24] nor is the depiction of Jesus Christ,[25] nor are questions about concentration and monopolization in the grain and beef industries.[26] In one case the FCC declined to decide on homosexuality.[27] The commission was forced to reconsider its stand later, but there still appear to be few cases in which the FCC would challenge a broadcaster's decision as unreasonable.

There is also an apparent misunderstanding that the FCC will scrutinize and crack down on unfairness in particular news reports. Perusal of the public files turns up many letters complaining about slanted or biased news reporting. But unless a viewer can produce testimony from a station insider showing intentional falsification of the news, the FCC policy is to do nothing. The policy requires implication of top management at the station, or in its news department, before the FCC takes any action.

This kind of evidence is called "extrinsic" evidence. Justification of the FCC policy is found in Form 8310-80, which is mailed out to those who complain about news coverage:

*FCC Not the Arbiter of "Truth" in News*

In the absence of such extrinsic evidence, the Commission has stressed that it cannot properly intervene. For example, the complaint is frequently received that "Commentator X has given a biased account or analysis of a news event" or that the true facts of the news event are different from those presented. In a democracy, dependent upon the fundamental rights of free speech and press, the FCC cannot authenticate the news that is broadcast nor should it try to do so. The Commission is not the national arbiter of the "truth" of a news event or judge of the wisdom, accuracy or adequacy with which it may have been handled on the air. Absent extrinsic evidence of deliberate distortion, the

FCC cannot properly investigate to determine whether an account or analysis of a news commentator is "biased" or "true."

In one case the FCC rejected a complaint that ABC's coverage was biased in favor of the PLO. The complainant had no extrinsic evidence and the FCC refused to order access to ABC news personnel, so the complainant had no chance to gather the evidence he needed. Martin Dann, Ph.D., had complained about the fall 1978 ABC "News Closeup" show titled "Terror in the Promised Land." Dann detailed 35 instances of error and said the show contained "gross and *deliberate* distortions" (emphasis in original), presenting only the PLO side of things:

> The film placed terrorism by the PLO in a more sympathetic context; only in Mr. [Frank] Reynolds' closing remarks, a brief, last-minute addition, was terrorism condemned. The adoption of the film by the PLO for their "Palestinian Solidarity Day" at the United Nations (in place of another film produced and financed by the UN) indicates the extent to which the film represented the case for the PLO.

Dann wrote the FCC in February 1979, attaching the correspondence between himself and ABC, and said, "I believe there is a violation of the 'fairness doctrine' in the response of ABC to my letters and I would appreciate it if you would investigate this matter." The FCC wrote back saying that it would not investigate, rejecting Dann's complaint for lack of extrinsic evidence. Dann tried again and was rebuffed by the FCC again. Finally, on June 4, 1979, Dann wrote to the FCC for help in uncovering extrinsic evidence about (among other things) any deals ABC might have had with the PLO relating to the content of "Terror in the Promised Land:"

> I have tried unsuccessfully to arrange an appointment with someone at ABC to discuss this program. They have been able to rebuff me, but I was hoping that the Commission would be able to provide such access.

> In my previous letter I raised several questions of what I believe to be, at least, improprieties. In view of the fact that I have been denied access to ABC's personnel, would it not be possible for the Commission to direct ABC to answer these questions specifically and directly?

The FCC ruled on July 27, 1979, against Dann:

> We cannot take any action on a claim of distortion in the absence of extrinsic evidence and it would be improper for us to even assist a complainant in attempting to obtain the evidence necessary to support a claim. Providing such assistance would merely be doing indirectly that which we stated we will not do directly.

Accordingly, the burden is on you to present extrinsic evidence that ABC deliberately distorted the news. In the absence of such evidence, it would not be appropriate for us to assist you in your investigation of this matter. . . . no further action is warranted on your complaint.

Two cases from the 1960s show what is still the FCC attitude. In 1968 the FCC received numerous complaints about ABC's coverage of riots at the Democratic National Convention in Chicago, including allegations of biased reporting. The commission declared it would not investigate the "truth" of what happened.[28]

In 1969, the FCC dealt with a complaint of news "staging" by WBBM-TV in Chicago, involving a story on pot parties at Northwestern University.[29] The report included film giving the impression that the reporter had managed to catch a party on camera. The party was actually put on for the reporter's benefit, at his request. The FCC even noted that the reporter had encouraged the commission of a crime, but refused to discipline the station or reporter, arguing that it was the media's duty to restrain their overly zealous newspeople, and broadcasters should be left to do so without government interference.

## Proof Is Hard to Come By

Getting the information to prove a complaint is a major hurdle that is not limited to complaints about news coverage. The FCC will do nothing to help a complainant obtain proof of his or her accusations. Unless the complainant already has the evidence to sustain the complaint, he or she is out of luck. There is no procedure like the discovery afforded litigants in civil court suits. In the case mentioned above, where a Texas station, KCOS, aired a misleading show in which county employees acted the part of county jail prisoners, a complaining group demanded a copy of the taped show, but KCOS refused. The FCC supported the station's refusal.

In 1973, the Wilderness Society complained that ABC-TV aired commercials favoring a certain way of cutting timber, without giving time to opponents of the method. The Wilderness Society couldn't prove ABC hadn't aired the other side. The FCC said, "ABC has no obligation to provide you with past programming information," and threw out the complaint for lack of proof.[30]

This inability to get information plays a large part in the failure of individual complaints, especially in light of the need to prove that a station's *overall programming* about an issue lacked balance.

The overall programming requirement was set out in the *Allen C. Phelps* case.[31] Phelps and the Federation of Citizens' Associations of the

District of Columbia opposed the 1969 renewal of WTOP-AM-TV licenses, alleging Fairness Doctrine violations as well as biased news and editorial coverage reflecting the view of the station owners. Phelps claimed that WTOP news was controlled by the Washington Post and that ownership of both the Post and WTOP had violated antitrust standards. The FCC called the Fairness Doctrine complaints "vague and general charges" of unfair coverage relating to public schools, crime, home rule, and allegations of police brutality in D.C. Phelps cited some interviews by Martin Agronsky as examples of attempts to advance partisan views. But the FCC denied the complaint because Phelps failed to provide "documentation or any other evidence to support a conclusion that in its overall programming the licensee has not attempted to present a contrasting view"[32] on the issues.

The Fairness Doctrine is in a sense misnamed. If it were called the "Overall Balanced Programming Doctrine," perhaps the public would better understand it, and fewer, or at least better-framed, complaints would be lodged.

Because of *Phelps,* what folks in their armchairs consider an "unfair" program will not generally qualify as the basis for a successful complaint, especially if the subject matter is treated on other programs aired by the broadcaster. It is all right for a station to air a one-sided piece as long as other programs on that issue balance that bias.

Because the station had no obligation to supply information about its overall programming, the complainant must monitor a station for a substantial period of time. As Geller points out:

> Many complainants understandably will not undertake the nuisance of such extensive monitoring. The probable result is that (1) the usual complainant— say, one who has heard scores of spots on one side of a ballot issue—will continue to find his complaint dismissed and (2) the complainant who retains a knowledgeable communications lawyer will simply recite whatever it is the FCC prescribes (e.g. that he has listened for $x$ period of time to $x$ (news/public affairs) programs of the station, and to the best of his knowledge never heard the contrasting viewpoint). A policy that frustrates the average citizen or amounts to just "turning the crank" for the few "in the know" is highly questionable.[33]

This "highly questionable" result is precisely what now occurs under the Fairness Doctrine. Some organized groups can (and do) monitor stations for lengthy periods to gather evidence of overall imbalance. For an individual, of course, this is a much more difficult exercise.

Some programming information does have to be made public, in the form of program logs, but these are sketchy and of little use except when counting paid advertisements on an issue. In any event, logs do not have to be made public until 45 days after the programs are aired.

Most individuals simply do not have the tenacity to follow through on a complaint to the FCC. For rulings issued in 1981, the average time between airing of the complained-about program and the FCC ruling was more than a year. If courts get involved, of course, the process takes even longer.

Documenting a complaint demands a lot of effort and knowledge of FCC policies. Virtually every word of the doctrine has been subjected to legal interpretation, and criteria have been established to measure the applicability of each word to any given complaint. In the course of a complaint against WNAC-TV in Boston, Dr. Richard Wilson (a professor of physics at Harvard and a pronuclear advocate) was trying to gain access to reply to the "No Nukes is Good Nukes" show. His frustration with the FCC system was apparent in one letter:

> It would, however, be improper for you to assume that because the information you need is *not* in the original complaint that it does not exist. The whole procedure of public complaints would be nullified if you have procedures and desires for information that you keep to yourselves.

Wilson's comment seems almost prescient. The FCC rejected his complaint for a specific lack of evidence "before" the commission:

> Although you identify the organization that you represent (SENSE) as an independent group "who often explain nuclear power to the public," you do not provide us with information to establish that your organization, "Prof. David Rose of MIT for SE$_2$," or "Mr. Campbell for the Mass. Voice of Energy" represent significant contrasting viewpoints. Accordingly, we cannot conclude that the licensee was unreasonable in not choosing to air those viewpoints.

For individuals who are not attorneys, it seems almost impossible to prosecute a complaint successfully. The FCC cannot award attorney's fees to a successful complainant. So if an attorney is hired, there is no way fees paid by an individual can be recovered, even if he or she wins.

In sum, it takes a lot of time, money, effort, and tenacity to pursue a complaint. And even then the chances of success are slim to none. So why such controversy over the Fairness Doctrine? Because the doctrine has been used by some well-organized interest groups to pressure broadcasters into providing access so their representatives can get on the air. It is outside Washington that the successful battles for access are often waged by those who seek airtime. To understand the impact of the regulation, one must leave the FCC's headquarters in downtown Washington, and look South, North, and especially West.

## *References*

1. Form 8330-FD is available from the Federal Communications Commission, Washington, D.C. 20554.
2. Broadcast Procedure Manual, 39 Fed. Reg. 32288, 32290 (1974).
3. Geller, *The Fairness Doctrine in Broadcasting* (Santa Monica, Calif., Rand, 1974), p. 132.
4. Simmons, *The Fairness Doctrine and the Media* (Berkeley, University of California Press, 1978), p. 15, note 28.
5. Quoted by Friendly, *The Good Guys, the Bad Guys, and the First Amendment* (New York, Vintage, 1975), p. 81. See *Brandywine-Main Line Radio, Inc.,* 27 FCC 2d 565 (1971), aff'd 473 F. 2d 16 (D.C. Cir. 1972), *cert. denied* 412 U.S. 922 (1973).
6. For a detailed examination of the *United Church of Christ* case, see Friendly, op. cit., pp. 89–102.
7. *United Church of Christ* v. *FCC,* 425 F. 2d 543 (1969).
8. Geller, op. cit., p. 5.
9. Interview of Stephen Nevas, First Amendment Counsel, NAB, September 15, 1982.
10. Geller, op. cit., pp. 33–34.
11. 31 FCC 2d 729 (1971).
12. Simmons, op. cit., pp. 210–211.
13. Telephone calls were included and 36,000 of the complaints were against one program, "Guns of Autumn."
14. Several hundred of these complaints were about the program "Defense of the Nation."
15. June 3, 1981, FCC decision.
16. January 2, 1981, FCC decision.
17. Letter to the FCC from Rep. Edward Madigan, January 22, 1981.
18. April 10, 1981, FCC Broadcast Bureau Decision.
19. Interview, September 8, 1982.
20. 1974 *Fairness Report,* 39 Fed. Reg. 26372, 26379 (1974).
21. Reconsideration of the *Fairness Report,* 58 FCC 2d 691, 696–697 (1976).
22. Id. at 697. See *DNC* v. *FCC,* 460 F. 2d 891, 903 (D.C. Cir. 1972), *cert. denied,* 409 U.S. 843 (1972).
23. 460 F. 2d at 903.
24. NBC and Roger Langley, August 7, 1979.
25. NBC and Rev. Carl McIntyre, August 31, 1979.
26. WCCO-TV and Iowa Beef Processors, Inc., June 16, 1982.
27. WFAA-TV and Rev. James Robison, March 30, 1980.
28. 16 FCC 2d 650 (1969).
29. 18 FCC 2d 124 (1969).
30. May 9, 1973, FCC decision.
31. 21 FCC 2d 12 (1969).
32. Id. at 13.
33. Geller, op. cit., p. 55.

# FOUR

# The Informal Handling of Fairness Issues

BEYOND THE POTOMAC, the Fairness Doctrine is taken more seriously than the record of decisions at the FCC would seem to merit. Although the odds are low for the success of a formal fairness complaint at the commission, the rule has a very real impact on broadcasting. Many fairness complaints never even reach the FCC, but are resolved informally, between the station and the complainant. Others that do reach the FCC end up requiring hardly any FCC involvement; they too are settled between the parties. In fact, the doctrine's impact on broadcasting is barely reflected in the formal process. It is *informally* that the doctrine has come to affect broadcasting.

Like so many things, California has set the trend for vigorous use of the regulation on an informal basis. That's partly true because the Pacific states have led the way with ballot referenda; and advertising about propositions that will be put to the voter seems invariably to trigger fairness complaints. So in the West the struggle over broadcast fairness is being waged most vigorously.

It is a different picture than the one in Washington, D.C., where, as Steven Simmons has noted, only one-third of one percent of Fairness Doctrine complaints result in sanctions against a broadcaster. Henry Geller has stated that the procedural and substantive barriers to bringing a successful fairness complaint to the FCC are almost insurmountable. But even unsuccessful complaints impose financial burdens on broadcasters, who must defend themselves before the FCC. The result, Geller suggests, is a chilling effect on broadcasters, who shy from controversial issues for fear of entanglement in a Fairness Doctrine dispute.

Organized interest groups that defend the Fairness Doctrine argue that it is their principal tool in negotiating for balanced coverage of issues in the electronic media. The Media Access Project (MAP) describes itself as a public-interest law firm specializing in fairness cases. MAP's executive director, Andrew Jay Schwartzman, said in a September 1982 interview:

> It is dangerous to try and measure the success of the Fairness Doctrine by what happens at the FCC, by the number of suits filed or whatever. Most of the dealings with the Fairness Doctrine are informal, the more informal the better so that the local groups get to establish an ongoing relationship with the news people or local station.

Schwartzman said most disputes are not confrontations that give rise to lawyers' involvement or lawsuits. Rather, he said, they occur after some "breakdown of communication between a reporter or news director or station manager and a local group." Most inquiries to MAP are resolved by one or two letters or telephone calls, Schwartzman said. "Ninety to ninety-five percent of the serious inquiries received by MAP are satisfactorily worked out without going to the FCC."

Schwartzman says most of the problems arise with small-market broadcasters who unintentionally run afoul of the doctrine. "The incidence of stations going ahead and doing something that they're aware will cause Fairness Doctrine problems but do it anyway is really low in 10,000 licensees." Cases like the one in Ohio three years ago are rare. In that case, "Station managers and owners of three radio stations were on the steering committee for a bond issue and the opposition didn't get on the radio. MAP moved in and got some well-deserved redress."

Schwartzman says that when the Fairness Doctrine is working well, "it is invisible," and that "the measure of success is the relative absence of a lot of suits at the FCC."

MAP has obtained free airtime to respond to paid issue advertising. The FCC's *Cullman* decision required stations to provide free time to opposing groups if they could not afford to purchase time to respond to issue advertising.[1] Schwartzman says, "As a matter of law and policy [this access] is perfectly acceptable to achieve a balance of frequency and total time. When the other side is entitled to a minute of unedited time, you learn something that way." He says the public benefits from the informal resolution of fairness matters, receiving better coverage of all sides of important public issues.

Given the 1-in-2,000 odds of bringing a successful Fairness Doctrine complaint through the FCC, one would expect the group of successful users of the doctrine to be very small.

It's not. People use the doctrine to great effect each week. But they don't deal with the FCC. They "settle" before that. These users are organized groups that can afford, or at least have access to, expert legal counsel.

Politicians fall into this category, and they frequently seek to influence TV programming either by claims under the Personal Attack Rule or by pleas of poverty coupled with requests for free time to rebut opponents (outside the formal campaign period). According to NAB sources and others who have been involved in politically oriented Fairness Doctrine cases, the politician's complaint often aims to force the opposition off the air, as much as to get on the air himself. "Politicians" in this sense include political action committees (PACs), party committees, and other clearly partisan entities.

Single-issue pressure groups are apparently the most frequent and successful users of the Fairness Doctrine. Small, local groups, or local chapters of national organizations, approach broadcasters for a chance to air their views. Local groups can easily monitor stations and be in a position to jump when something airs that appears to deal with "their" issue.

Large national organizations use the rules this way as well, but representatives of broadcasters and pressure groups agree that most of the users are small, local chapters or groups. These local groups have access to sophisticated legal counsel and expertise beyond their own financial resources. Through Washington-based organizations such as the Safe Energy Communication Council,[2] the National Citizens Committee for Broadcasting,[3] the Media Access Project, and Citizens Communication Center, local groups learn how to deal with broadcasters. If attempts at negotiation fail, legal counsel will be provided free of charge.

The Media Access Project is funded primarily by foundations. Some idea of who uses the doctrine can be gained by reviewing a nonexhaustive MAP's 1980 client list:

| | |
|---|---|
| Environmental Defense Fund | National Abortion Rights Action |
| United Auto Workers | League |
| Citizens to Tax Big Oil | FUSE |
| Californians for Smoking and Non- | Public Media Center |
| Smoking Sections | Center for Renewable Resources |
| Energy Action Foundation | Critical Mass Energy Project |
| Citizen/Labor Energy Coalition | Solar Lobby |
| Maine Nuclear Referendum | Environmental Action Foundation |
| Committee | Friends of the Earth |
| National Organization for Women | Nuclear Information and Resource |
| (NOW) | Service |

National Gay Task Force
Dallas Gay Political Caucus
Alaska Conference on Human
  Sexuality
American Friends Service
  Committee
Arkansas Consumer League
Bakery and Confectionery
  Workers
California Public Interest Research
  Group
California Renters and Owners
  Organized for Fairness
Center for Defense Information
Center for Law in the Public
  Interest
Committee Against Registration
  for the Draft
Concerned Mothers of San Luis
  Obispo
Connecticut Citizen Action Group
Coulee Region Energy Coalition
Friends of the Earth, D.C. Chap.
Institute for Policy Studies
International Association of
  Machinists
Interreligious Instruments for
  Peace (Syracuse, NY)
Jonesboro, Ark., Chap. NOW
Massachusetts Public Interest
  Research Group

Michigan Public Interest Research
  Group
National Center for Law and the
  Deaf
National Coalition for Central
  American Human Rights
National Organization for the
  Reform of Marijuana Laws
New Jersey Sea Alliance
New Jersey Solar Energy Assoc.
Ohio Public Interest Campaign
Oklahomans for Fair Utility Rates
Proposition 11 Committee
  (Missouri)
Reading CA., Unitarian
  Universalist Fellowship
Righter for Congress Committee
Rural America
SANE
South Dakota Committee for
  People's Choice
St. Louis Broadcast Coalition
Students for Economic Democracy
U.S. Committee in Solidarity
  with the People of El Salvador
U.S. Department of Education,
  Office of Civil Rights
Young and Associates
Citizen Soldier
Citizens Party of Illinois
Coalition for Fair Utility Rates

Many groups and individuals use the doctrine to get their people on the air, often to oppose a viewpoint stated on a paid commercial or broadcast. This is the major goal of many interest groups. They want to "speak with their own unedited voices."[4]

In general, the Fairness Doctrine is not, and was never intended to be, an access mechanism. The FCC has said repeatedly that a broadcaster will *not* be ordered to let a particular person or group use its licensed airwaves. This extreme and last-resort remedy is available only in cases involving personal attacks, political editorials, and the Equal Opportunity political broadcasting rules.

Not only do interest groups want their points of view aired, but they also want to be the ones stating those views. In 1980, KXTV aired paid advertisements in favor of a California ballot initiative, Proposition 10, that would have repealed existing rent control laws in the state. Californians Against Initiative Fraud (CAIF) wanted to air its own advertisements against the initiative, and filed a complaint with the FCC. The TV station said enough of the CAIF side had been aired already. As part of a complex calculation of anti-Proposition 10 programming, the station included 15-second summaries written by station staff and read by station announcers. The summaries were read as part of 30-second spots, including 15 seconds of arguments in favor of the proposition. These were aired 30 times.

CAIF argued that the 15-second spots were virtually useless in presenting its side of a complex ballot issue, and that the summaries were not what CAIF would have said, or how CAIF would have said it. The FCC refused to go into the quality of the station-prepared summaries. The time was included as balancing time, and the complaint was rejected.[5] The station had given time for the CAIF viewpoint and the group couldn't complain just because it did not get enough airtime itself. Even though CAIF lost this case at the FCC, the group garnered thousands of dollars of free time from other stations.

The number of advocates wanting access to the airwaves for their presentations seems to be growing. And a large, and increasing, number of groups are using the Fairness Doctrine to gain that access. That can include corporations that feel they've been treated unfairly on the air.

In one instance, negotiations between Kaiser Aluminum and ABC took 16 months to reach a satisfactory conclusion. On April 3, 1980, ABC aired a "20/20" segment on the dangers of aluminum wiring. An announcer introduced the piece this way:

> Tonight you may have a time bomb in the walls of your home that you may not even know about. If it hasn't already burned your home down. Aluminum wiring. Was the danger covered up for 10 years? Or was it just good business? Geraldo Rivera, with a special report—"Hot Wire."

Later in the program, Kaiser Aluminum was accused of covering up the dangerous nature of aluminum wiring, after clips of burned homes and fire victims were shown:

> [Kaiser] failed to adequately warn the public of the hazards. And apparently they later withheld results of their tests from the government . . . Kaiser's own tests warned of the potential hazards.

Kaiser demanded 10 minutes on "20/20" to respond to the "Hot Wire" show. ABC refused, arguing that Kaiser's views were sought before the program aired, but that Kaiser had refused to be interviewed. In effect, ABC said Kaiser was given a chance, but blew it. Kaiser responded that it had no obligation to submit to a hostile interview that would be edited beyond its control, and that ABC had an obligation to present contrasting views and had failed to do so.

After much negotiating, ABC finally agreed to give Kaiser four minutes on "20/20." At the last moment, ABC changed its mind and withdrew the "20/20" time, offering instead an appearance on the half-hour "ABC Nightline" show at 11:30 p.m.

Kaiser rejected the proposal for three reasons: (1) Kaiser did not want to submit to what it called "Trial by TV." Kaiser wanted to reply to the attack with its own unedited voice, (2) "Nightline" was unacceptable because it played to a different and much smaller audience than the prime-time "20/20," and (3) ABC had already agreed to give up time on "20/20" and should keep its word.

Kaiser filed a Fairness Doctrine complaint with the FCC to force ABC to comply with its original agreement. The dispute generated a two-inch-thick file at the FCC, including 12-page letters from attorneys involved. Both sides spent a lot of money. ABC told the FCC that Kaiser's refusal to be interviewed before the show let ABC off the hook. But Kaiser replied, "The mandate of the Fairness Doctrine is not satisfied by inviting a proponent of opposing views to step into the lion's den."

Kaiser and ABC finally agreed to an appearance on ABC's prime-time "Viewpoint" program at 10 p.m. on July 24, 1981. On July 29, after the program had aired, Kaiser withdrew the FCC complaint.

Andrew Schwartzman, of the Media Access Project, maintains that because of the way journalists work, all kinds of groups, from the "establishment" Kaiser Aluminum Company to the "activist" clients of MAP, want to get on the air and be heard with their own unedited voices on the issues they feel are important. Schwartzman points out, for example, that nobody is happy with the way broadcasting treats issues related to the business community. This inadequate treatment results not from newsroom bias, he suggests, but a result of journalistic ignorance or naiveté. Schwartzman says it is a radicalizing experience to be interviewed at length by a reporter and then see only a snippet included in the final story. After watching his or her presentation cut to the bare bones and possibly taken out of context, the interview subject wants to get on the air unedited next time.

These groups have won both paid and free time. Naturally, free reply time is sought most by special interest groups. Both broadcast industry representatives and interest-group spokespersons generally acknowledge that free time is often granted. The enthusiasm with which this statement is made, of course, varies dramatically with its source.

Broadcasters sometimes view grant of free access as caving in to pressure akin to extortion, i.e., the threat of FCC action that will cost the station a lot of money. Interest groups describe access as a form of good community relations between local groups and TV and radio stations.

The form of access can vary: editorial reply time; spots on programs such as CBS's "Letters;" appearances on talk shows, call-in programs, or debates; airing of taped 30-second commercial-style spots (produced locally, possibly with help from the station, or professionally produced by a national or parent interest group); public service announcements; news stories using a local group's spokesperson; and airing of more programming on an issue. An example of the last option was the "No Nukes is Good Nukes" show which countered Mobil's "Energy Options for Tomorrow." Schwartzman says he wants to establish a "working relationship" between the local broadcaster and the interest group so that access will be ongoing and amicably arrived at, rather than forced upon the broadcaster as a "one-shot deal" under threat of FCC complaints. Schwartzman contends the doctrine is used to persuade, not intimidate.

## Winning Access

The evidence is overwhelming that negotiation is the key to obtaining access to the airwaves. Nobody really wants to deal with the FCC—certainly not the broadcaster, who fears government red tape, legal expenses, and possible FCC sanctions. And the access-seeker wants to avoid an FCC battle both because of the time and money involved and because the odds are overwhelmingly against a complaint succeeding. Even if the complainant wins, the FCC might not order the station to put him or her on the air. No matter who wins, both sides will spend money—money that even the winner will not recapture. So the incentive is for informal resolution of fairness complaints.

In its 1982 annual report, the Media Access Project points to the experience of the "Yes Committee" of St. Louis as a "particularly successful case study of how the Fairness Doctrine can be used as an access tool for citizen groups."

The Yes Committee opposed construction and licensing of new nuclear power plants in Missouri. When the local utility, Union Electric (UE), began running a series of advertisements promoting nuclear power in late 1981, the Yes Committee contacted the Safe Energy Communication Council (SECC), which referred the Yes Committee to MAP.

MAP advised the Yes Committee to contact local television and radio stations that had run the UE ads. All four radio stations involved agreed to provide airtime to the Yes Committee, in a ratio of approximately one spot announcement for the Yes Committee to each four UE commercials.

So the stations provided one free spot for an antinuclear message for every four paid spots promoting nuclear power.

One of the three television stations promptly offered considerable spot-ad time to the Yes Committee, but the remaining two stations balked. With MAP's assistance, a complaint was filed with the FCC in April 1982. The complaint met the threshold requirements and the FCC sent inquiries to the stations. Negotiations then resumed, with one station agreeing to provide 50 one-minute spots to the Yes Committee. The complaint against that television station was withdrawn.

The other station, KTVI, held out. On December 1, 1982, after the election, the commission agreed KTVI had been reasonable when it determined that the power company's ads had no obvious and meaningful relationship to the Yes Committee's ballot referendum. But while the case dragged out at the FCC, the Yes Committee managed to appear on four radio stations and two other television stations. MAP estimated the broadcast time and exposure the Yes Committee received was worth at least $100,000.[6] And in the KTVI case, the FCC in its December 1 letter asked the station to further explain how it would present the issue of utility rate increases—in effect urging the station to be more forthcoming in dealing with the Yes Committee in the future. The hint was obvious.

In many cases, negotiations are conducted in an atmosphere of misunderstanding about exactly what the Fairness Doctrine says and means. According to the National Association of Broadcasters (NAB), some broadcasters, particularly owners of small stations, think an FCC Fairness Doctrine investigation could cost them their license.[7] Even NAB publications fuel this fear. One NAB pamphlet urges broadcasters to use their airwaves to build public support for repeal of the Fairness Doctrine. The pamphlet contains this statement:

> In-depth reporting of delicate, often complex developments affecting candidates or issues is often restricted for fear of governmental reprimands for non-compliance or perhaps *even loss of license.* (Emphasis added.)[8]

Small broadcasters feel threatened, especially when a group demands free time by citing laws and cases a station general manager never heard of. Some station executives do not realize that the way the FCC handles cases is more likely to help broadcasters than complainants. Indicative of the FCC attitude is that the commission has stopped sending copies of all complaint letters to the stations involved, apparently because there was some feeling that letters from the FCC struck fear into the hearts of broadcasters.

Also, many access seekers frequently are confused about what they are entitled to under the rules. They tend to demand ''equal time'' access for themselves, apparently confusing the Equal Opportunities Rule (covering candidates for public office) with the Fairness Doctrine and the personal attack and political editorializing rules. It is a confusing legal landscape, one that only experts can successfully traverse.

Public misunderstanding may result partly from inaccurate press reports about the Fairness Doctrine. Two examples from the *Washington Post* illustrate the point. An October 9, 1982, story stated in part:

> A Norman Lear-backed political organization is launching a television campaign attacking the Moral Majority and similar groups for what it says is religious and political intolerance reminiscent of "witch hunts, slavery, (and) McCarthyism." . . . An angry Jerry Falwell, head of the Moral Majority, rejoined that "This is the typical dishonest, irresponsible type-programming that has become vintage Lear." Falwell said "every TV station in America" has been warned that Moral Majority will seek *equal time* if they air the program. (Emphasis added.)

On October 12, the *Post* reported that President Reagan asked the major networks for a half-hour of free airtime to talk about the economy, apparently in response to news of a 10.1 percent unemployment rate. The 1982 elections were only 20 days off, and the Democratic National Committee (DNC) urged the networks to reject Reagan's request. The *Post* reported that:

> [DNC Chairman] Manatt also urged all Democrats running for the Senate and House to request separately that they be given *equal time* to respond to Reagan's address, on the grounds that it constitutes a free *campaign message* that is being aired to the voters in their states. The Democrats argue that each candidate should be allowed the time to respond under the Federal Communications Commission's *Fairness Doctrine.* (Emphasis added.)

In fact, under the Fairness Doctrine, Democrats would only be entitled to have a contrasting opinion aired. The broadcasters would have no obligation to provide equal time.[9] In 1980, KGO-TV in San Francisco aired paid advertisements against a ballot initiative that would have levied a 10 percent surtax on profits of oil companies. For every 5.4 ads, the station also aired one free spot in favor of the surtax, and this 5.4-to-1 ratio satisfied the Fairness Doctrine.[10] That's not a very equal ratio.

Even if the broadcaster agrees to air additional material, he can choose almost any spokesperson. Under the general Fairness Doctrine, no one has the *right* to time for himself. A station manager could quite legitimately tell an access-seeker to go home, watch TV, and quit bothering him. But in practice, if a serious fairness matter is raised, the broadcaster usually gives the complainant the access he seeks, although this does not usually result in equal time.

Because the doctrine is misunderstood both by the people subject to it and the people trying to use it, much free airtime is given out by broadcasters. Who can blame stations for capitulating? It has been noted that complaints can be expensive, drawn-out affairs that discourage individuals from pursuing them. But this is a two-edged sword, wielded by interest groups seeking access. The NAB estimates that negotiations involving attorneys in even a minor Fairness Doctrine matter can cost $1,000 to $3,000. Thus, it is obviously cheaper to "cave in" and give away some airtime.

Henry Geller writes of the Washington state station, KREM, which spent about $20,000 in legal fees and 480 executive and supervisory manhours defending itself against a complaint from someone who was refused airtime to reply to an editorial.[11] This was back in the early 1970s. Comparable attorney's fees today would cost even more. The licensee of KREM pointed out that the 480 hours spent on the complaint was "a very serious dislocation of regular operational functions and far more important in that sense than in the simple salary-dollar value."

Sometimes a station's attorney will provide what is called "bottom-line" advice. That is, the attorney tells the station, "You are right; the law, facts, and FCC policy are all on your side, but it will take months and a lot of money before you are vindicated. Therefore, in the interests of the bottom line on your balance sheet, you're better off to offer the complainant some free airtime." Part of the bottom-line analysis is a recognition that running, say, 30 paid spots on one side of an issue and 10 free spots on the other side still means more revenue for the station than not running *any* spots; and a 3:1 ratio easily satisfies FCC policy about "reasonable opportunity for contrasting views." But this financial incentive only holds when unsold commercial time is available. Local stations usually can always find room for one more ad.

This does not generally apply to networks, because the amount of unsold advertising time available on the networks is limited in a way that local station time is not. As will be discussed in Chapter 8, the networks reject most advertising that promotes views on issues.

It should be noted that local stations are responsible for whatever goes out over their channels. This includes programming originated by a network, so even if a network program is the basis of a Fairness Doctrine claim, the local station can be approached. Major market stations are usually more intransigent about granting access than small-market stations. It is not clear whether this is because the major stations have more money at stake, and more money to fight complainants, or whether they are more sophisticated and realize a Fairness Doctrine complaint has a poor chance of success. But interest groups report few refusals outside the major markets when free time is requested in response to paid issue advertising.

## *Organizing for Access*

The key to winning access through the Fairness Doctrine appears to be vigorous organizing and pressing of requests upon broadcasters. The groups which succeed usually focus their activities on hot issues—nuclear power, the environment, defense-related matters, and the like. These are the kinds of subjects that often end up on state and local ballots as referendum questions. When stations accept ads on these ballot issues, they bear an almost automatic duty to provide contrasting points of view. Very often the paid ads are sponsored by industry groups attempting to defeat propositions directed at taxing or regulating them. In such cases activist reformers often pounce with requests for free time. They virtually need only assert that they have no funds to purchase the airtime to qualify for free time under the Cullman Principle. Some broadcasters complain that groups will expend their funds on newspaper and billboard ads then show up at the stations with empty pockets seeking free time.

A spokesman for one such group, Michael Gendler, concedes that broadcasters "get very upset if they know you have spent money elsewhere." He noted that one station manager in Fresno, California, when confronted with a request for time, "made it sound like we were stealing his groceries." Gendler, who was interviewed by phone in October 1982, was active in a group called "Yes on 15," which supported a ballot proposition to register and restrict handguns in California.

Gendler claims groups with an interest in gun sales poured more than $700,000 into a campaign to defeat Proposition 15. Gendler contacted station after station requesting—and receiving—free time on 70 radio stations and 10 TV stations. Most negotiations took a week and he usually won pledges of receiving one free spot for every three or four paid ads which ran. He estimated his group got $40,000 to $50,000 worth of free airtime. He viewed his role as preventing monied interests from "buying the election." Most stations "were very good about it and understood their responsibilities under the Fairness Doctrine," Gendler said, "although they didn't like it very much."

Barbara Joy, of the antinuclear organization, Safe Energy Communication Council (SECC), says most stations with which she deals are amicable and aware of fairness obligations. Generally, they offer free time (in a 1:5 ratio to paid advertising time bought by pronuclear forces).

In a typical Fairness Doctrine matter, a local group would monitor a radio or TV station, then talk to the station executive about getting on the air to rebut what had already aired. Since it might not have a 24-hour monitoring operation, the group asks to look at station broadcast logs to see how many spots have been aired.

Usually equal time and format are requested. If the programming prompting the request was on prime-time TV or drive-time radio, then reply time is sought in equivalent times. What follows is a form of horse trading over what type of access is to be granted, and when it will air. Instead of running a prepared, taped 30-second spot against another series of spots, the station might prefer to run three or four "Speak-Out" responses of one-and-a-half to two minutes.

Groups such as SECC say their goal is both immediate access and a long-term relationship to ensure future access without time-consuming confrontation. Apparently they are most successful when countering paid advertisements advocating positions on ballot propositions.

MAP's Schwartzman states that California broadcasters "have recognized they have a Fairness Doctrine obligation. Typically, California [interest] groups get the MAP materials and then call up to say 'They [the stations] have offered this. Should we take it?'" He notes that California is a ballot-initiative-oriented state with a population easily and economically reached through the electronic media, "so a lot of sophistication has developed out there."[12]

Even if an interest group considers a station's access offer unsatisfactory and complains to the FCC, the FCC may decide that the original offer was reasonable. Thus, the group's earlier refusal may cost it any access at all. So both sides have something to lose in going to the FCC, and both are interested in successful negotiations.

An ability to prove the extent of overall programming is always key in Fairness Doctrine matters. But monitoring a station is not as important when paid advertising spots are at issue, because stations log all spots, and these logs are available to the public. The pro-Equal Rights Amendment (ERA) lobby took advantage of this fact during Virginia's consideration of the ERA. The pro-ERA lobbyists blanketed all radio and TV outlets in the state with form letters requesting lists of all anti-ERA spots aired, who paid for them, how often they were aired, and information about time purchased for future ads. Demands for free, equivalent response time were made. NAB counsel Stephen Nevas described the letters as "menacing, with an implied threat" of FCC action. Use of this technique may well increase in future state-wide referendum battles. In California and Maine, where there are numerous referenda, such letters have apparently been used to good effect.

The ERA campaign provides one example of what the NAB describes as the doctrine's "chilling effect." Nevas asserts that one station canceled some ERA ads after selling the time, but before the ads aired, because of demands for free response time.

A number of documents are available to help local groups pursue free airtime on "their" issue. The National Citizens Committee for Broadcasting published a 21-page "Citizens' Primer on the Fairness Doctrine" describing the doctrine and advising how to use it. The Primer includes a sample letter requesting free airtime, and detailed instructions on how to document a request.

Part of the letter, drafted by the Media Access Project, is reprinted here:

Dear Broadcaster:

I am writing on behalf of [name of organization(s) with footnotes giving brief explanation of nature and purpose of organization(s)], concerning your broadcast, throughout the day and night, of several [name of company] ads that present but one viewpoint on the controversial issue of public importance concerning immediate commercial construction of nuclear power plants and use of nuclear power. These ads claim that nuclear power is environmentally clean, safe, practical, and economical. Numerous residents of [state or community], including members of these organizations, who have been regular listeners to your station over a lengthy period of time, have informed us that they have heard no other programming on your station which presents any opposing viewpoints on this issue.

* * *

While it is true that no one group or individual has an absolute right of access to radio airwaves, a licensee must, under the Fairness Doctrine, provide a reasonable opportunity in its overall programming for the presentation of contrasting viewpoints on controversial issues of public importance. Moreover, the Federal Communications Commission has continuously recognized that various factors must be considered under the Fairness Doctrine in determining what constitutes a reasonable opportunity for response when a licensee has presented programming expressing only one side of a controversial issue of public importance. These "signposts" of reasonableness include not only the total amount of time afforded to each side, but also the frequency with which each side is presented, the size of the listening audience during the various broadcasts, the time period over which the one-sided broadcasts have appeared, and the reaching of different audiences.

In light of your broadcast of the [name of company] nuclear power ads throughout the day and night, including during periods of maximum listening, and in light of your failure to provide any adequate access for the presentation of contrasting views, according to frequent regular listeners of your station, you are invited to immediately air such contrasting views. While we are financially unable to purchase airtime for such presentation, we will be happy to provide you with pre-recorded material, prepared on behalf of nuclear power opponents, which we feel would help you satisfy your Fairness Doctrine obligations if aired a sufficient number of times.

If you feel you have met your fairness obligation in some manner we have been unable to determine, please inform us of the specific times and substance of any contrasting programming which you have aired. Otherwise, in order to avoid our filing a formal complaint with the Federal Communications Commission, let us know exactly how you plan to meet your obligation, including whether you wish to receive our pre-recorded spots. We view this matter as extremely serious and are confident that working together we can insure a fully-informed citizenry on the issue of nuclear power.

Sincerely yours,

The American Federation of State, County and Municipal Employees (AFSCME) puts out a 40-page booklet titled "Gaining Access to Radio and TV Time: A Union Member's Guide to the Broadcast Media."

The AFSCME introduction argues that public approval of unions has shrunk to its lowest level in 43 years because "organized labor has been the consistent victim of neglect and bias on the part of both commercial and public broadcasters for many years. Fair and honest coverage of labor is a myth." The booklet encourages union representatives to seek access to the airwaves by using the Fairness Doctrine.

Like other advocates for special interest groups, AFSCME urges "pleasant, informal, continuous contact" with broadcasters.

If confrontation becomes necessary, the booklet contains a four-page sample letter, complete with citations of FCC and court cases. An excerpt follows:

> We note that your station has presented programming in the form of (State number or "numerous"), (State type of program) which urge voters to cast a ballot (for or against) the referendum. The FCC has made it clear that in such circumstances a station *must* provide groups which hold opposing views a reasonable opportunity to respond, considering total time, frequency and total time exposure . . . See *King Broadcasting*, 23 FCC 2d 41.
>
> Unfortunately, we are unable to purchase airtime for such a presentation; nonetheless, the FCC has made it clear that even when one side *buys* time, and no responsible spokesperson for the other side can afford to buy time then *free* time must be given to the other side. *Cullman Broadcasting*, 40 FCC 576 (1963). In such cases, a licensee should not investigate the good faith presentation by an underfinanced citizens group, *Council on Energy and Employment v. FCC* USLW, 1st Circuit, (1978), but *should provide free time.* . . .

In 1980, Maine held a referendum on the closing of the Maine Yankee Nuclear Power Facility. An antinuclear citizens' group called the Maine Nuclear Referendum Committee negotiated free airtime on almost every radio and television station in the state—time worth $200,000 to $300,000.

The nuclear power issue has spawned many citizens' groups that have developed an expertise in Fairness Doctrine matters. Antinuclear forces have won free airtime for their presentations across the country, from California to New Mexico to New York.

The Safe Energy Communication Council is a coalition of several groups against nuclear power, including the Sierra Club and Ralph Nader's Critical Mass Energy Project. The SECC's raison d'etre is to assist local groups in getting airtime for the antinuclear position, principally by countering advertisements sponsored by the nuclear power industry. SECC efforts won an estimated $100,000 of free time from 1979 to 1981. In just a few months of 1982, SECC was instrumental in securing almost as much free time as in the previous two years. This is evidence of the antinuclear lobby's growing expertise with Fairness Doctrine matters.

In 1981–1982, SECC held five media workshops in regions covering all of the United States east of the Mississippi. Representatives of local groups spent a day and a half learning about media relations, including use of the Fairness Doctrine.

SECC has eight professionally produced spot ads available for airing on local stations. And the organization is becoming known in the broadcasting community. At the beginning of a pronuclear ad campaign in Grand Rapids, Michigan, a producer at WOTV called SECC to ask if any spots were available for airing, to balance the paid campaign.

Grand Rapids was chosen as a test market for a Committee for Energy Awareness (CEA) pronuclear campaign. The CEA, funded by the nuclear power industry, spent approximately $270,000 from February to May 1982 for about 250 spots on each of three TV stations and five radio stations in the Grand Rapids area.[13] The ads were of three types. One ad stated that scientists in 15 nations, including the United States, were developing safe ways to store nuclear waste, and pictured waste being wrapped in metal containers and placed in geological formations such as salt domes. The tag line was to the effect that "Most people aren't aware of that, so that's why we're bringing you this message—to set the record straight."

Other ads minimized the dangers of radiation from nuclear power plants. The ads showed someone flying a plane and standing by the Lincoln Memorial while the script told that people receive more exposure to radiation from natural emanations and a plane trip to Colorado than from a power plant. The third type of ad demonstrated the benefits of nuclear power, with shots of cities, battleships, and laboratories. With SECC assistance, the Grand Rapids-Kalamazoo Citizens for Safe Energy negotiated free airtime on two of the three TV stations and most of the radio stations. The airtime was worth about $50,000.

WOTV, which voluntarily aired the antinuclear spots, now is more hesitant about accepting additional issue ads. Marvin Chauvin, WOTV's

General Manager, said in an October 1982 telephone interview for this study that before accepting the paid pronuclear ads "we realized it triggered some legal, if not moral responsibility" to air the other side. But he found it a costly episode. If WOTV accepts issue ads again, he said, "it will be on a more controlled, limited basis. . . ." Chauvin added,

> Categorically, the Fairness Doctrine inhibits. We are very reluctant to put any issue on the air because of what it triggers—outside of news which is more traditionally balanced.

Chauvin is not alone in the industry in his evaluation of the effect of the rule. The Chairman and General Manager of KSTP-TV in Minneapolis, Stanley Hubbard, says his station "practiced fairness before there was a Fairness Doctrine." In an October 1982 telephone interview he noted that his father started broadcasting in 1923. Concepts of fairness have long applied to his station's news operation but he says the rule has discouraged KSTP from doing other types of controversial programming.

In one episode KSTP gave airtime to the Vietnam Veterans for a Just Peace but denied reply time to an antiwar group, Laymen and Clergy Combined, because, Hubbard said, the station's programming had been weighted on the antiwar side. A complaint was filed by the antiwar group. Hubbard said that even though the station's judgment was upheld by the FCC, "it cost us $50,000 for that one."

The General Manager of WZZM-TV in Grand Rapids, George Lyons, described this problem as "a can of worms." In a telephone interview he said, "You want to serve the public, and do, but this is a business, too."

Activist groups such as SECC see it differently. SECC calls recent attempts to abolish the Fairness Doctrine "the single most important issue threatening all activist groups alike in this country" because the doctrine is "an integral part of the strategy for every major cause which is working within the political system and cannot afford to purchase extensive advertising time."[14]

Though the doctrine is useful to these groups, free airtime is not always so easily obtained. When Pacific Gas and Electric placed pronuclear ads on 24 northern California TV stations, only 12 stations bowed to requests and agreed to run free responses. A complaint against six of the holdouts was launched by the Environmental Defense Fund, but the FCC threw it out. The stations maintained the ads addressed no controversial issue, and the FCC agreed.[15]

This short survey of the Fairness Doctrine as it really operates indicates that the formal complaint process is almost completely useless to the general public. And even specialized groups with legal expertise are rarely successful in their complaints. Because of the formal system's failure and its expensive, time-consuming nature, it has become something for everybody to avoid. This, in turn, has led to *informal* methods for resolving disputes about broadcasters' coverage of controversial issues. The informal arrangements generally result in organized groups getting access to the airwaves. The Fairness Doctrine was never designed to accomplish this particular end, although it does satisfy one general aim of the doctrine: presenting a contrasting viewpoint.

The FCC has recommended that Congress abolish the doctrine—a reflection of the general antiregulatory climate in Washington. Groups that use the doctrine as a negotiating tool report that lately the FCC appears even more unsympathetic toward complaints, even complaints from respected sources such as MAP. MAP sees this as also "reflecting the increased clout of the broadcast industry."[16] The FCC's Milton O. Gross, branch chief in charge of Fairness complaints, with 14 years of experience in the area, denies this. He maintains that as long as the law remains unchanged, the FCC's proposed abolition of the doctrine does not affect how it is administered.[17]

One of the major reasons given for recommending repeal of the Fairness Doctrine is that it has a "chilling effect" on broadcasters, making them avoid programming about controversial issues for fear of an expensive FCC fight or of being forced to give away free airtime. If this is the impact of the rule, it defeats the doctrine's original purpose of encouraging more robust coverage of controversial issues.

## References

1. *Cullman Broadcasting Co.,* 40 FCC 576 (1963).
2. See pp. 81–86 for a discussion of this organization's activities.
3. It's also called Telecommunications Research and Action Committee (TRAC).
4. September 9, 1982, interview with Andrew Jay Schwartzman, MAP executive director.
5. *KXTV and Robert De Vries* (CAIF), May 28, 1980, FCC decision.
6. Media Access Project, *1982 Annual Report,* p. 21.
7. Theoretically it could. But in practice, as we have seen, the record of Fairness Doctrine enforcement suggests that license revocation is highly unlikely.
8. National Association of Broadcasters, *Government Control of Broadcasting—The First Amendment.*
9. The DNC complaint is discussed more fully in Chapter 9.
10. *KGO-TV and Citizens to Tax Big Oil,* June 23, 1980, FCC decision.
11. Geller, op. cit., p. 134.
12. For more on the question of issue advertising, see Chapters 7 and 8.
13. Interview, October 22, 1982, with S. Burton on Winner/Wagner & Associates, representative of Committee for Energy Awareness.

14. Interview, October 7, 1982, with SECC representative Barbara Joy; May 19, 1981, SECC correspondence with Media Access Project.
15. *KERO-TV, KEJO, KMST, KECR-TV, KRON-TV, and KTXL,* April 17, 1981, FCC decision.
16. Media Access Project, *1981 Annual Report,* p. 6.
17. September 8, 1982, interview.

# FIVE

# The Uneasy Truce: Regulators and Journalists

THE WARFARE BETWEEN broadcasters and regulators seems to have abated, at least for now. This is due partly to the political composition of the Federal Communications Commission. The deregulatory philosophy of the Carter and Reagan administrations, particularly the latter, seems to be taking hold. But this has come after a protracted period of administrative and judicial contests that have shaped a regulatory milieu that has proven almost impossible to alter.

Even in the heyday of regulatory zeal there was a recognition within the FCC of the dangers of applying the Fairness Doctrine in too heavy-handed a way. Section 326 of the Communications Act prohibits government censorship, and the line between censorship and regulation is not always clear. Those entrusted with applying the rules often exercised restraint. Henry Geller, former general counsel of the FCC, stated that the "basic problem" in assuring fairness is that if the FCC "intervenes unduly or inappropriately to assure that the broadcaster is fulfilling his public trustee obligation by not being one-sided, it may well thwart the goal of robust debate. Thus a difficult and delicate 'tightrope' balance is called for."[1]

The government has tried, overall, to tread lightly when scrutinizing that type of programming most likely to deal regularly with the elements of "robust debate," news programming.

When the question of fairness is raised, most people think immediately of television and radio news. But the Fairness Doctrine has come to apply to news both more and less than the public might expect. The rules affect more than just newscasts; they also affect station editorials, public affairs programs, talk shows, and even commercials. Yet in some respects the rules involve TV and radio news less than might be assumed. The FCC is cautious about holding journalists to strict formulas of fairness, yet is more rigorous in applying its rules to other types of programs.

FCC handling of complaints about news fairness shows how an uneasy truce has been declared. It is not all quiet; skirmishes still erupt on this front, especially over the way television treats controversial subjects.

This chapter examines public attitudes about broadcast news to discern why people sometimes believe it is unfair. It then examines how the FCC has refused to become the judge of what is accurate on the news. Then it looks at FCC policies designed to force stations to air controversial issues. Finally it examines the often inconsistent decisions on what actually constitutes a Fairness Doctrine issue. The goal is to assess whether the regulations are relevant to the public concern about what is sometimes perceived as unfair news coverage.

Although television news enjoys wide viewership across the land, there is widespread uneasiness about the fairness of what is portrayed on news programs. A 1980 poll by the Public Agenda Foundation revealed broad concern about fairness, not only on television but in newspapers as well. More than 80 percent of those surveyed believed that television and newspapers should be required to give major candidates for public office the same amount of coverage. More than 70 percent favored laws requiring television and newspapers to give opponents of a controversial policy as much coverage as proponents.

That survey showed a lack of public support for the autonomy of the news media, and a desire for regulation to assure that diverse points of view would be presented in newspapers, radio, and television. Other polls have indicated much the same sentiment. A Gallup Poll conducted for a 1980 First Amendment Congress found that public opinion is "indifferent and to some extent even hostile to the cause of a free press in America."

One of the cofounders of the Public Agenda Foundation, public opinion analyst Daniel Yankelovich, concluded that many Americans are more concerned that the media, not government, may restrict freedom of expression because the media have the power to select the information to be transmitted to the public. "What is paramount to the public is the ability to hear all significant points of view," Yankelovich found. Fairness, he concluded, is the "primary value. Media freedom is secondary."

Opinion surveys have painted an unclear, confused picture of how the question of media bias is viewed by the public. "Since not even the antagonists and protagonists agree on whether the news media are guilty of anti-business bias, it should surprise no one that public opinion seems similarly split over the controversy," according to Frank Kalupa of the University of Georgia.[2] He notes some surprising survey results on how the public perceives bias. In one study involving over 1,500 "middle class adults," about 60 percent believed the media to be somewhat biased or very biased in business coverage.[3] The remaining 40 percent thought the media generally unbiased, but what was surprising was the breakdown within the majority who felt there was bias. Of the respondents who thought news coverage of business issues was biased, about half perceived it to be probusiness and the other half perceived it to be antibusiness. As Kalupa pointed out, these findings tend to confirm an observation that "news bias is less a function of reporters' accuracy or fairness and more a function of what readers and viewers think the situation is or ought to be."[4]

Moreover, the leaders of the news profession often use the First Amendment, which was designed to protect against government interference, as an all-purpose shield against any criticism from any quarter. Lester Markel remarked on this phenomena:

> The press, pretending to believe that there is no credibility gap and asserting its near-infallibility, countenances no effective supervision of its operation; it has adopted a holier-than-thou attitude, citing the First Amendment and in addition the Ten Commandments and other less holy scripture.[5]

While journalists should quite properly resist any government attempts to dictate what is reported, the First Amendment does not render the press unaccountable to its audience. Much of public concern about unfairness in the news stems from the arrogant attitude of some editors and producers when confronted with complaints about poor coverage.

Among business leaders, television is most often cited as the worst media offender. A Louis Harris poll printed in the October 18, 1982, issue of *Business Week* found that 73 percent of the executives surveyed believed that business coverage on television is prejudiced against business. (Just under 40 percent felt the same way about newspaper coverage of business.) Executives of those industries and businesses subjected to intense media scrutiny were most outspoken in their criticism.

Ronald Rhody, vice president for public relations of the Kaiser Aluminum and Chemical Corporation, equates being interviewed for a network news program with going on trial, where the news production team is the accuser, judge, and jury. "Under the rules of this court," Rhody says, "the 'accused' may speak only through the prosecutor, and the prosecutor has the exclusive right to decide what portions of the 'accused's' defense the jury will be allowed to hear, and in what manner that defense will be presented."[6] Under such circumstances, Rhody asks, why should a business that finds itself "accused" on television submit to interrogation?

It should be noted that criticism of television news for being unfair usually results from disagreement with the story theme and conclusions reached in the news report. As in the case of Kaiser Aluminum, the target of the report is usually offered a chance to tell its side of the story. What is perceived as unfair is the thrust of the report, rather than a reporter's failure to seek out divergent points of view.

In fact, if anything, television news is confrontational. News reporters, producers and editors see it as their duty to find and report disputes, conflicts, and arguments. The drive to find spokespersons with varying viewpoints goes beyond the ethical duty of journalists to "get the other side of the story." Almost by definition, a good story must have more than one side. Agreement is dull; confrontation is exciting. The unfairness that many people perceive in the news stems not from the absence of contrasting views, but in fact may be partly due to the clash, the near cacophony, of viewpoints.

A common attitude among news personnel is that the Fairness Doctrine has almost no impact on their daily work. They may oppose the rule on ideological grounds as an infringement of First Amendment rights, but in actual practice the Fairness Doctrine rarely forces them to do something they had not already wanted to do: present contrasting views. It is the nature of news coverage, as practiced nowadays, to highlight dissension, the unusual, and the unsettling. Once a topic is deemed newsworthy, opponents are sought out to dramatize the differences.

One example is telling: When William P. Tavoulareas, president of Mobil Corporation, testified in 1979 before a congressional committee about the long lines at gasoline stations, he spent several hours explaining Mobil's views on price controls and the proposed windfall profits tax. During the hearing, Democratic Congressman Andrew Maguire of New Jersey held up a poster for the cameras covering the event. "No decontrol," the sign read. Maguire proceeded to accuse Mobil of price gouging and profiteering. Tavoulareas tried to defend his company but finally, exasperated, he stalked from the hearing room. That night's coverage on ABC's "World News Tonight" ignored the substance of Mobil's testimony while the tape of the confrontation between Maguire and

Tavoulareas was highlighted. As often happens, television's attention focused on the exciting, the visual, and the confrontational.[7]

Had ABC only run Maguire's comments, there might have been a Fairness Doctrine problem with its coverage; but this incident dramatizes how the perceived unfairness does not stem from a failure to present contrasting views as much as from overemphasis on what is contrasting. No wonder companies like Mobil and Kaiser resist television news interviews, and seek to control their messages by demanding unedited airtime or by purchasing advertising time for issue-oriented messages.

Rhody's Kaiser Aluminum requested an unedited appearance on ABC's "20/20" program to respond to that show's attack on the company, but was refused. After much negotiation, ABC invited Rhody to appear on its "Viewpoint" program to discuss the issues first aired on "20/20." That arrangement proved satisfactory to the company, because even though it faced questioning on the program, the answers would not be subjected to editing.

But such arrangements are rare, and under the Fairness Doctrine, a complainant has few grounds on which to object after he has refused an invitation to be interviewed for a broadcast. Once such an invitation has been declined, the complainant will find little sympathy from the FCC; after all, the station need only provide a reasonable *opportunity* for presentation of contrasting views. The rule does not mandate the actual presentation, only that stations provide an opportunity.

## Ethics and Fairness

Most journalists, even those who disagree with the idea of government regulation, agree with the values embodied in the Fairness Doctrine. Good reporters want to focus on public issues and tell all sides of the story. Moreover, ethical standards for journalists go beyond the twofold duty to present significant issues and provide contrasting viewpoints. First among the standards that good journalists voluntarily follow is the requirement that reports be accurate.

Nowhere is the dichotomy between a voluntary ethical standard and government regulation more stark. The Fairness Doctrine does not require that stories be accurate. The way the Doctrine has been defined and other rules have been applied has left the public largely unprotected from a broadcaster who might air untruths. This is not to argue that the FCC *ought* to be a watchdog—only that public perceptions that it *is* are unfounded. The FCC itself is responsible for some of the misconception that it acts to keep the media honest.

The FCC has stated that deliberate distortion of the news is a most serious matter that could reflect on the basic character qualifications of a licensee. The FCC has denounced slanting of the news and staging of events in no uncertain terms.[8] The Fairness Doctrine is not the tool to ferret out such practices; it deals with sins of omission, the failure to present issues or contrasting viewpoints. Slanting, staging, or distortion are sins of commission, which are beyond the scope of the Doctrine.

The FCC has indicated that hard evidence of deliberate distortion would reflect on whether a licensee possesses the requisite character to hold a license from the FCC. Thus, even if the Fairness Doctrine had never been invented, the FCC could reprimand or revoke the license of any station found to have slanted the news. As the commission stated in evaluating the CBS program "Hunger in America,"

> Rigging or slanting the news is a most heinous act against the public interest—indeed there is no act more harmful to the public's ability to handle its affairs. In all cases where we may appropriately do so, we shall act to protect the public interest in this important respect.[9]

But having denounced distortion, the commission proceeded to make it next to impossible to prove and punish any transgression. In the program "Hunger in America," the FCC refused to take action against CBS for misrepresenting the cause of death of an infant. Early in the documentary this moving sequence was presented:

> Hunger is easy to recognize when it looks like this. This baby is dying of starvation. He was an American. Now he is dead.

There was only one problem with the CBS report. Doctors who treated the infant said later that the child had been born prematurely and had died of complications, not starvation. Even so, the commission refused to intervene to determine whether CBS had "engaged in sloppy journalism or was recklessly indifferent to the truth. . . ."[10] The commission decided it was not the arbiter of truth where the complainant had not come forward with evidence that went beyond what was presented on the air, namely, extrinsic evidence of deliberate distortion. Such evidence could consist of testimony of a station employee that he had been instructed to falsify a report, or an incriminating memo to show that the owners or top management of the station had ordered slanting of a story. In short, the words and pictures on the TV screen were not enough; slanting could not be inferred from the program alone. Distortion could only be proved with a "smoking gun." However, because the commission's rules do not provide for discovery of such incriminating evidence (unless a strong threshold showing of a prima facie case is made) the evidence usually would be beyond the reach of a complainant under the Fairness Doctrine.

Such a heavy burden on a complainant is justified, the commission said, because in a democracy, "no Government agency can authenticate the news, or should try to do so."[11] The FCC decided to "eschew the censor's role, including efforts to establish news distortion in situations where Government intervention would constitute a worse danger than the possible rigging itself."[12]

This is a wise policy, but not an entirely consistent one. The FCC has portrayed itself as a vigorous foe of slanting, staging, and unfairness in the news, yet it does very little to police such conduct. If the myth of enforcement were dispelled, nongovernmental market forces, including public criticism of news gathering might increase—proving more effective than the bureaucrats in scrutinizing the media. Examples abound of how the FCC has been unable to come to grips with the problem.

In dismissing another Fairness Doctrine complaint against CBS for its program "Selling of the Pentagon," the commission rejected evidence that the network had edited film to distort the meaning of those who had been quoted. In one instance, a statement by a Marine colonel had been edited so that he appeared to be espousing views that he actually had quoted from the prime minister of Laos. In a second instance, an interview with an assistant secretary of defense was edited so that answers were rearranged, and remarks made in response to one question were seen following a separate, different question. Once again the commission noted that stations must require honesty of their news employees and must take reasonable precautions to see that the news is "fairly handled," but the FCC declined to decide if the editing was deliberate distortion.[13] Lacking extrinsic evidence of slanting, the commission declined to investigate.

> It would be unwise and probably impossible for the Commission to lay down some precise line of factual accuracy—dependent always on journalistic judgment—across which broadcasters must not stray. As we stated in the *Hunger in America* ruling, "the Commission is not the national arbiter of the truth" (20 FCC 2d at p. 151). Any presumption on our part would be inconsistent with the First Amendment and with the profound national commitment to the principle that debate on public issues should be "uninhibited, robust, [and] wide open" (*New York Times Co. v. Sullivan,* 376 U.S. 254, 270). It would involve the Commission deeply and improperly in the journalistic functions of broadcasters.[14]

Without extrinsic evidence of deliberate distortion, the commission avoided the "impenetrable thicket" of the editing process. The FCC indicated it would intervene in only the most extreme case, as when a "yes"

answer to one question had been used to replace a "no" answer to an entirely different question.[15] Failing such a clear-cut transgression, the commission required that a complainant prove his case with extrinsic evidence before he would be granted a hearing.

Although slanting has been condemned in no uncertain terms, the commission has avoided second-guessing broadcast editors. Even where extrinsic evidence has been produced, the FCC has shied from evaluating the broadcaster's conduct. After a viewer submitted a quote from a station manager that he had been ordered not to cover certain stories "because the wrong people would look bad," the FCC rejected the complaint alleging news suppression because the licensee's actions could have been based on private interests instead of public concerns.[16]

The scope of the alleged staging is important. When the Black Producers Association accused ABC News of staging certain fight scenes in the documentary "Youth Terror: The View from Behind the Gun," evidence included an audio tape of interviews of four persons who appeared in the broadcast and a statement from a member of the production staff of the program. But the complaint was rejected partly because the fight scenes involved only about 38 seconds of the hour-long documentary.[17]

This is not to say that the commission is powerless to act if testimony or documentary evidence indicated that an owner or a member of senior management ordered the news staff to perform in an overtly biased way. The punishment could be as severe as loss of license. But bias, by definition subjective, is usually implicit in the report rather than explicit in the preparation, and thus proof of the kind the FCC requires would rarely be available.

So the commission's role in the news area—as in other facets of programming—really has been to shout about problems but do very little to correct them. Given the potential threat to free expression implicit in any government crackdown, it is entirely proper for the FCC to keep hands off news content. But its practice of yelling about what stations and networks ought to do, its policy of intimidation, often has a major impact on broadcasters. It does not get to the heart of what bothers many observers about news fairness, however.

Most Fairness Doctrine litigation falls back to the twofold test of issue coverage and presentation of contrasting viewpoints. Such issues do not involve the accuracy, objectivity, or plausibility of the story in question. The FCC simply looks at whether a variety of viewpoints has been aired in a station's overall programming. Such a narrow view of fairness precludes examination of what common sense suggests are the essential elements of fairness: the truth, accuracy, and impartiality of a report. These dimensions of fairness are alien to the day-to-day application of the Fairness Doctrine.

## What Must a Station Cover?

Even if the Fairness Doctrine is largely irrelevant to most journalistic endeavors and fails to address the roots of perceived unfairness in the news, it has had an impact on broadcasting. Some hard-fought cases have narrowed broadcasters' discretion to decide which issues are newsworthy and which trigger the duty to provide contrasting viewpoints. The expense and sometimes inconsistent outcome of litigation indicates the risk a broadcaster assumes if he either ignores or aggressively spotlights controversial issues.

The first part of the Fairness Doctrine, requiring presentation of significant issues, has been called the "forgotten half" of the doctrine.[18] The 1949 *Report on Editorializing* stressed the importance of informing the public about "news and ideas concerning the vital public issues of the day."[19] The FCC emphasized a licensee's duty to devote airtime for the discussion of issues, including a "reasonable percentage" of time for news and other issue-oriented programming. This general duty to carry issues produced little enforcement. There are only a few cases involving a station's responsibility to air specific issues.

In 1950 a representative of the United Auto Workers of America complained that a radio station refused to permit discussion of a strike because the auto manufacturers would not take part in the program. The FCC criticized the station for failing to air an issue the station had conceded was "of paramount importance," but the commission took no punitive action.[20] That same year an FCC administrative law judge criticized a licensee for shortcomings in discharging "its overall public service responsibilities" because the station had a policy of avoiding all discussions of controversial issues, political matters, pending legislation, and the like.[21] During the 1950s and 1960s the duty to present programming about public issues was not considered a major component of the Fairness Doctrine; most complaints involved alleged imbalance *after* a station had presented an issue.

There was increased interest in using the Fairness Doctrine's forgotten part in the 1970s, when interest groups were clamoring to buy time for issue-oriented advertising or demanding free time to counter views raised in paid commercials. In a case involving the Democratic National Committee, the FCC was asked to rule that a station could not refuse to sell time to responsible groups for comment on public issues.[22] The FCC refused to order stations to sell time for issue ads, but noted that there had been no claim that the station had failed to fulfill its duties under the Fairness Doctrine to air major controversies. The Supreme Court upheld the FCC position, but said stations were obliged to provide "full and fair coverage of public issues."[23]

In a case involving an activist group called Friends of the Earth, the FCC denied a complaint seeking airtime to rebut automobile and gasoline commercials, but did state that licensees "have an obligation to inform the public to a substantial extent on these important issues."[24]

What has occurred is a mixture of two FCC policies: the Fairness Doctrine requirement to present major controversial issues, and the programming requirement that a station air material relating to the needs of the community it serves.[25] In one license renewal hearing where it was alleged that a station ignored a black group and other local news, the FCC emphasized the station's duty to air "major local problems" and "keep the public informed of important local news and to promote the discussion of substantial local issues."[26] But rhetoric aside, the consequence of FCC handling of this matter has not mandated much public issue programming.

Until 1975, the FCC had never ruled that a station had failed to live up to the requirement to cover important issues. In its 1974 *Fairness Report,* the commission described the obligation as the "most basic requirement" of the Fairness Doctrine, but left it to the individual broadcaster to choose which news items and issues to present.[27]

The FCC changed its hands-off approach to issue selection in the *Patsy Mink* case. Mink, a member of Congress, helped prepare and promote an 11-minute tape about pending strip mining legislation. She asked stations that had run a program prepared by the U.S. Chamber of Commerce to air her tape as a contrasting viewpoint to the Chamber's broadcast. But station WHAR in Clarksburg, West Virginia, declined to air Mink's tape, explaining that it had not broadcast the chamber's program, or *any* programming on strip mining.[28] Attorneys for the Media Access Project took Mink's complaint to the FCC, arguing that strip mining was of "extraordinary controversiality and public importance to WHAR's listeners."[29]

The commission sided with Mink and the Media Access Project, concluding that strip mining was so important in the region served by WHAR, and was so highly controversial, that WHAR could not ignore the issue.[30] While the FCC said it had "no intention of intruding on licensees' day-to-day editorial decision making," it found WHAR in violation of the Fairness Doctrine.[31] The station was required to state within 20 days how it intended to meet its Fairness Doctrine obligations, that is, how it would present programming on strip mining.

Despite dicta about not wishing to interfere with a station's editorial selections, the *Patsy Mink* decision opens the door for exactly that kind of second-guessing by government regulators. Given that WHAR's avoiding a major issue was indefensible on journalistic grounds, the case may prove to be a unique exception to the FCC's general unwillingness to dictate which issues stations must carry. But the precedent exists for an expanded role, if the FCC decides in the future to be more aggressive in monitoring compliance with its rules. As Bill F. Chamberlin noted, the coverage requirement is potentially dangerous because it encourages government interference in specific program content.[32] The FCC asserted that it has the last word on which issues must be aired. Chamberlin said the commission "moved towards taking the more active, and sinister, role of determining the subject of discussion, which is but one step from determining that which is said."[33]

Even aggressive regulatory action along the lines of the *Patsy Mink* case might fail to supply the remedy complainants seek from the government. As Steven J. Simmons has pointed out, the original complaint against WHAR was filed in September 1974, but the FCC decision was not adopted until June 1976.[34] Twenty-one months had elapsed, Congress had passed strip mining legislation, but the people of Clarksburg had received no information on the subject from WHAR. Such after-the-fact regulatory action hardly filled the void created by the station's indifference.

The *Patsy Mink* decision creates uncertainty as to which issues are so critical, important, and vital that a station must provide coverage. The FCC has said that stations must not ignore contemporary "burning issues,"[35] but it has failed to come to grips with how to assure compliance without intruding deeply into daily editorial decisions of broadcasters. In fact, in the years since the *Mink* decision the trend has been toward deregulation. The active "sinister role" that Chamberlin warned against has not been adopted by the FCC, but the precedent exists for it to intervene in the future. And there's pressure on broadcasters to air news and public affairs, despite deregulation.

When the FCC was considering modest proposals to lighten the regulatory burden on radio stations, FCC Commissioner Abbott Washburn appeared before a congressional subcommittee to argue that it was necessary and desirable that stations carry some news. "They had a terrible tornado down there in Texas this week," he testified. "Young people listening to a rock station in Wichita Falls might have had no warning of the danger if we didn't require the licensee to provide a minimum of news."[36] Congressman Lionel Van Deerlin, the subcommittee chairman, said that this comment revealed the mindset of the Washington bureaucracy; "it conjured up the picture of a disc jockey diving under a studio table, clutching his microphone but saying nothing about the roaring black cloud outside because Commissioner Washburn and cohorts hadn't told him he must."[37]

In 1981 the FCC voted to "deregulate" some aspects of commercial AM and FM radio, including commercial time rules, log requirements, and formal ascertainment procedures.[38] Radio stations were relieved of the requirement to air minimum amounts of nonentertainment programming, such as newscasts. But stations were still required each year to prepare a list of 10 or fewer important local issues that had been aired, giving examples of the programs that addressed those issues. Percentage guidelines on news and public affairs had been lifted, but radio licensees were not freed of the requirement to air significant issues and provide contrasting viewpoints under the Fairness Doctrine. The U.S. Court of Appeals upheld radio deregulation but told the FCC it ought to give further consideration to retaining some requirements for program logs so that citizens will have information to challenge a station when it seeks to have its license renewed.[39]

### Which Issues Are Fairness Doctrine Issues?

The uncertainty created by FCC policies mandating coverage of significant issues is mild compared to the confusion generated over another line of cases. The most hotly contested Fairness Doctrine cases involve deciding which issues, *once they have been carried by a station,* are so controversial and of such public importance that the station must present contrasting viewpoints. This second part of the doctrine accounts for most of the litigation.

If a complaint is filed alleging that a station has not provided contrasting viewpoints in its coverage of an issue, the first task is to ascertain precisely what issue was raised in the broadcast. Then that issue is examined to see if it is truly controversial and of public importance. At first glance, this may seem a simple matter of looking at a tape or script of the program, spotting the subject matter, and judging its controversiality and importance. But the FCC has turned this into one of the most complicated and convoluted exercises.

Consider, for example, these varying determinations: An "NBC Nightly News" series on the problems of air traffic safety and congestion indicated that a major factor was the presence of private pilots in the skies. When the Aircraft Owners and Pilots Association complained that this had been raised as a subissue, the FCC's Broadcast Bureau staff ruled that NBC would have to program pro-private-pilot viewpoints to counter the negative statements made in the series. The full commission rejected the rationale, ruling that the "thrust of the program" had been congestion at large airports.[40] NBC did not have to provide additional viewpoints from the private pilots because, the FCC said, "If every statement, or inference from statements or presentations, could be made the subject of a separate and distinct fairness requirement, the doctrine would be unworkable."[41]

But the commission came to a different conclusion regarding a complaint lodged by Accuracy in Media, Inc. (AIM) against a Public Broadcasting Service program, "Justice." AIM said the program's discussion of the trials of Angela Davis and the Soledad brothers raised an issue about those trials and had failed to provide contrasting viewpoints. PBS said the only issue raised was how well the law enforcement system, including the courts and prisons, were functioning. The FCC rejected both definitions of the issue, deciding on its own that the program had raised two subissues—whether blacks receive justice in the United States and whether prisons can rehabilitate criminals.[42] As Simmons has noted, the commission offered no rationale or evidence from the text of the program to justify this conclusion.[43]

These decisions indicate how difficult it is to determine just what the issue is. One broadcaster asserted that a program entitled "Hunger: A National Disgrace" did not raise the issue of whether hunger is indeed a national disgrace, and the FCC said that was a reasonable conclusion![44]

Sometimes an issue is only implicitly addressed, as in an entertainment program or a commercial. In news programming, issues are usually explicitly addressed, but often subissues are raised or other issues are mentioned briefly. The commission has had difficulty grappling with these cases, and deciding which subissues or related issues trigger the Fairness Doctrine requirements for contrasting views.

Even where the issue seems clear-cut, there's always the problem of deciding if it's truly controversial and of public importance. Not all issues are controversial, and not all controversies affect the public. Those issues that fail to meet the test propounded in the 1974 *Fairness Report* may be presented in whatever way the broadcaster wishes, with or without contrasting viewpoints.[45] In deciding which issues trigger the rule, the *Fairness Report* test asks first whether an issue is of public importance. Three factors are considered: how much media coverage it has received, how much attention it has received from public officials and community leaders, and "a subjective evaluation of the impact that the issue is likely to have on the community at large."[46] Of these, the third test, looking to the likely impact of an issue, is the most important.[47]

There is no impact test in determining the controversiality of an issue, and hence the judgment can be made in a more objective manner. But some of the same tests used to determine public importance are used to consider controversiality, namely, the amount of attention given the issue by the media and government and community leaders. If an issue is the subject of wide debate and generates significant opposition, then it usually is controversial.

These are rather vague guidelines, purposely so, for the FCC in its *Fairness Report* said it would rely on a licensee's reasonable, good-faith judgment in deciding which issues are of such controversy and public importance that he must present contrasting viewpoints. But in the event of a complaint, the FCC can reevaluate that judgment, reversing those that are found not to have been reasonable or made in good faith. As former FCC Commissioner Benjamin Hooks told Simmons, evaluating whether an issue is controversial and of public importance is "almost like pornography; I may not be able to define it, but I know it when I see it."[48] On such nebulous standards are fairness questions determined.

Among the topics the FCC has said are *not* controversial issues of public importance are bullfighting in Spain,[49] atheism,[50] theories of curved space,[51] and amoral sexual relationships.[52] When a complaint was filed against CBS after a "60 Minutes" report criticized the private guard industry, the FCC ruled that the network had not raised an issue of public importance.[53] A casual observer might wonder why "60 Minutes" would explore an issue if the network felt it was not of public importance.

Several recent decisions will show how the commission addresses complaints about imbalanced programming. In a case involving the NBC miniseries "Holocaust," a complaint alleged that NBC had only presented one side about the "allegation of a German policy of Jewish extermination during the Second World War."[54] The complainants wanted NBC to air a contrary view, that the Holocaust had not occurred. But the FCC rejected the complaint, agreeing with NBC that the network could reasonably conclude that the Holocaust program did not raise a current controversial issue of public importance.

In September 1982 the FCC rejected a complaint brought by the Joint Council of Allergy and Immunology against ABC for an item broadcast on "World News Tonight." The story discussed new ways of treating allergies, and the council felt it failed to show that traditional treatment methods are safe and effective. ABC responded that the topic was newsworthy, but not a controversial issue of public importance. ABC also pointed out that some criticism of the new treatment method had been included in the same broadcast, and that four times allergists had appeared to discuss the topic on "Good Morning America." The FCC held that ABC was reasonable in concluding that the topic was not a controversial issue of public importance.[55]

In March 1980, WCCO-TV of Minneapolis aired a documentary "The Moore Report—Feast of the Giants," which criticized the allegedly illegal actions of some grain-exporting companies, and growing monopolization of the grain and beef industries. The Iowa Beef Processors Inc. filed a complaint alleging that the report gave only one side of the issue. WCCO replied that the issue of competition and control in the food industry was not a controversial issue of public importance under the Fairness Doctrine. The station's response also pointed out that it had sought repeatedly to obtain an interview with a spokesperson of the Iowa Beef

Processors, and had invited one to participate in a follow-up "Town Meeting" discussion.

The Iowa Beef Processors submitted a lengthy record showing media attention and debate by public officials and community leaders. But the FCC sided with WCCO. The commission said the question is not whether the FCC thinks the issue raised is a controversial issue of public importance, but whether the station acted reasonably, in good faith, when it ruled on that question. Additionally, the FCC noted that WCCO's invitation to the Iowa Beef Processors to appear in interviews and on the "Town Meeting" program fulfilled any requirement under the Fairness Doctrine to afford a reasonable opportunity for presenting contrasting views.[56]

The fact that the FCC deferred to the judgment of the broadcasters in this sampling of cases should not obscure several points. First, in defending against each complaint, the broadcaster was forced to devote employee time, and pay for legal help. Second, the broadcaster was forced to argue that while newsworthy, the topics discussed were not really controversial or of public importance, something that presumably the station would be loath to do during its newscast. Just imagine a news anchor reading a story that began, "We have an exclusive report tonight on an issue that is not controversial or important. . . ." Third, and most important, the broadcaster was forced to account for his decision. Perhaps such accountability appeals to some who see media power as unbridled, but have these cases shown that media power actually was checked by regulation?

The FCC will discount the fact that a broadcaster has devoted airtime to a topic in assessing the public importance of the matter aired. When a complaint was filed after a one-hour program on the United Nations resolution equating Zionism with racism, the commission criticized the complainant for not demonstrating that there was any substantial debate in the United States as to whether Zionism is a form of racism.[57]

If the purpose of the Fairness Doctrine is to assure that the public is not left uninformed,[58] then one may question why the FCC requires complainants to make a threshold showing that an issue *already* is "the subject of vigorous debate with substantial elements of the community in opposition to one another."[59] If a vigorous debate is already underway, how likely is it that the public would be uninformed about the issue? If a complainant could meet the FCC's test by showing this element of public importance, presumably he would have demonstrated that the purpose of the doctrine already was being met—at least in part—and there would be less reason for concern that the public was left in the dark.

In any event, it seems strange to require a showing of vigorous public debate on a matter in order to surmount a procedural hurdle and advance to the substantive question of whether the public needs more information so it won't be left uninformed. It is those *other* types of issues, the under-reported, overlooked festering problems that merit attention; the Fairness Doctrine is no tool to shed light where darkness prevails.

## *Broken Promise or Controversial Public Issue?*

Nowhere has the problem of issue been tackled with such vigor as in a case involving one such overlooked problem area. The dispute arose after an NBC documentary "Pensions: The Broken Promise," was broadcast in 1972. The program highlighted problems in private pension plans, focusing on aging workers who were left without pensions despite a lifetime of work. The program won a George Foster Peabody Award, a Christopher Award, a National Headliner Award, and a Merit Award of the American Bar Association. But Accuracy in Media, Inc. (AIM) complained that the program had violated the Fairness Doctrine by presenting "a one-sided documentary that created the impression that injustice and inequity were widespread in the administration of private pension plans."[60] The program was a hard-hitting exposé of inadequate pension protection, featuring tragic cases of the elderly left without benefits. The program discussed the need for reform legislation. The little commentary that was favorable toward the private pension industry came in a brief reference near the end of the program when narrator Edwin Newman said, "This has been a depressing program to work on but we don't want to give the impression that there are no good private pension plans. There are many good ones, and there are many people for whom the promise has become reality."[61]

After AIM filed its complaint, NBC defended the program as presenting only a "broad overview" of "some" of the problems in "some" pension plans. The network argued that since it was clear that some problems did in fact exist in some plans, the program had not raised a controversial issue of public importance.

In many respects this was an astonishing claim. NBC had produced an award-winning documentary that revealed major shortcomings in an industry that had received almost no attention. It was a first-class journalistic product; it spurred controversy, and it addressed a matter of public importance. But in order to fight off the fairness complaint, NBC insisted its program had not raised an issue of controversy and public importance.

The FCC ruled that NBC had been unreasonable in its determination. The commission said the program's "overall thrust" was criticism of the entire pension system, including proposals that it be regulated.[62] NBC quickly appealed the unfavorable ruling to the federal appeals court in the District of Columbia.

A three-judge panel of the court found in favor of NBC, and reversed the FCC's ruling. The decision, by Judge Leventhal, said that since NBC was reasonable in viewing the topic of the broadcast as "some problems in some pension plans," the commission could not substitute its judgment on the question of what issue had been raised.[63] The court said the FCC had to abide by its rule of letting the broadcaster decide such questions as long as the broadcaster's determination was reasonable and made in good faith.[64]

> In the absence of extrinsic evidence that the licensee's characterization to the Commission was not made in good faith, the burden of demonstrating that the licensee's judgment was unreasonable to the point of abuse of discretion requires a determination that reasonable men viewing the program would not have concluded that its subject was as described by the licensee.[65]

The court concluded that the commission may have started on the "wrong path" when it undertook to determine for itself whether the program did raise a controversial issue of public importance. To overturn a licensee's judgment the commission had to find that judgment was unreasonable or made in bad faith. In the *Pensions* case it had failed to meet this burden.

The majority opinion was vigorously attacked in a dissent by Judge Tamm, and again in a dissent by Judge Bazelon when the full appeals court was deciding whether to rehear the case. The dissenters said that the FCC had not ignored the standard of reasonableness nor had it substituted its own judgment for the network's. The FCC acted properly, the dissenters said, in evaluating what issues the broadcast raised to determine if NBC's version was reasonable. NBC's conclusion that the program was not about a controversial issue of public importance was an unreasonable conclusion, according to the dissent.

NBC had won a clear-cut victory from the three-judge appeals court, but it was short-lived. The full appeals court decided to vacate that decision and rehear the case *en banc,* according to Fred Friendly, because of concern the initial decision had gone too far in weakening the Fairness Doctrine.[66] But two weeks before the full appeals court was scheduled to hear oral arguments, a majority of judges voted to drop the case, out of concern that the controversy had vanished from the pension reform issue with passage of the Employment Retirement Income Security Act of 1974, thus rendering the *Pensions* case moot.[67] In his dissent, Judge Bazelon blasted his colleagues for ducking the constitutional issue and rejected the idea that the matter was moot.[68] But the full court sent the matter back to the three judges of the original appellate panel that heard the case. It issued a decision that pleased neither NBC nor Accuracy in Media. Although the network won, the court's second opinion did not include a decision on the merits; instead it returned the matter to the FCC for burial, with the implication that the controversy was moot in light of passage of the pension law. As Friendly concluded:

> The Court of Appeals of the District of Columbia, which is regarded as the upper house of the FCC, had again demonstrated how splintered and contentious its members are when faced with the vagaries of the Fairness Doctrine.[69]

Throughout the entire litigation, as far as Friendly could ascertain, not one of the members of the FCC or the appeals court ever viewed the "Pensions" show, when it first aired or on tape. Every decision was based on a transcript of the program, ignoring the visual content of our most visual medium.

The *Pensions* case points up the difficulty under the Fairness Doctrine of deciding who decides. A common-sense viewing of the program suggests that NBC intended to produce a documentary about an important public matter that deserved to be the focus of scrutiny and controversy. NBC's effort to avoid an adverse Fairness Doctrine ruling seems convoluted. The commission's evaluation of the issue seems on the mark, but it thrust the FCC deep into the editorial process of the network. The Court of Appeals sought to protect the independence of the editorial decision-making process, but brushed aside the sound logic applied by the FCC.

Despite the impression that a neutral reading of the "Pensions" transcript would require a conclusion that the program was not balanced, the ultimate outcome of the case was justified by a concern that the FCC had intruded too much into the journalistic function. NBC had performed a public service by exposing the pension problem, then it had been forced to expend more than $100,000 battling the Fairness Doctrine complaint. Had it been required to present additional programming, against its will, providing free access to defenders of pension plans, it would have been much more careful in the future either to include heavy doses of contrary views or to ignore controversial issues altogether.

Incidents like the *Pensions* litigation provide a strong disincentive to networks and stations interested in tackling tough issues. But has the Fairness Doctrine chilled journalistic endeavor? Or on the other hand, has bias been pervasive in broadcast news despite the regulation?

## References

1. Henry Geller, *The Fairness Doctrine in Broadcasting* (Santa Monica, Calif., Rand, 1973), p. 11.
2. "Public Attitudes Show Surprising Split on Whether TV News is Anti-Business," The Media Institute, *Business-Economic News Report* (December 1982/January 1983), p. 6.

3. Robert Peterson, George Kozmetsky, and Isabella Cunningham, *Journalism Quarterly* (Autumn 1982).
4. Quoting Robert Stevenson and Mark Greene, "A Reconsideration of Bias in the News," *Journalism Quarterly* (Spring 1980).
5. Lester Markel, "Watching the Press," *New York Times,* February 2, 1973, p. 31.
6. Speech to the Media Institute Business/Media Luncheon Series, April 15, 1981.
7. This incident and other examples of press conduct were described in an excellent series of articles on the news media by A. Kent MacDougall in the *Los Angeles Times* on February 3-7, 1980.
8. *CBS, "Hunger in America,"* 20 FCC 2d 143 (1969), *CBS, "The Selling of the Pentagon,"* 30 FCC 2d 150 (1971).
9. 20 FCC at 151.
10. 20 FCC at 147.
11. 20 FCC at 151.
12. Id.
13. 30 FCC at 153.
14. 30 FCC at 152.
15. 30 FCC at 153.
16. *Melvin Pulley,* 58 FCC 2d 1224-1226 (1976).
17. *The Black Producers Association,* 70 FCC 2d 1920 (1979).
18. Kurnit, "Enforcing the Obligation to Present Controversial Issues: The Forgotten Half of the Fairness Doctrine" 10 *Harvard Civil Liberties—Civil Rights Law Review* 137 (1975).
19. *Editorializing by Broadcast Licensees, Report of the Commission,* 13 FCC 2d 1246, 1248 (1949) [hereinafter, *Report on Editorializing*].
20. *Evening News Association,* 40 FCC 441 (1950); see Bill F. Chamberlin, "The FCC and the First Principle of the Fairness Doctrine: A History of Neglect and Distortion," *Federal Communications Law Journal* 361, 363 (1979).
21. *Morrisville Broadcasting Co.,* Pike & Fischer, 6 *Radio Regulation* 77 (1950).
22. Democratic National Committee, 25 FCC 2d 216 (1970), reversed sub nom. *Business Executives' Move for Vietnam Peace* v. *FCC,* 450 F.2d 642 (D.C. Cir. 1971), reversed sub nom *CBS* v. *DNC,* 412 U.S. 94 (1973).
23. 412 U.S. 94, 129 (1973).
24. *Friends of the Earth Concerning Fairness Doctrine* re Station SBNB-TV (Gary Soucie), 24 FCC 2d 743, 750 (1970), *reversed on other grounds,* 449 F.2d 1164 (D.C. Cir. 1971).
25. Report and Statement Re: Commission en banc Programming Inquiry, 44 FCC 2302, 2312-2314 (1960).
26. Application of Radio Station WSNT, 27 FCC 2d 993, 995, 999 (1971); see 31 *Federal Communications Law Journal* 361, 383 Note 98 (1979).
27. FCC, *Fairness Doctrine and Public Interest Standards, Fairness Report Regarding Handling of Public Issues,* 39 Fed. Reg. 26372, 26375 (1974). [1974 *Fairness Report*]
28. 59 FCC 2d 987, 996 (1976). WHAR later said some coverage of the strip mining controversy was carried on newscasts, but it appears from the record that coverage was skimpy at best.

29. Id. at 987–988.
30. Id. at 995–997.
31. Id. at 994, 997.
32. "The FCC and the First Principle of the Fairness Doctrine: A History of Neglect and Distortion," 31 *Federal Communications Law Journal* 361, 363 (1979).
33. Id. at 409.
34. *The Fairness Doctrine and the Media* (Berkeley, University of California Press, 1978), p. 171.
35. *Friends of the Earth,* 24 FCC 2d 743, 750 (1970).
36. Lionel Van Deerlin, "The Regulators and Broadcast News" in Marvin Barrett (Ed.), *Broadcast Journalism* (New York, Everett House, 1982), p. 206.
37. Id. at 207.
38. *Report and Order* in BC Docket 79–219, 46 Fed. Reg. 13888 (1981).
39. *Office of Communication of the United Church of Christ* v. *FCC,* Nos. 81–1032, 81–1463, 81–2127 and 81–2134 (D.C. Cir. 1981).
40. *National Broadcasting Company,* 25 FCC 2d 735, 737 (1970).
41. Id. at 736.
42. *Accuracy in Media, Inc.,* 39 FCC 2d 416 (1973), *affirmed on other grounds,* 521 F.2d 288 (D.C. Cir. 1975). PBS was found to have provided balance on these issues in its overall programming.
43. Simmons, op. cit., p. 149.
44. Discussed in Simmons, id. The case is *American Conservative Union,* 23 FCC 2d 33 (1970).
45. 1974 *Fairness Report,* 39 Fed. Reg. 26372.
46. Id., p. 26376.
47. *Arkansas Cable Television,* 58 FCC 2d 192 (1976); see Note, "The Fairness Doctrine: Fair to Whom?" 30 *Cleveland State Law Review* 485, 502 (1981).
48. Simmons, p. 179, note 56.
49. *The Clarin,* 28 FCC 2d 313 (1971).
50. *Madalyn Murray,* Pike & Fischer, 5 *Radio Regulation* 2d 263 (1965).
51. *Morton Schwartz,* 52 FCC 2d 596 (1975).
52. *Thomas J. Houser,* 52 FCC 2d 477 (1975).
53. *Security World Publishing Co.,* 59 FCC 2d 107 (1976).
54. *Ridgewood Group,* FCC 80–436, July 31, 1980.
55. Letter from FCC to Joint Council of Allergy and Immunology, September 10, 1982.
56. *In Re Complaint of Iowa Beef Processors, Inc.,* #13875, June 16, 1982.
57. *Douglas J. Allan,* 58 FCC 2d 181 (1976).
58. *Green* v. *FCC,* 447 F.2d 323, 329 (1971).
59. *Security World Publishing Co.,* 59 FCC 2d 107, 108 (1976); see 30 *Cleveland State Law Review,* 485, 503 (1981).
60. *Accuracy in Media, Inc.,* 40 FCC 2d 958, 963 (1973), *application for review denied,* 44 FCC 2d 1027 (1974), *reversed sub nom, National Broadcasting Co.* v. *FCC,* 516 F.2d 1101, *reversal vacated and rehearing en banc granted,* 516 F.2d 1156, *second reversal vacated as moot and remanded with direction to vacate initial order and dismiss complaint,* 516 F.2d 1180 (D.C. Cir. 1974). As

the case citation suggests, the federal appeals court had some difficulty deciding how to dispose of this case, with some judges concluding the matter had become moot with congressional passage of pension legislation, and others basing the remand on equity principles.

61. 516 F.2d at 1101.
62. 40 FCC 2d at 966.
63. 516 F.2d at 1117–1118.
64. 516 F.2d at 1117–1122.
65. 516 F.2d at 1121.
66. Fred W. Friendly, *The Good Guys, the Bad Guys, and the First Amendment* (New York, Vintage, 1976), p. 161.
67. Id. at 163.
68. Id. at 153–166.
69. Id. at 166.

# SIX

# The Cold War:
# News Fairness

IN THE MID-1970s a major complaint was lodged against one of the three television networks alleging pervasive bias in news reports about national security issues. An examination of the case tells as much about the government's enforcement of fairness regulations as it reveals about the alleged lack of objectivity. This chapter begins with that specific example, surveys more recent complaints of unfairness in the news, then evaluates the news profession for clues as to the nature of bias in journalism. It concludes with a discussion of whether government regulation is a viable tool in assuring balanced news coverage.

Most complaints that come to the FCC involving journalists start with the premise that a news program raised a controversial issue and then failed to present contrasting views. A major consideration in such cases is whether the issue actually was raised on the air, and if so, whether the issue really was an important public controversy.

In the most ambitious assault ever mounted against network news, the commission addressed a different question: whether the complaint had sufficiently specified the issue allegedly raised in news programming.

The case, *American Security Council Education Foundation*,[1] involved a lengthy study undertaken of coverage on the "CBS Evening News" during 1972 and 1973 of various national security matters. Included were U.S. military and foreign policy, Soviet military and foreign policy, Chinese military and foreign policy, and Vietnam affairs. The

ASCEF study was coordinated by Dr. Ernest W. Lefever of the Brookings Institution.[2] "CBS News" was chosen as the subject because CBS had the most viewers. ASCEF used "viewpoint analysis" to judge whether an opinion had been expressed by a reporter or person being interviewed during the newscast. It divided these opinions into three classes:

> Viewpoint A holds that the threat to U.S. security is more serious than perceived by the government, or that the United States ought to *increase* its national security efforts;
> Viewpoint B holds that present government threat perception is essentially correct, or U.S. military and foreign policy efforts are adequate. . . .
> Viewpoint C holds that the threat to U.S. security is less serious than perceived by the government, or that U.S. national security efforts should be *decreased.*[3]

The ASCEF study concluded that less than 4 percent of the items it studied reflected Viewpoint A, approximately 35 percent reflected Viewpoint B, and about 62 percent reflected Viewpoint C.[4] The study conceded that concern about the Vietnam war accounted for much of the tilt toward Viewpoint C, but that even when items about the war were excluded, the ratio of C views to A views still was 3 to 1.[5] The study concluded that CBS had slanted its news broadcasts in favor of "dovish" views, and against "hawkish" views.[6]

After ASCEF published its study in 1974, it called on the network to redress the imbalance, but CBS denied there was any such bias in its broadcasts. ASCEF filed a Fairness Doctrine complaint with the FCC, requesting that CBS be ordered to allow ASCEF to present Viewpoint A programming. In 1977 the FCC denied ASCEF's complaint, declaring it had failed to present prima facie evidence of a violation.[7]

The commission faulted ASCEF on several grounds. It said the national security issue encompassed too many subjects to be a well-defined, particular issue.[8] The classification scheme of viewpoints provided no explanation for the arbitrary assignment of some news items into particular categories.[9] And the FCC noted that ASCEF had only looked at the "CBS Evening News," rather than the network's overall programming.[10]

ASCEF appealed to the U.S. Court of Appeals for the District of Columbia and won a reversal from a three-judge panel.[11] The divided court said the FCC had abused its discretion because the national security issue was explicit and precisely formulated.[12] The issue, according to the court, was "plain as day: whether this nation should *do more, less or the same* about perceived threats to its national security."[13]

The appeals court granted a rehearing, *en banc,* and in a 6-to-3 decision changed the outcome, affirming the FCC's decision to dismiss the ASCEF complaint.[14]

The appeals court's final ruling upheld the FCC because the court said national security was too vague to meet the prima facie requirement of a specific, well-defined issue.[15] ASCEF's four subissues were too tangential to each other, and the complaint had failed to focus on a single topic.[16] While the court conceded that "there is no doubt that most of the issues aggregated by ASCEF under the umbrella of 'national security' are controversial issues of public importance,"[17] it declined to require that the FCC consider the alleged imbalance regarding the subissues.

The appeals court stated that enforcement of the Fairness Doctrine must take into account the "delicate balance" between the First Amendment rights of the broadcasters and the public's right to hear conflicting viewpoints.[18] To order a broadcaster to answer complaints based on amorphous issues would "unduly burden broadcasters without a countervailing benefit to the public's right to be informed."[19]

The court found that endorsement of the issue as formulated by ASCEF could create precedent that might affect news programming by causing broadcasters to forgo coverage of controversies.[20] Journalists might be "required to decide whether any of the day's newsworthy events is tied, even tangentially, to events covered in the past," and whether a report upset the balance in coverage.[21]

But in condemning ASCEF's "blunderbuss approach" of using an "umbrella issue" to seek redress for perceived imbalance, the appeals court turned its back on a more lenient approach to complaints it had previously employed. In dissent, Judge Willkey stated that the dismissal on grounds of issue ambiguity was almost unprecedented.[22] Both the FCC and the Court of Appeals had shown a tendency in prior cases to search inartful complaints to ascertain their meaning. The appeals court in *Green v. FCC* looked beyond the complaint's stated issue of "military recruitment" to evaluate five subissues.[23] While it ultimately ruled against that complaint, the court was willing to cull the complainant's evidence to try to help frame the issue.[24] The FCC in one case had rejected a complaint attacking coverage of the "Middle East" issue because the complaint failed to specify a particular aspect of the general topic.[25] But when another complaint described a "children's advertising" issue in three different ways, the commission treated all three descriptions as saying basically the same thing.[26] On these occasions, the commission has been willing voluntarily to extract subissues from complaints which seemed very general.[27] The dissent in the *ASCEF* case offered other examples of the commission's willingness to accept issue definitions advanced by complainants in cases involving abortion,[28] cigarette advertising,[29] and women's liberation.[30] After the rejection of the ASCEF claim of pervasive bias, it is questionable if any multifaceted issue would ever meet the prima facie test.[31]

In his dissent Judge Wilkey accused the court of turning the prima facie procedural question into an open-ended tool for the commission to avoid hard cases.[32] Calling the court's unwillingness to discern the issue "willful obtuseness," Wilkey warned if the FCC refuses to consider complaints with an umbrella issue it would be hard to make *any* major matter the subject of a fairness complaint.[33] The dissent asserted that the ruling could foreclose complaints aimed at countering pervasive imbalance on television and radio.[34]

In evaluating whether the *ASCEF* ruling properly balanced the public's right to know, which the Fairness Doctrine is supposed to promote, against the broadcasters' need to be freed of undue regulatory burdens,[35] it is important to note that the court seemed to alter the balancing test by weighing the benefit to the public against the broadcaster's burden of contesting a complaint.[36] To assist the broadcaster, the appeals court held that the complaint must provide him with "a clear understanding of the issue."[37]

Procedural questions aside, did ASCEF make a convincing showing of pervasive bias in one network's coverage of national security topics? Even if the FCC or the appeals court had accepted the issue of national security as capable of adjudication under the Fairness Doctrine, it might still have rejected the claim that CBS's coverage was imbalanced.[38] Complaints are supposed to allege that a broadcaster has "presented only one side of the question," in the words of the FCC's 1964 *Fairness Primer*.[39] Enforcement practice has given great editorial discretion to stations to meet "minimal standards of fairness."[40] Given the absence of a specific formulation for balance, ASCEF's findings of a 3-to-1 ratio of dove-to-hawk viewpoints, even if accepted, might not be so imbalanced as to require redress. In short, even accepting ASCEF's data would not mandate a ruling against CBS.

But the ASCEF study itself can be criticized for the kind of bias the group accused CBS of displaying in its coverage. First, as any good advocate recognizes, the way a question is posed often predetermines its answer. The assumptions underlying the ASCEF study reveal a simplistic view of a complicated set of topics. For example, national security means different things to other people, and it is not clear whether improved relations between the United States and China are a sign of weakening American resolve to combat communism or a shrewd diplomatic show of strength against the Soviet Union. In a tripolar contest, there are more variables and options than the ASCEF study recognized. The shortcomings become even more obvious when one considers the North-South debate in world affairs.

Moreover, the analytical methods in the ASCEF study were designed to guarantee the results the group intended. By devising Viewpoint B (that the U.S. defense effort is adequate) so that it coincided with the views of President Nixon, the secretary of defense and others in the government during the bombing of North Vietnam and Cambodia, the authors assured that only the most extreme hawks would fit into the A category.[41] For instance, when Senator Barry Goldwater said on CBS, "I'm for bombing them and bombing them and bombing them, and keeping it up until they come to the table and say, 'I want to quit,'" ASCEF labeled that as a B viewpoint.[42] So as the Nixon administration became more hawkish, its policy remained the determinant of Viewpoint B, shrinking the potential number of A viewpoints and expanding the body of opinion that would constitute a C viewpoint.[43] All those who supported the war but opposed the massive bombing of the North would thus be put in the C category.

The study originally included a Category D, which was deleted from the final report. If a story on CBS presented no viewpoint on whether the U.S. effort should be increased, decreased, or stay the same, it was classified as a D viewpoint. The study initially considered 1,396 news items. But when the items presenting no viewpoint were eliminated, the number of stories dropped to only 274.[44] By deleting 80 percent of the news items about national security, the ASCEF study ignored those most likely to be neutral or more objective than the ones surveyed.

Besides ignoring the neutral reporting on national security issues, the study was flawed by relying on abstracts and indexes. Fred Friendly faults ASCEF researchers for failing to look at tapes of actual broadcasts during 1973 while relying on abstracts prepared at Vanderbilt University.[45]

And the ASCEF study overlooked the political context in which national security matters were discussed in 1972 and 1973. Nixon was running for reelection and geared his campaign to present himself as the centrist candidate; his opponent, George McGovern, clearly occupied the left side of the spectrum. None of the major candidates expressed what ASCEF called A viewpoints. Had the survey been taken during 1964, when Senator Goldwater mounted a challenge from the right against Lyndon Johnson, presumably one would find more coverage of right-wing views. In 1972, CBS may only have reflected the composition of the political debate that was unfolding.[46]

In his concurrence in the *ASCEF* case, Chief Judge Wright argued that the methodological shortcomings of the ASCEF study rendered it "useless" as evidence of imbalance.[47] He disputed the idea that the Nixon policy (Viewpoint B in the study) actually represented the middle point on the political spectrum. He also noted that there are many more than just three views on national security:

If [ASCEF's] world is populated by "hawks," "sparrows," and "doves," the real world, as I understand it, is an aviary of inexhaustible variety.[48]

But ASCEF was not the only critic of the media's role in reporting military issues in general and the Vietnam war in particular. Edward J. Epstein showed that the three networks all began describing the war in negative tones after the 1968 Tet Offensive.[49] In a lengthy study of the press, Peter Braestrup came to similar conclusions about war coverage.[50] John P. Roche said the Braestrup study indicated "a shameful episode" by the media.[51] Press coverage made what was a significant military victory for anticommunist forces seem a demoralizing loss. James Reston indicated the power of the coverage when he concluded that maybe "the reporters and cameras were decisive in the end. They brought the issue of the war to the people, before Congress and the courts, and forced the withdrawal of American power from Vietnam."[52]

Perhaps the media only *reflected* the divisions over the war that had been manifested in public debate. No one would fault that role in reporting on the controversy. But some critics believed the press was *creating* the divisions. Max Kampelman stated that there is "substantial evidence that television became a potent influence in turning public opinion against the Vietnam War."[53] Although ASCEF's study suffered from conceptual and methodological flaws, it confirmed a suspicion held by many nonscientific observers of television news—that it had tilted against U.S. military policy.

The ASCEF complaint was one of the most thorough and vigorous ever mounted against news programming. Its failure reflects the concern of the FCC and appeals court about shielding electronic journalists from procedures that could chill news coverage and inhibit the robust, wide-open debate essential in a democracy. In his concurring *ASCEF* opinion, Judge Bazelon stated:

This case vividly illustrates the substantial constitutional perils inherent in the fairness doctrine. Unlike the personal attack and political editorial components of the fairness doctrine upheld in *Red Lion*, applying the fairness doctrine to daily news coverage poses a serious threat to the independence of the broadcast press.[54]

The *ASCEF* decision did not exempt daily news coverage from fairness regulation, but it did increase the procedural barriers to bringing a successful Fairness Doctrine complaint. Presumably a better-designed, more inclusive study buttressing a more cogent, well-specified issue alleging pervasive bias, could survive the prima facie test enunciated in the *ASCEF* case. But there's little doubt the decision curtailed use of the Fairness Doctrine by complainants.[55] Had the court's decision gone the other way, the FCC and the networks might have been faced with a torrent of complaints from those dissatisfied with overall media treatment of their issues.

## The Balancing Act

During the Vietnam war, ABC refused to televise the halftime show of a college football game presented because antiwar activists at the school planned to stage an antiwar show. During halftime the cameras were turned away from the field. ABC justified the decision because the show had "definite political implications."[56] A complaint was filed suggesting ABC Sports feared alienating potential customers of the sponsors buying airtime during the game.

But several weeks later when ABC televised the Army-Navy game, the network carried that halftime show, even though it featured military drills and an appeal for support for prisoners of war in Southeast Asia. ABC said the Army-Navy program had no political viewpoint.[57]

Despite the seeming imbalance, the FCC turned down the complaint, saying ABC's refusal to carry a particular program was within its discretion; the commission warned, however, that ABC would fulfill its obligations if it "arbitrarily and discriminately refused to broadcast valid ideas which are controversial."[58]

And the FCC has been willing to intervene in other programming decisions, including the politically charged controversy over the Vietnam war. In 1970 it adjudicated a complaint objecting to five televised addresses to the nation by the president about the war.[59] There was no question that the networks had presented contrasting viewpoints in overall programming, but the complaint suggested there was an inherent imbalance in having one outstanding spokesman with such a great podium overwhelm several opponents featured in shorter interviews. The commission agreed, saying it would be unreasonable for a broadcaster to fail to give opponents of the Vietnam policy an *uninterrupted* opportunity for an appropriate spokesperson to respond.[60]

Mandating a specific-reply opportunity ran counter to the FCC's statement the prior year that the Fairness Doctrine does not "prescribe the presentation of a news item or viewpoint nor does it specify any particular manner of presentation."[61] It made that assertion in turning down complaints directed against the coverage by all three networks of events surrounding the Democratic National Convention in 1968. The accusations included failure to cover speeches at the podium, excessive floor coverage, failure to air views of Chicago officials regarding allegations of police brutality, and failure to show violence started by antiwar protestors.[62] The networks responded that they had provided fair and balanced coverage of the issues despite the tumult and violence that marred the convention. Two networks objected to the FCC inquiry into news coverage, with NBC stating:

> [F]ew spectres can be more frightening to a person concerned with the vitality of a free press than the vision of a television cameraman turning his camera to one aspect of a public event rather than another because of a concern that a governmental agency might want him to do so, or fear of Government sanction if he did not.[63]

The FCC, however, said the Fairness Doctrine was an exception to the rule that the agency does not "review the broadcaster's news judgment, the quality of his news and public affairs reporting, or his taste."[64] There seemed to be plenty to review in the coverage of the 1968 Democratic Convention. "Television," according to Ernest B. Furgurson of the *Baltimore Sun,* "came to Chicago in a bad mood."[65] The Democrats had refused to accommodate the networks by holding their convention in Miami Beach after the Republicans had finished there. Chicago authorities refused to permit broadcast trailers to park near major hotels. There was a telephone strike in Chicago.

Both conventions were marred by violence. In Miami six persons were killed and riot areas were put under curfew. But it was in Chicago, where there were no deaths, that the media focused on violence in the streets. The Democrats were portrayed as unfit to cope with dissension. According to Drew Pearson and Jack Anderson, the networks decided to highlight the Chicago disturbances:

> In Chicago they played up the violence which they had virtually ignored in Miami. . . . anyone who watched the two conventions on television might think that Chicago was exploding with violence while Miami was comparatively peaceful. The result was an outrageously biased picture of the events in Chicago.[66]

After CBS's Dan Rather was punched by a security guard, the networks decided to "avenge him by sending their wrath on every security agent, every policeman," according to Theodore White.[67] Furgurson reported there was a "vindictive, near hysteria on the air," making it seem that Hubert Humphrey "was being nominated by the force of police clubs."

Despite such charges of network misconduct, the FCC backed off the case. The commission rejected all the complaints because there was insufficient evidence that the networks had imbalanced coverage. But it did say that allegations that reporters had staged incidents would remain open for further consideration if evidence was brought forward.[68]

Even though the commission has been much less aggressive in pursuing complaints about news imbalance in recent years, these cases indicate how easily a more activist FCC membership could delve deeply into the editorial judgments of broadcasters. Nor should one overlook the potential political impact simply of launching an inquiry, not to mention the dramatic effect of an adverse ruling. Would not future coverage of antiwar protests, convention violence, presidential addresses, and the like be affected by memories of an FCC probe of past conduct?

As we have seen, the Fairness Doctrine applies to newscasts, news interviews, live news coverage, and news documentaries. Coverage of football halftime shows and national political conventions is not exempt. However, most of the litigation over the Fairness Doctrine involves not the news, but paid advertising about issues, demands for reply time, and political contests. So in viewing the impact of the regulation on news coverage, one must look beyond the formal cases to the everyday impact on how broadcast journalists perform. This is not simple to assess, because news reporters voluntarily seek to provide contrasting opinions about the controversies they cover.

Because journalists want to cover what is most controversial, it is hard to assess the day-to-day effect of the Fairness Doctrine on news coverage. Most would-be complaints never arrive at the Federal Communications Commission; that formal process is avoided, instead, by the broadcaster's own desire to present opposing viewpoints on the news. Some rather mundane examples illustrate how controversies are routinely handled.

In January 1982, WDVM-TV in Washington, D.C., aired a news story suggesting that the facilities for the handicapped were inadequate at George Mason University in northern Virginia. According to the university's vice-president for student affairs, Donald Mash, the WDVM crew came to do a story on financial aid but ran across a paraplegic professor who complained about lack of facilities for handicapped persons. The resulting news coverage referred to federal regulations being violated at George Mason. The story had shots of a trailer blocking access to handicapped parking spots and featured an interview with a handicapped student who had to go to the third or fourth floor each day. According to Mash, the story did not mention that there was an elevator in the building. Mash wrote the station, pointing out these inaccuracies, complaining of a lack of balance, and suggesting a follow-up story comparing George Mason with other institutions in the area. He felt the university, housed in a new facility, would compare favorably. Mash said in an interview that the station immediately called and offered to do a follow-up story.

In September 1982, station WJLA-TV in Washington, D.C. aired a report on its "5:30 Live" news about the local Jewish community's reaction to events in Lebanon, particularly the massacre of civilians in Palestinian refugee camps. The reporter, Chris Gordon, said later in an interview that he had talked with his producer about including some Arab reaction as well. But the producer felt that previous stories had already dealt with that side of the issue. When one person being interviewed on the program said that media coverage of the Mideast was anti-Israeli, Gordon ad-libbed the following:

> Other people feel the press is anti-Arab. Channel 7 in other shows has had interviews and done stories on the Arab and Palestinian point of view to provide balance in our overall programming on this issue.

For such a statement to be spoken extemporaneously on a live broadcast suggests a knowledge of the Fairness Doctrine; it was an instant and excellent defense of the station's conduct. But Gordon denied in an interview for this book that he was worried about potential Fairness Doctrine complaints to the FCC. Rather, he said, his concern was that neither the station nor he give the appearance of unbalanced news coverage. Even so, he said he still received eight or nine telephone calls that day, even after the on-air disclaimer.

Gordon stated that the station's assistant news director, Ken Middleton, had circulated a memo reminding the staff that the Arab/Israeli conflict was very emotional and that accuracy and sensitivity were called for. Middleton said in an interview that the memo had nothing to do with the Fairness Doctrine, but that it was just good journalism.

It's hard to tell if WDVM would have been as eager to do a follow-up story about handicapped facilities were there no Fairness Doctrine. Or would WJLA have shown such sensitivity in the absence of the regulation?

Perhaps so. After all, a station's credibility—and its ratings—depend on its reputation for serving its community and playing fair with its audience. But broadcasters cannot operate without appreciating that disgruntled viewers may complain to the FCC, and that government regulators may double-check the reasonableness of editorial decisions.

## A Chilling Effect?

It is not possible to document whether the effect of the Fairness Doctrine and other FCC content regulations severely inhibit journalistic endeavor. Stephen E. Nevas, who served as First Amendment Counsel for the National Association of Broadcasters, said the NAB had no hard statistical evidence of a chilling effect, but started a survey "to see if the anecdotal evidence holds up." Nevas said it is hard to find broadcasters willing to speak on the record about specific issues in which they have felt "chilled" from airing a program or topic. It's hard to document, he said, because "no one wants to lay bare a particular instance to public scrutiny." By going public, a broadcaster might face a Fairness Doctrine complaint. "It's an acknowledgment that it is controversial and they ducked it, and they have an obligation to deal with the major controversial issues of the day," Nevas said in an October 1982 interview for this book.

Nevas also said broadcasters "have become so accustomed to content regulation that the inhibitions and self-censorship have become internalized." Moreover, most broadcasters would be ashamed to admit they were afraid to air some program. To concede there had been a chilling effect in a given instance might open the broadcaster to ridicule as a coward, Nevas said. Additionally, money is a factor because, Nevas estimates, the average Fairness Doctrine complaint costs from $1,000 to $3,000 to defend. "There is a price tag on controversy," he said. It is one that broadcasters in small and medium markets may not want to pay.

The NAB denounces the Fairness Doctrine as having a chilling effect. One NAB position paper put it this way:

> [Broadcasters] are subjected to a subtle, continuous and strong incentive to avoid the experience entirely by sticking entirely with the safe and the bland, depriving the public of the kind of journalism that a truly free press is able to provide. The problem is greatly magnified where the station is small and management lacks the resources with which to defend its journalists against constant harassments by complainants who are able to invoke the power of the FCC.

The Supreme Court, in affirming the constitutionality of the Fairness Doctrine, considered a possible chilling effect, but stated the "possibility is at best speculative."[69] The Court added,

> If experience with the administration of those doctrines indicates that they have the net effect of reducing rather than enhancing the volume and quality of coverage, there will be time enough to reconsider the constitutional implications. The fairness doctrine in the past has had no such overall effect.

The decision stated that if stations should prove timorous, "the Commission is not powerless to insist they give adequate and fair attention to public issues."[70] But if regulation were shown to produce broadcast timidity, would more regulation cure that defect? Or would increased exercise of FCC power be even more chilling?

In its 1974 *Fairness Report* the FCC considered whether the rule inhibited coverage, and found that it expanded and enriched debate instead.[71]

Journalists, however, often insist that there is a chilling effect.

Richard Salant, who has headed CBS News and worked as a top executive at NBC, said that content regulations "do have a chilling effect":

> They create a brooding omnipresence, which limits robust journalism. Reporters and editors, like anybody else, can't do their best work sitting under the sword of Damocles. [Section] 315 and the fairness doctrine constrict, not expand, the flow of information. They put in the hands of government the coercive power, which history has shown government has sought to use, to manipulate and control.[72]

Salant, who offered no specific examples, said that "important and valid stories" have been "spiked," or killed, because of the Fairness Doctrine. He condemns the regulation for vesting in a political body the responsibility for deciding questions of what is fair, what should be covered, and to what extent.

The Radio Television News Directors Association says that broadcasters are "ensnarled in volumes of regulations and legal interpretations," and are "unable to present as forcefully as they should the great issues of our time."[73] The RTNDA publication lists the following "concrete examples":

> It took NBC four years, two full-scale court hearings and eight separate judicial opinions to beat off a fairness complaint in which the FCC *had not even viewed* the documentary it held to be in violation.

> To defend a single editorial favoring EXPO 74 cost KREM-TV Spokane $20,000 in legal fees, 480 hours of executive time and a delay in license renewal.

> A Roanoke city councilman being interviewed suddenly declared himself a candidate for mayor. The station thought it prudent to offer time to all other candidates, including an 18-year-old highschooler and the publicity-seeking operator of a massage parlor.

> This is Fairness? One side in a state referendum controversy in Maine spent all its money on newspaper ads, then, being broke, demanded free time from the broadcasters who'd carried the other side's commercials.

> You've heard of the "chilling effect?" A Pennsylvania radio broadcaster killed a B'nai B'rith series because, "Airing these programs would open the floodgates to a paranoid response from 'nut' groups."

> It took two and a half years to let NBC off the hook after a fairness complaint against the classic documentary, "Holocaust." The complaint alleged there'd never been a deliberate Nazi effort to exterminate the Jews.

> It took twice that long for the regulators and courts to dispose of a complaint against 12 California broadcasters who sold spots to the nuclear power industry.

The RTNDA publication includes other examples of problems posed by the various regulations, and urges a repeal of content rules.

Hard statistical evidence about any chilling effect is inconclusive, however. Published surveys focus mainly on broadcasters' attitudes toward the Fairness Doctrine generally, and do not deal with whether anything specific has been chilled. One NAB survey presented to the Senate Committee on Interstate and Foreign Commerce in 1968 reported that 60 percent of broadcasters wanted the doctrine repealed. The committee's own survey of 5,245 stations indicated that only 22.3 percent wanted the doctrine repealed. A 1974 survey of Florida news directors concluded that those surveyed had problems with the doctrine as presently formulated, but the survey "did not indicate strong feeling for repeal of the Doctrine as found in the NAB study."[74]

During the 1982 annual meeting of the Radio Television News Directors Association, the author conducted an informal, unscientific series of discussions to ascertain attitudes about the regulation. News directors who were questioned had few day-to-day problems with the Fairness Doctrine. But many expressed fear that the expense and trouble of defending against potential complaints would be overwhelming. Moreover, most news directors who commented felt concerned about the First Amendment consequences of broadcast regulation. In sum, they feared the doctrine on a theoretical basis, rather than because of bad experiences with application of the law.

The Fairness Doctrine does possess potential to intrude into daily journalistic efforts of broadcasters, and to punish those judged by the FCC's bureaucrats and political appointees to transgress the rule. That the FCC has generally refused to enter this thicket is commendable, but not eternally guaranteed. The conflicting decisions in past cases create uncertainty about what the commission would do in any future case. The possibility of political misuse of the commission is always present as long as content regulations are on the books.

## Combating Bias in the News

Whatever the dangers of regulation, a key question that must be addressed is whether regulation can be an effective deterrent to bias, imbalance, and partisanship, and if so, whether the benefits to the public outweigh the costs to broadcasters. Bias is difficult to examine, partly because it is in the eye of the beholder, requiring subjective determinations of someone else's motives. Empirical extrapolations even from a large data base can be flawed by initial conceptual shortcomings, as evidenced in the ASCEF viewpoint analysis of national security coverage.[75]

Moreover, news bias is hard to judge because those who know first-hand of it—news reporters, producers—and editors—are likely to deny flatly that it exists. Most journalists claim to be objective. It is a worthy goal, but elusive. Like every person, a news reporter must view the world through the prism of his or her own mind-set, relying on personal attitudes and preconceptions to process new information. It has been said that everyone is entitled to one's own opinion, but not one's own facts. But facts are like marbles, the kind children play with. Hold a marble up to the light and you will see different hues and tones depending upon the light in which it is viewed.

Subjectivity in the news is most apparent in the selection of items deemed newsworthy enough for a newscast or a newspaper. A network anchorman once was quoted as saying, "News is what I say it is." As arrogant as that may sound, it is fundamentally correct. News is what the news professionals say it is. At its best, news is selected from sound journalistic judgments as to an item's importance, relevance, and interest to the audience. But such judgments are rarely scientific or impartial. They often reflect the gut feelings of those making the news decisions. At its worst, the selection of items can reflect "pack journalism," where coverage is mandated by the intense interest competing news organizations have in a subject.

Despite some assertions to the contrary, the author's experience in the press corps has produced little hard evidence that the media, both print and electronic, are gripped by partisan bias. Many reporters are liberal, and that seems the predominant mood of the Washington press corps. But partisanship or ideological fervor is rare. The predominant attitude is more difficult to define. The post-Watergate, post-Vietnam outlook of the press corps reflects a distrustful view of authority, any authority.[76] Such a view is, of course, a bias—it just seems to be applied in a nonpartisan fashion against, for example, every recent occupant of the White House.

Some recent studies have demonstrated that news elites are liberal in their outlook but often manage to keep their reporting from reflecting this bias. Robert Lichter and Stanley Rothman showed rather persuasively that the media elite—at the top of the journalism profession—was more liberal in its thinking than its national audience.[77] More than half the media elite labeled themselves liberal, double the proportion in the public at large. But this does not mean that personal views dictate how stories are written and edited. Michael Robinson and Margaret Sheehan scrutinized news coverage of the 1980 election campaign and found almost no evidence of bias in the reporting.[78] They surveyed all three networks, two wire services, and three newspapers, concentrating on CBS and UPI. Some 6,000 stories were tested, and Robinson concluded, "we failed to find that UPI or CBS (or any of the other six sources) behaved very ideologically in covering 1980 politics. They were cynical, yes; but liberal, no."[79]

In his thoughtful study of the news profession, Herbert J. Gans suggests that "the news is not so much conservative or liberal as it is reformist; indeed the enduring values are very much like the values of the Progressive Movement of the early 20th century."[80] He sees liberal tendencies coexisting with traditional values, including some of these elements: support for responsible capitalism, competition, individualism, nonbureaucratic government and honesty; opposition to bigness, monopolies, political machines, populist demagogues, socialism, and hypocrisy.[81]

Gans says most journalists seem to support "the social order of public, business and professional upper-middle-class, middle-aged, and white male sectors of society."[82] The point should be emphasized: such values are perpetuated in much news reporting. Journalism reflects the values of journalists. Gans suggests that like Progressives of an earlier era, news persons see themselves as rising above partisan politics and regard themselves as independents.

Political candidates are viewed with a healthy skepticism that borders on unhealthy cynicism. The bias is not "I like Ike" or JFK or LBJ. The author's impression is that it more closely resembles "I don't trust Reagan," or Carter, or Ford, or Nixon, or Johnson. Such attitudes are entirely plausible, given the credibility gaps created by the misleading statements of public officials during the Vietnam war and Watergate. But if this impression of media bias (admittedly unscientific) is accurate, then it colors the work product of journalists in ways that most reporters will not concede, and that some, convinced of their own objectivity, will staunchly deny.

The first step for reporters who seek to be fair is to confront their own biases rather than hide behind the slogans of objectivity. Good journalists seek to evaluate information in a detached and impartial way. Even those who produce commentary or editorials or who advocate solutions to specific problems should remain open-minded to evidence or opinion that contradicts their preconceived points of view. But some journalists make up their minds before they've gathered all the facts. Television news reporting, with its emphasis on theme, is especially prone to sliding down the slippery slope of subjectivity. Because the time for presenting facts is very limited, the selection of those items and spokespersons to be included in a report often depends on whether they advance the thematic message of the report. Important information that detracts from the story line often ends up on the cutting room floor as the electronic journalist strives for a product that conveys a strong message.

No amount of government regulation, short of the kind of censorship currently prohibited by Section 326 of the Communications Act, would remedy the problems of such subjectivity. Should government watchdogs monitor the press to see if stories are being selected because they further Progressive values? Express nihilistic doubts? Jump to rash conclusions? Play upon catchy themes? Such intervention would be especially intrusive. In addition to failing to cope with subjectivity, regulation as practiced now does little to remedy the other shortcomings of television news—shallowness and sensationalism. Such shortcomings contribute to an impression that the news media often are unfair.

Shallowness results from the common failure in broadcasting to hire or train reporters who are specialists in the subjects they cover. It is compounded by a career ladder that rewards generalists who know a little about a lot of subjects. It is accentuated by editors who prefer to use reporters on a general assignment basis, shifting personnel frequently from subject to subject. It is aggravated by the success of investigative reporters who spend more time looking for things to expose than learning about the subjects they cover. Moreover, television, unlike newspapers, usually places junior personnel in gatekeeper functions, such as the assignment desk. While a print reporter may view a shift to the editor's desk as a promotion, television reporters rarely consider this a career goal, preferring an anchoring job on a newscast instead. The less one knows about a subject, the more often he must "fly by the seat of his pants," quickly distilling information on an ad hoc basis.

Because broadcasting rewards reporters who can end their reports with a snappy phrase telling the audience "what it all means," shallowness is a major handicap. Many reporters do not know the meaning of what they are covering, but feel compelled to tell the audience something that sounds momentous anyway.

The most dramatic news stories are the ones that convey impressions. Never mind if they are short on information; if the material is sensational it will be judged newsworthy. Some news events are truly sensational. The release of the U.S. hostages from Iran, the first trip to the moon, and the Israeli capture of West Beirut come to mind. But sensational events do not happen every day in time for the evening's news. Some reporters are tempted to hype stories to make them seem more sensational.

Many factors account for the shortcomings of subjectivity, shallowness, and sensationalism in news reporting, and none are susceptible to cure by government intervention. Here is a short list of common problems:

First, the media are in a hurry. There never seems to be enough time to do all the research possible when a reporter must produce stories on deadline.

Second, the media are competitive. Scoring a beat or a scoop is rewarded. Doing a better story after a competitor has broken it rarely commands the same kind of praise.

Third, peer group pressure is intense. Because news is what news organizations say it is, reporters constantly compare stories after they appear (not, as Spiro Agnew once alleged, before they appear). If a reporter has prepared a report that is similar to his competitor's version, his judgment as to what was newsworthy is reinforced. If he takes a different tack, he faces the possibility his boss will question why he didn't include some of the same material his competitor did.

Fourth, information must be compressed for inclusion into a news story. Compression alters reality.

Fifth, even where reporters are assigned to beats, or specialties, they often fail to develop technical expertise. For example, the most sought-after assignment in Washington is White House correspondent. It is a glorified general assignment job, with a multitude of events and issues orchestrated by the White House press office.

Sixth, the press is indebted to news sources. People, not documents, are the most frequent sources of information. And reporters rely on sources who seem to be the most disinterested. This evaluation of motive often means locating someone who appears to have no economic or political interest in the information divulged. In some instances people who have the most facts—government officials or business executives—are assumed to have motives for distorting the truth while relatively uninformed protestors are perceived as disinterested and, hence, reliable.

Seventh, the media are relatively status-quo-oriented. This may seem to contradict the image of a left-leaning, nihilistic press corps, but it is consistent with mainstream middle-class mores. Most reporters are firmly middle-class in their outlook, with attitudes that reflect the values of the Progressive Era, favoring economic competition, small business enterprise, consumer protection, and clean government, while exposing corruption, monopolistic practices, windfall profits, consumer rip-offs, and the like. This is not necessarily bad, but it is inhibiting. The media are notoriously uninterested in new ideas, be they espoused by the New Left or neoconservatives.

Eighth, the media are more interested in clashes between people than in clashes between ideas. Reporters are more skilled in covering disagreements between people than reporting on trends. Consequently, newscasts often feature opponents disagreeing, without clarifying their points of disagreement. We get heat, not light. It may be balanced coverage, but the contrasting points of view are reduced to slogans. When confronted with a new, complicated debate, the media often oversimplify the issue. Moreover, as journalists Jude Wanniski and Robert L. Bartley have observed, the media can become a captive of their own "Initial Simplistic Explanation," adjusting their coverage of the new issue to their own simplistic evaluation of what is at stake.[83]

Ninth, the media often trivialize the events, issues, and people they cover. The nightly television news with its barrage of short, one-minute stories is the prime offender in reducing serious matters to seeming trivia. Herbert Schmertz, the Mobil Oil executive who has been outspoken against the media for its coverage of business, talks of the "tyranny of the 25-second bite," the penchant of TV reporters to edit any statement down to less than half a minute in length. Imagine the chagrin of a person who has sat before a camera for a 20-minute interview only to see about 20 seconds run on the newscast. What usually vanishes is the patient explanation, careful qualification, or thoughtful discourse; what is most often selected is the snappiest characterization, colorful quote, or (double chagrin for the interviewee) stumbling answer to the toughest question.

Tenth, the news must be interesting. In some cases this means it must be entertaining, especially on commercial television where entertainment lures the large audiences advertisers crave. Daniel Schorr, the former CBS correspondent now with Cable News Network, once wrote in *Washingtonian* magazine how entertainment values help shape the news:

> Television news itself—obliged to coexist with its entertainment environment, seeking to present facts with the tools of fantasy—ends up with a dramatized version of life. Everything that goes into making a well-paced, smoothly edited "package" subtly changes reality into a more exciting allegory of events. The confusion is compounded by the use of (1) "cinema realite" techniques in fictional dramas, (2) the modern forms of fact-and-fiction "docudramas," and (3) "reenactments" of events.

Other journalists and media observers may dispute this somewhat subjective list of shortcomings. Despite all the problems, the free press performs well, overall. Most reporters, editors, and producers are well-meaning professionals who strive for excellence. On the whole, Americans are well served by the media, both print and electronic. The point here is not to harp on the failings of the media, but to examine the roots of why the media's product is sometimes criticized as unfair. Even this cursory examination indicates that government regulation is no cure for what ails the news profession. Rules such as the Fairness Doctrine appear irrelevant to improving the quality of news coverage.

One reason is that the Fairness Doctrine looks to quantity, not quality. Stations must devote "a reasonable percentage" of time to covering issues and must afford "an opportunity" for presenting contrasting viewpoints. A station that has failed to meet its Fairness Doctrine duties is deficient in a quantitative way, with an insufficient percentage here or an inadequate number of viewpoints there. Such a doctrine cannot grapple with the real causes of unfairness that may exist in the electronic media.

The Supreme Court, alert to the shortcomings of newspersons, nonetheless has warned against the danger of overregulation by the government:

> For better or worse, editing is what editors are for, and editing is selection and choice of material. That editors—newspaper or broadcast—can and do abuse power is beyond doubt, but that is no reason to deny the discretion Congress provided.[84]

## *References*

1. 63 FCC 2d 366 (1977).
2. Lefever, *TV and National Defense: An Analysis of CBS News, 1972-73* (1976).
3. Id., p. 78.
4. *American Security Council Educational Foundation* v. *FCC,* 607 F.2d 438, 442 (D.C. Cir. 1979).
5. Id.
6. ASCEF offered the avian metaphor.
7. 63 FCC 2d 366 (1977).
8. Id. at 368.
9. Id at 368–369.
10. Id. at 369.
11. *American Security Council Education Foundation* v. *FCC,* Pike & Fischer, 44 *Radio Regulation 2d,* 193 (D.C. Cir. 1968), [also reported at 4 *Media Law Reporter* 1516.].
12. Id. at 204.
13. Id. at 203.
14. 607 F.2d 438.
15. Id. at 448.
16. Id.
17. Id. at 450, n. 38.
18. Id. at 444–446.
19. Id. at 448.
20. Id. at 451.
21. Id.
22. Id. at 446.
23. 447 F.2d 323 (D.C. Cir. 1971).
24. Id. at 329.

25. *Hakki S. Tamimie,* 42 FCC 2d 876 (1973).
26. *Council on Children, Media and Merchandising,* 59 FCC 2d 448 (1976).
27. *Accuracy in Media,* 39 FCC 2d 416 (1973), aff'd, 521 F.2d 288 (D.C. Cir. 1975).
28. *Michael McKee,* 49 FCC 2d 1258 (1974); *Voice for Innocent Victims,* 42 FCC 335 (1973).
29. *WCBS-TV,* 8 FCC 2d 381 (1967).
30. *Females Opposed to Equality,* 42 FCC 2d 434 (1973).
31. Note "Communications Law—FCC Fairness Doctrine Procedures," 2 *Western New England Law Review* 775, 783 (1980).
32. 607 F.2d at 460 (Willkey, J., dissenting).
33. Id. at 465–467.
34. Id. at 463.
35. See "Federal Communications Commission—Fairness Doctrine—Requirement that a Fairness Doctrine Complaint Establish a Prima Facie Case Defining a Specific Issue," 25 *Villanova Law Review* 386, 399 (1979–80).
36. Note "The Fairness Doctrine: Fair to Whom?" 30 *Cleveland State Law Review* 485, 499 (1981).
37. 607 F.2d at 451.
38. Note "The Fairness Doctrine and Claims of Systematic Imbalance in Television News Broadcasting: American Security Council Education Foundation v. FCC," 93 *Harvard Law Review* 1028, 1035 (1980).
39. Page 600.
40. 1974 *Fairness Report* at p. 9.
41. For a lengthy treatment of the defects in the ASCEF study, see Fred W. Friendly, *The Good Guys, the Bad Guys, and the First Amendment* (New York, Vintage Books, 1976), pp. 167–191.
42. Id. at 177.
43. Id.
44. Id. at 175.
45. Id. at 181
46. 93 *Harvard Law Review* 1028, 1037 (1980).
47. 607 F.2d at 456.
48. 607 F.2d 455 (Wright, C.J., concurring) (footnote omitted).
49. Edward J. Epstein, *Between Fact and Fiction: The Problem of Journalism* (New York, Vintage Books, 1975), pp. 210–232.
50. Peter Braestrup, *Big Story: How the American Press and Television Reported and Interpreted the Crisis of Tet—1968 in Vietnam and Washington* (Boulder, Colo., Westview Press, 1977).
51. *Washington Star,* July 27, 1977, p. A15.
52. *New York Times,* April 30, 1975, p. 41.
53. 6 *Policy Review* 7, 20 (Fall 1978).
54. 607 F.2d at 459.
55. See, Note, "American Security Council Education Foundation v. Federal Communications Commission: An Increased Burden of Proof in Fairness Doctrine Complaints," 29 *American University Law Review* 181, 188 (1979).

56. *Student Association of the State University of New York,* 40 FCC 2d 510, 511 (1973).
57. See, Note, "The Fairness Doctrine: Fair to Whom?," 30 *Cleveland State Law Review* 485, 516–517 (1981).
58. 40 FCC 2d 510, 516 (1973).
59. *Committee for the Fair Broadcasting of Controversial Issues,* 25 FCC 2d 283 (1970), reversed on other grounds pub nom., *CBS* v. *FCC,* 454 F.2d 1018 (D.C. Cir. 1971).
60. 25 FCC 2d 283, 297 (1970).
61. *Network Coverage of the Democratic National Convention,* 16 FCC 2d 650 (1969).
62. 30 *Cleveland State Law Review* 485, 517 (1981).
63. Id. at 518; 16 FCC 2d 650, 654 (1969).
64. Id.
65. Quoted in Max Kampelman, "The Power of the Press: A Problem for Our Democracy," 6 *Policy Review* 7 (1978).
66. *Washington Post,* September 6, 1968, p. B13.
67. *The Making of the President—1968* (New York, Atheneum, 1969), p. 285.
68. 16 FCC 2d 650, 659.
69. *Red Lion Broadcasting Co.* v. *FCC,* 395 U.S. 367 (1969) at 393.
70. Id.
71. *Supra* note 20, at p. 26374.
72. Speech to the National Press Foundation/National Press Club Forum, December 16, 1981.
73. Radio Television News Directors Association publication, "It's Not Fair."
74. Meeshe and Handberg, "News Directors' Attitudes toward the Fairness Doctrine," *Journalism Quarterly* (1975), p. 126.
75. *Supra* note 2.
76. This view of the media, defined as including reporters, editors, producers, photographers, and news management for newspapers, magazines, radio, and television, is shaped by the author's 18 years as a reporter, 14 in Washington.
77. Robert Lichter and Stanley Rothman, "Media and Business Elites," *Public Opinion* (1982).
78. Michael Robinson and Margaret Sheehan, *Over the Wire and on TV: CBS and UPI in Campaign 80;* see also Michael Robinson, "Just How Liberal Is the News? 1980 Revisited," *Public Opinion* (February/March 1983), p. 53.
79. Id., p. 56.
80. Herbert J. Gans, *Deciding What's News: A Study of CBS Evening News, NBC Nightly News, Newsweek and Time* (New York, Pantheon, 1979), p. 68.
81. Id., pp. 68–69.
82. Id., p. 61.
83. "The Limits of the Press Corps in a Political/Technical Debate," University of Chicago, 1974.
84. *Columbia Broadcasting System* v. *Democratic National Committee,* 412 U.S. 94, 125 (1973).

# SEVEN

# The Minefield:
# Special Cases

IN THEORY, THE FAIRNESS DOCTRINE should be a powerful tool to assure the broadcast of a wide variety of viewpoints on important issues. But in practice, the Federal Communications Commission and the courts have usually deferred to the broadcasters' discretion in the absence of a showing of unreasonableness or bad faith by a licensee. This is not to say that the scope of regulation has not been extended beyond regular news programming and imposed with more zeal in some circumstances; it has. And the impact has been complex and confusing.

One fresh example indicates the difficulty of resolving fairness questions. In January 1983, CBS News broadcast a report entitled "The Gospel According to Whom?" It aired on "60 Minutes" and created quite a stir in some Protestant denominations. The report alleged that the National Council of Churches and several denominations supported Marxist-Leninist causes, guerrilla movements, and the leftists in Nicaragua, Vietnam, and Cuba. It indicated that church leaders had misled their members about where contributions were flowing.

When CBS refused a request for airtime to reply to the criticism, a fairness complaint was filed with the FCC by the United Church of Christ, the United Methodist Church, the United Presbyterian Church in the U.S.A., the Christian Church (Disciples of Christ), and the Episcopal Church. They alleged that CBS had broadcast a personal attack on their groups. If so, the Personal Attack Rule would require CBS to notify the churches, provide transcripts, and offer a reply opportunity.

Several points are worth noting about this complaint. First, the truth of CBS's allegation is irrelevant. While most viewers might wonder, first and foremost, if the report is true, the FCC has decided that it shall not become the arbiter of truth. As noted previously, the Fairness Doctrine only requires stations to provide a reasonable opportunity for the airing of contrasting views on certain types of controversies.

Second, the regulations covering personal attacks are complex. Criticism of the rightness or wrongness of a policy, something the viewer might be expected to ponder, is not what's covered by the Personal Attack Rule. It applies only to attacks on someone's honesty, character, integrity, or a like quality. It does not apply to criticism of one's wisdom. The churches allege that CBS accused them of lying, something that could be covered by the rule.

Third, while the Fairness Doctrine applies to "60 Minutes," the doctrine's subpart, the Personal Attack Rule, does not apply to most news programming. The attack rule exempts newscasts, news interview programs, on-the-spot coverage of news events and commentary on regular newscasts. There is no exemption from the Personal Attack Rule for documentaries. "60 Minutes" is described on the air as a "news magazine" program, and is not exempt from the rule.

Fourth, if the rule does apply to "60 Minutes" and a personal attack, in fact, was aired, then CBS would have to comply with more strict requirements for providing access to the airwaves than under the general Fairness Doctrine. The network has less discretion in presenting contrasting views; the churches have a greater right of access to get their side across.

Fifth, for the rule to be triggered, the attack would have to have occurred during discussion of a controversial issue of public importance. CBS argued that the issue raised involved possible disparity between moral philosophy and religious fundraising, and therefore was not a public controversy. The FCC agreed that CBS could reasonably make such a determination and it dismissed the complaint of the church leaders.[1]

In this regulatory context, the primary concerns of the audience (and presumably of the network and churches), namely whether the report was true and the church policy wise, take a backseat to other technical considerations. To wit, was it really a personal attack? And is the news broadcast exempt from the specific rule? The rule sidesteps the central elements of what constitutes fairness while focusing on access mechanisms.

In general, the Fairness Doctrine provides no specific, personal right of access to the airwaves. Broadcasters have an obligation to air contrasting viewpoints, but they may choose the spokespersons, format, time, and program on which to air a point of view. The emphasis is on balance in a station's overall programming. Within this broad rule, the FCC has created subcategories, such as the Personal Attack Rule, where the broadcaster's discretion is more limited and specific access may be compelled. While the broadest leeway is provided for news programming—a reflection of the policy of not intruding too deeply into the journalistic function—special categories have been carved out for more vigorous regulation.

Besides personal attacks, the special cases include political editorials and some advertisements. The Political Editorializing Rule requires a station that endorses or opposes a candidate for public office to afford airtime to all opposing candidates who were not endorsed. The so-called Cullman Principle involves commercial advertisements; a station must present contrasting viewpoints on important public controversies raised in advertisements, even when there is no sponsor willing to pay to present the other side.[2]

The two rules addressed at length in this chapter, the Personal Attack Rule and the Political Editorializing Rule, are being re-evaluated by the FCC as of this writing. In 1983 the commission sought comments on whether it should abolish these rules. While the FCC cannot act on its own to eliminate the entire Fairness Doctrine—it was enacted by Congress—the commission could modify enforcement of part of the rules. One problem for a deregulatory-minded commission is the fact that the landmark *Red Lion* case, in which the Supreme Court upheld the Fairness Doctrine, involved a personal attack. With *Red Lion* as precedent, any court reviewing FCC changes to these rules might conclude that the commission was overstepping its bounds in the absence of congressional approval.

The Appeals Court has sent a strong signal to the FCC not to act too decisively. In upholding limited radio deregulation in 1983, the author of the court decision, Judge Skelley Wright, warned that the "tidal wave" of deregulation should be enacted by Congress, not by the FCC. The "unrepresentative bureaucracy and judiciary," Wright said, should not take the lead in "grossly amending" the system of regulation.

No matter what the outcome of the reconsideration of these rules, a look at how they evolved is instructive in evaluating the proper role of government in assuring broadcast fairness.

Like the Fairness Doctrine in general, these subcategories are designed to keep the public informed about differing sides of important public matters. The theory is that if someone is attacked during discussion of an important controversy, society would benefit by hearing his or her rebuttal. If one candidate is endorsed in a station editorial, the public would benefit by hearing the opponents. If some group buys airtime to take a stand on a public controversy, the public would profit from hearing the other side, even if the station has to give away airtime for the reply.

That's the theory. In practice the Personal Attack, Political Editorializing, and Cullman rules have operated as access tools for those seeking exposure on the air. They have been used by persons and groups to demand airtime to advance their views. While the rules operate to prevent either a station or its sponsors from using the scarce airwaves to monopolize discussion of an issue, the subcategories hardly afford access to all viewpoints. Instead the rules provide some protection for those harmed in certain ways by a broadcast, someone who has been attacked, opposed in an editorial, or stung by issue advertising. Herein lie the seeds of uneven regulation. On one hand, the rule is theoretically supposed to protect the public's right to know. On the other hand, in practice the rule provides an access right to one who has been attacked or whose views stand to be drowned out by a station's editorials or advertising. Predictably, the tension between goals has resulted in unpredictable rulings and complicated standards for enforcement.

In the 1940s the FCC put broadcasters on notice that stations and sponsors could not dominate discussion of major issues to the detriment of some individuals or groups. In a 1946 case involving the refusal of a station to sell time for commercials advocating abstinence from alcohol, the commission indicated that some forms of advertising could trigger Fairness Doctrine obligations.[3] Just because the controversy was raised in the advertising of a product does not diminish the duty of the broadcaster to treat it as an issue, the commission stated.[4] In 1949, station editorials were recognized as having the potential of spurring a right of reply where "elementary considerations of fairness may dictate that time be allocated to a person or group which has been specifically attacked over the station. . . ."[5]

These subcategories developed in the 1960s as the FCC began expanding the Fairness Doctrine from a general requirement to a specific access tool.[6] In a complaint against the owner of a Florida radio station who was a candidate for a state senate seat, a group of local and state officials alleged that the station had attacked their character and integrity by accusing them of dictatorial tactics and political dirty tricks. The FCC concluded that where "the attacks are of a highly personal nature which impugn the character and honesty of named individuals, the licensee has an affirmative duty to take all appropriate steps to see to it that the persons attacked are afforded the fullest opportunity to respond."[7]

The FCC added more detailed procedures in a 1962 case involving a Montana radio station that broadcast editorials criticizing the general manager of a rural electric cooperative. The FCC required the station to provide copies of specific editorials to the person attacked either before or at the time of the broadcast so the person could have a reasonable opportunity to reply.[8]

In a case involving the 1962 gubernatorial campaign in California, a Los Angeles television station broadcast some 20 commentaries criticizing incumbent Governor Edmund Brown and the Democrats, and commending his opponent, Richard Nixon and the Republican party.[9] When the Democrats complained, the FCC sent a telegram to the station stating that the two replies afforded the Democrats were not adequate, that where a candidate is attacked or his opponent endorsed the station must send a transcript to him immediately and offer a comparable opportunity for a spokesman to answer the broadcast.[10] The candidate who was not endorsed was given "a substantial voice in the selection of the spokesman" to make the rebuttal on the air.[11] When the station objected that such procedures would deter news coverage of the campaign, the FCC partially relented and exempted newscasts from the strict requirements.[12]

While news programs enjoyed some relief from the stricter rules, other programming did not. In one case the FCC made it clear that a station must follow personal attack procedures even where the attack is made by a party not employed by the station.[13]

In 1963 the commission warned stations that commercials that editorialize on issues could create Fairness Doctrine obligations because "the Commission looks to substance rather than to label or form."[14] The FCC asserted that it is "immaterial" whether the viewpoint is expressed in a paid announcement.[15] And that same year the commission indicated in the *Cullman* case that the Fairness Doctrine could require stations to provide time free to groups to reply to paid issue advertisements.[16] Under the Cullman Principle, the station must bear the cost of reply programming if paid sponsorship is not available.

Within a few years the commission was deeply involved in cases where individuals and groups claimed a right to reply to attacks, respond to editorials, and produce countercommercials. The wide discretion afforded broadcasters under the general Fairness Doctrine for such things as newscasts was supplemented with complicated procedures and rules where the station had less control over who could reply and the format for the reply.

## Personal Attacks

When the honesty, character, or integrity of a person or group has been attacked during a broadcast on a controversial issue of public importance, the Fairness Doctrine imposes very specific requirements on the station that aired the attack. These procedures were first outlined in the 1964 *Fairness Primer*.[17] The FCC limited the scope of the personal attack regulation in several ways:

1. It is applicable only when the attack is made in connection with a controversial issue of public importance.
2. It concerns only attacks on "integrity, character, or honesty or like personal qualities."
3. It is not triggered by mere references to a person or group or mere disagreement about an issue.
4. It is not applicable to attacks on foreign leaders.

In 1967 the commission specified the precise rules for personal attacks.[18] They required the station within one week after the attack to notify the person or group attacked of the date, time, and title of the program in which the attack was aired, to send the person a script or tape (or accurate summary if a script or tape was not available), and offer the person or group a reasonable opportunity to answer the attack over the station. The same rule applied similar notification and reply procedures to editorials endorsing candidates, but with a shorter time frame.

The 1967 Personal Attack Rule specifically exempted attacks by candidates on other candidates. In other words, if a station broadcasts a personal attack delivered by a legally qualified candidate or his or her spokesperson against an opponent or persons associated with the opponent in the campaign, the station is under no obligation to notify the person attacked and offer reply time. Thus, the Personal Attack Rule does not apply to paid political broadcasts, which are covered instead by the Equal Opportunities Rule. This is important, because if the Personal Attack Rule covered paid broadcasts, every time a candidate bought airtime to attack an opponent's character, the opponent would be entitled to free time to reply. Instead, the Equal Opportunities Rule mandates that stations treat candidates equally, providing free time to all candidates only when one candidate for the same office is given free time.

But the exemption from the Personal Attack Rule only applies when the attack is made by one candidate upon another candidate; there is no exemption from the rule when the station attacks a candidate or when a candidate attacks someone who is not associated with a rival's campaign. Thus if a candidate purchases airtime and attacks a noncandidate or a person or group not associated with another campaign, the one who was attacked may qualify for free reply time on the station. Because stations are prohibited by law from censoring the remarks of candidates on paid political broadcasts,[19] the station may find itself obligated to provide free time to the target of the candidate's ire.[20] The attacked party is entitled to airtime even if he cannot pay for it.[21]

It is important to note that personal attacks are not prohibited. The FCC has told stations they may criticize individuals and groups. But if personal attacks are broadcast, the notice and reply requirements *must* be observed.

In 1967 the commission formally exempted certain types of news broadcasts from the personal attack requirements.[22] The FCC reluctantly made news exempt; it had withheld this exemption when the initial set of rules about personal attacks were issued earlier in 1967. The exemption was granted during controversial litigation. The federal courts were considering the constitutionality of the Personal Attack Rule and Fairness Doctrine, including the *Red Lion* case.[23] The Radio Television News Directors Association, CBS, and NBC promptly filed suits in federal court seeking to overturn the regulation; within a few days the FCC amended its regulations to exempt newscasts and on-the-scene news coverage.[24] Shortly thereafter, news interview programs were exempted, along with commentary on regular newscasts.[25]

As finally promulgated, the rule relieved stations of the obligation to notify and provide a reply opportunity when a person was attacked on a bona fide newscast, news interview program, or during on-the-spot coverage of a bona fide news event. The logic for this exemption was that the usual journalistic practice was to get the reaction of someone who was criticized publicly. Moreover, the imposition of strict procedures was seen as inhibiting news coverage and involving the FCC unduly in day-to-day editorial decisions. Note, however, that two important types of news programs were not exempted from the rule: editorials and news documentaries.

Thus while commentary or analysis during a regular newscast will not trigger personal attack obligations,[26] an attack during an editorial or documentary will oblige a station to follow the strict notice and reply procedures. The commission opined that there had been shortcomings in providing reply opportunities to answer editorials and attacks aired on documentaries.[27] But the result of the differing treatment for various news programs could be inconsistent enforcement. For example, CBS commentator Bill Moyers can criticize the honesty of those lobbying for a new gas pipeline during a "CBS Evening News" broadcast without fearing he will trigger the Personal Attack Rule. But when Moyers anchors a "CBS Reports" documentary on the impact of Reagan's budget cuts, the network must take care that if it airs a personal attack, the notification and reply procedures are followed.

Similar problems might occur if the commentary Moyers delivers on

"CBS Evening News" is taped for rebroadcast on radio. Suppose it is not aired on a radio newscast, but as a "First Line Report," "Newsbreak," or "Spectrum" feature? Suppose it airs during the "all-news" programming of the stations owned and operated by CBS? Commentary aired outside of a regular newscast is not exempt. The identical commentary would receive different regulatory treatment depending on when and where it was aired.

Does it make sense to require stations to meet different standards when a personal attack occurs in an editoral rather than a commentary in a newscast? During a documentary rather than a regular news interview program? And does the person on the receiving end of the criticism really care if it aired on a talk show or during spot news coverage? Is the public less entitled to hear a reply because the criticism is aired on an exempt news program? Are the distinctions irrational?

As for those news programs that are exempt from the Personal Attack Rule, the FCC has made it clear that the general Fairness Doctrine requirement still applies. Thus the station must present contrasting viewpoints on important public controversies covered in its newscasts.[28] So if a personal attack occurs on a newscast, news interview program, or during coverage of a news event, the station must air the contrasting viewpoint. Here, however, the general requirements for fairness apply, and the station may use its own personnel to state the contrasting view, rather than the one attacked. But if the station does not state the other side, then the "appropriate spokesman" to present the other side of the attack is the person or group attacked.[29] In sum, the rule seems to indicate that while attacks aired during certain news programs do not require a station to follow the precise notice and reply procedures, the station still has an obligation to air the other side. This generally means the one who was attacked should be informed and offered an opportunity to reply.[30] Of course, this is also standard journalistic practice.

As Simmons has pointed out, the Fairness Doctrine is generally "loose-fitting," but the rules tighten where there is a personal attack. This results in a "more direct opportunity to reply."[31] A station may not insist that the reply be made during a panel discussion where an interviewer can pose tough questions.[32] The opportunity to appear on a panel discussion would suffice under the general Fairness Doctrine, but not necessarily under the Personal Attack Rule. Additionally, while the Fairness Doctrine does not mandate equal time for differing views, the latitude afforded broadcasters narrows considerably in personal attack situations. So the reply must be afforded a comparable amount of airtime and the reply must be aired at comparable times of day.

It should be stressed that the truth or falsity of the attack is irrelevant to application of the rule. If there is a personal attack, the station has an absolute duty to comply with the regulation. Unlike libel law, truth is no defense to a failure to provide the notice and reply opportunity required by the FCC. The commission simply will not inquire into the accuracy of the attack.[33]

This does not mean the Personal Attack Rule has proven simple to interpret and apply. Stations have a variety of defenses they can assert for not observing the requirements, including:

1. The attack took place on an exempted news program.
2. The attack was not critical of honesty, character, integrity, or like personal qualities.
3. The attack was a general criticism, not one directed at an identified person or group.
4. The attack was a mere reference.
5. The attack was of a passing nature and was not germane to the subject matter discussed.
6. The attack was made during discussion of a private dispute that is not an important public controversy.
7. The attack was not made during discussion of a controversial issue of public importance.

Professor Benno Schmidt, Jr., has asserted that decisions in various cases seem haphazard and "hopelessly confuse any effort to figure out what general principles delineate the scope of the personal attack rules."[34] Where the attack questions the wisdom of a person or group rather than honesty or integrity, the rule does not apply.[35] References to a "garrulous grand dame" and "pistol-packing mamma" are not personal attacks.[36] But a statement that an official's "veracity leaves something to be desired" and that the electorate should "assess his integrity or lack of it" falls under the Personal Attack Rule.[37]

In his detailed examination, Professor Simmons evaluates the FCC's inconsistent decisions.[38] Allegations that a county board sold land illegally, and a commissioner took a "champagne flight" for personal gratification were not personal attacks.[39] The suggestions that a businessman may have dynamited his business to fraudulently collect insurance was a personal attack.[40]

Claims that a state legislator appeared to have a conflict of interest over his private dealings was not a personal attack.[41] The implication that a political candidate might be receiving money from crime figures was a personal attack.[42]

A claim that doctors and nurses are "incompetent" was not a personal attack.[43] A suggestion that a female news reporter got good interviews because of the way she positioned her legs was a personal attack.[44]

Labeling a person an "extremist" was not a personal attack.[45] But calling a group "subversive" and run by a "Communist" was a personal attack.[46]

Simmons, armed with even more examples, says the "pattern is extremely hard to follow and riddled with inconsistency."[47] One reason for inconsistent rulings is that the Personal Attack Rule is applied only where the attack occurred during discussion of a controversial issue of public importance. Thus if a station shows that the subject aired at the time of the attack was not an important public controversy, the rule will not apply.

The attack must come during actual discussion of the issue. The most revealing case of the pitfalls of trying to decide whether an attack occurred during presentation of a controversial public issue involved radio talk show host Bob Grant.[48] Grant had invited Congressman Benjamin Rosenthal to appear on his phone-in show to discuss a meat boycott. When Rosenthal declined to participate, Grant went ahead and took calls on the subject. Two hours after discussion of the boycott had ended, Grant was on another subject when a caller praised Grant, prompting Grant to state, "When I hear about guys like Ben Rosenthal . . . I wish there where a thousand Bob Grants 'cause then you wouldn't have . . . a coward like him in the United States Congress."[49] This spontaneous outburst prompted Rosenthal to complain. The FCC ruled that a personal attack had occurred. The station appealed to the U.S. Court of Appeals in Washington, which overruled the FCC, noting that the attack was "separated by a substantial time lapse from the issue discussion to which it supposedly relates."[50] The court chided the FCC for making its own judgment as to whether the attack had occurred during discussion of the controversial issue of public importance, rather than evaluating the reasonableness of the station's determination of that question.[51]

But does it make any difference to the victim of the attack if the attack occurred during discussion of an issue or not? Rosenthal was labeled a coward on the air, and even if a listener had just tuned in to Grant's program and had no idea what issue had been discussed, the insinuation is a nasty one.

Moreover, an attack may not fall under the Personal Attack rule even if it occurs during discussion of a controversial issue of public importance, if the attack is not central to the issue being presented. When CBS, in a program about disclosure of secrets by government employees, stated that Lockheed Aircraft had "robbed the taxpayers blind" in building the C5-A aircraft, the FCC held that the mention of Lockheed was incidental, peripheral to the subject, of a passing nature, and did not constitute a personal attack.[52]

Was it unfair to deny Lockheed and Rosenthal an opportunity to defend their reputations simply because an attack seemed peripheral to a major public controversy or occurred after discussion of the issue? The rationale for these decisions rests upon the idea that the regulation protects the public's right to know. The goal is to inform the public, not to provide a remedy for someone who is attacked. Thus fairness, as defined as letting an attack victim state a rebuttal, takes a back seat to the overall public interest in hearing contrasting viewpoints on important public controversies. In upholding the constitutionality of the Personal Attack Rule and the Fairness Doctrine, the Supreme Court said the First Amendment right of the viewers and listeners, not the right of the broadcasters, predominates.[53] Those attacked come third under such a scheme of regulation. For those truly damaged, an adequate remedy cannot be found under the Communications Act. A libel action, in a court of law, could not only vindicate the one who was attacked, but afford him or her payment for damages, something the FCC cannot order. Additionally, a libel case affords the station a defense it does not have under the Personal Attack Rule; if the report is shown to be true, the station wins the libel suit.

A dispute involving retired General William Westmoreland and CBS demonstrates how a libel action differs from the Personal Attack Rule. After CBS attacked Westmoreland in its documentary "The Uncounted Enemy: A Vietnam Deception," the network was stung by criticism. It offered airtime for Westmoreland to defend himself, but the general filed a libel suit against the network instead. The suit commanded more attention than a mere reply would have, and Westmoreland may win damages. As of this writing it has not been decided whether the network defamed him or not—the jury is still out, so to speak. In any event, CBS was forced through discovery to make public an embarrassing internal evaluation of problems in the program. Such discovery is possible only in a civil suit, not in the FCC complaint process.

While imperfect, the Personal Attack Rule does provide an outlet for some of those criticized on the air to rebut the charges. This sometimes degenerates into "name-calling exercises" lacking substantive discussion of underlying issues.[54] The broadcaster, however, dares not shirk his duty to obey these imperfect, complicated regulations. If a station refuses or neglects to comply with the notification and reply procedures of the Personal Attack rule, the FCC can impose a substantial fine on the licensee. Repeated violations can be grounds for nonrenewal or revocation of license. In one case the FCC has refused to renew a license for violations of the Personal Attack Rule and the Fairness Doctrine. In *Brandywine-Main Line Radio, Inc.,* the FCC pulled the plug on WXUR, a station that was deeply involved in controversial issues, had not provided an opportunity for airing opposing views, and had engaged in personal attacks without observing the notification and reply rules.[55] The station appealed to the Court of Appeals, which upheld the FCC's refusal to renew WXUR's license.[56] A central element in the decision was the licensee's broken promises to abide by the Fairness Doctrine.[57]

## Political Editorials

The FCC has never seemed enthusiastic about editorializing on the air; at one point it even seemed to ban editorials. In its 1940 *Annual Report* the FCC stated that "stations are required to furnish well-rounded rather than one-sided discussions of public questions."[58] In the *Mayflower* case the FCC insisted on balanced coverage of major issues.[59] *Mayflower* dealt with station editorials supporting political candidates and taking sides on various public controversies where "no pretense was made at objective, impartial reporting."[60] The FCC declared that licensees could not use their stations to advocate causes or support candidates.[61]

The Mayflower Doctrine effectively put the damper on editorializing by stations. Even though the apparent ban on editorials was rescinded in 1949, a majority of television and radio stations do not editorialize now.[62] Part of the reason for licensee reluctance to take a stand is the restrictive language contained in the 1949 *Report on Editorializing by Broadcast Licensees*.[63] Although the report made it clear that stations could editorialize, it imposed Fairness Doctrine obligations to assure that contrasting viewpoints were also aired. One member of the FCC at the time said the 1949 report left a licensee in need of "an involved academic legal treatise to determine what he can or cannot do in his day-to-day operation."[64]

The rules enunciated in 1967 helped clear up the confusion, but left broadcasters with the duty of presenting differing viewpoints if the station chose to endorse candidates or take stands on major public issues.[65] The Political Editorializing Rule was framed in this way:

> Where a licensee, in an editorial, (i) endorses or (ii) opposes a legally qualified candidate or candidates, the licensee shall, within 24 hours after the editorial, transmit to respectively (i) the other qualified candidate or candidates for the same office of (ii) the candidate opposed in the editorial (1) notification of the date and the time of the editorial; (2) a script or tape of the editorial; and (3) an offer of a reasonable opportunity for a candidate or a spokesman of the candidate to respond over the licensee's facilities: *Provided, however,* that where such editorials are broadcast within 72 hours prior to the day of the election, the licensee shall comply with the provisions of this subsection sufficiently far in advance of the broadcast to enable the candidate or candidates to have a reasonable opportunity to prepare a response and to present it in a timely fashion.[66]

The rule made clear that a station that editorialized against a candidate could provide reply time to the candidate's representative rather than to the actual candidate, because an appearance by a candidate could trigger the Equal Opportunities Rule, requiring the station to provide additional free time to all the other candidates in the race. The candidate's representative receiving reply time under the Political Editorializing Rule normally would be chosen by the candidate.[67]

Although this rule is often confused with the "equal time" provisions of the Equal Opportunities Rule, the candidate is guaranteed only a "reasonable opportunity to respond" to an editorial. While something less than equal time might suffice, the commission has required comparable time for a reply.[68] It has rejected as unreasonable a decision by a station that had aired seven editorial endorsements totaling 11 minutes, 24 seconds, but allowing the opposing candidate's spokesman only two replies totaling 4 minutes, 18 seconds.[69]

The commission has also rejected as unreasonable a station's airing 24 twenty-second editorials and offering the opponent only six 20-second replies.[70]

The Political Editorializing Rule does not impose a reply requirement for editorials endorsing or opposing ballot referendum issues in normal circumstances. The general Fairness Doctrine would apply where a station takes a stand on a ballot proposal, requiring that contrasting views be aired but leaving the broadcaster much more discretion in providing balance in his overall programming. As we will see, groups advocating positions on ballot issues often can obtain access under the Fairness Doctrine, but not normally under the strict procedures of the Political Editorializing Rule. But even in this arena, operation of the rules is complicated. When a station editorializes on an issue clearly associated with a candidate for office, the Political Editorializing Rule may spring into operation. In a 1975 case, the FCC held that even where the editorial did not mention a candidate's name, the station owes the candidate a reply opportunity if the editorial takes a "partisan position on a politically significant issue which is readily and clearly identified with" the candidate.[71]

Given that many candidates take positions on and become identified with issues, a station that editorializes on issues could find itself facing reply obligations from several candidates under the Political Editorializing Rule.

Several factors work to deter stations from editorializing on candidates and issues. First is the complexity of the rules. Second, substantial sanctions may be imposed for transgression of the FCC's rules. Third, stations lose revenue when they have to give away "free" airtime for replies.

Some comment on the third point is relevant. Many people assume stations have so much time that it would not hurt to give away a little of it. But the time available for commercials, and, hence, for sale by the stations, *is* limited. If a reply must be afforded, it must replace some other form of programming. The news must be shortened, an entertainment program abbreviated, an editorial dropped from the schedule, or a paid commercial replaced with the free message. Under some of these alternatives a station risks loss of its audience. After all, the popularity of political broadcasts and editorial replies has never been evidenced in the ratings. If the audience is driven away by programming it does not wish to hear, a station's overall standings in the ratings will decline along with its ability to command top dollar for commercial time. If it foregoes selling a spot commercial so it can run a free reply, the station suffers an immediate loss of income.

Just as there is no such thing as a free lunch, there is no such thing as free airtime. Ultimately the broadcasters bear the cost of time given away. Perhaps this is a price society can and should impose upon licensees for use of the public airwaves, but this indirect cost falls hardest on those stations that do the most to air controversial issues and discuss political matters. In any event, many stations shy away from controversies and candidates precisely because they want to avoid the problems of providing free reply time. In short, they want to maximize profits. They can do this by avoiding politics. The following exchange involving a broadcast executive appearing before a congressional subcommittee is instructive:

> MR. LAVERGNE: Any newspaper who wants to can fully exercise his freedom of the press. He can say: In conscience on behalf of the community, I believe so-and-so should be elected. Radio station owners have to hide that in the harbor of neutrality because we are not allowed to do that. And I am just wondering in this subcommittee meeting whether or not we are members of a free press.
>
> MR. JOHNSON: I think the record should be correct on that. There is no inhibition on your editorializing.
>
> MR. LAVERGNE: But a newspaper can report the news the same as I do and they can come in and give an editorial.
>
> MR. JOHNSON: You can, too.
>
> MR. LAVERGNE: No sir, I cannot, because I have to give equal time and they do not.
>
> MR. JOHNSON: Well, give the equal time.
>
> MR. LAVERGNE: But except I have some elections that have 20 people running.
>
> MR. JOHNSON: But don't make a flat statement that you cannot editorialize in support of a candidate when you know you can.
>
> MR. LAVERGNE: Yes, I can, but I cannot do it because I am—
>
> MR. JOHNSON: You can.

MR. LAVERGNE: No, wait a minute . . . I am in a system of free enterprise and I cannot do something . . . the government is not going to turn around and give me my money. They are not going to subsidize me. . . .[72]

As is evident from the exchange, broadcasters believe economic realities preclude them from incurring extensive obligations to provide reply time. It would cost them too much.

Whatever the reasons, a recent study by the National Association of Broadcasters reveals just how few editorials are aired.[73] The NAB study, conducted in cooperation with the National Broadcast Editorial Association and the Radio Television News Directors Association, polled every commercial radio and television station in the country to inquire about their editorial programming. Forty-three percent of the stations replied. Only 3.1 percent of the responding stations endorse candidates for public office. But 35 percent of those stations said they would endorse candidates if the Political Editorializing Rule was repealed.

Even more eye-opening than the statistic that only 3 percent of stations endorse candidates was the widespread absence of *any* kind of editorializing. Less than half the stations responding, 45 percent, reported editorializing in any form since 1980. And many that did run editorials ran them infrequently. About 59 percent of stations that editorialized aired a new editorial less than once a week. This means only about 18 percent of commercial broadcast stations air different editorials each week.

This empirical data support the claim that the regulations chill the expression of views. The NAB said the "results provide a compelling demonstration of the degree to which the political editorializing rule, contrary to the purposes of the commission and the Constitution, discourages over-the-air expression of political opinion."[74] By choking off broadcast editorials, the rules tend to deter robust debate and limit what the public hears about candidates for public office.

Once again, the comparison with newspapers is apt. Almost every paper editorializes in every issue; around election time there is little reluctance to endorse candidates. The public is free to reject the advice, of course. And many papers choose to allow vigorous dissent in their "Letters to the Editor" column, or on their op-ed page. In short, the public benefits from the publication of opinion. Not all information is transmitted in the seemingly objective front page or evening news. In fact, some very useful information is conveyed by the clash of opinion—something the unregulated newspapers have not shied from providing.

Many observers, however, fear that if broadcasters were relieved of the requirement to provide reply time they would exert enormous power to unduly influence the outcome of elections. The Political Editorializing

Rule complements the statutory language of the Equal Opportunities Rule requiring stations to treat candidates equally when selling or giving them airtime.[75] If freed of all regulation, some broadcasters might endorse certain candidates and blackball others, preventing their appearance on newscasts. Newspapers, of course, have this power now, but they are not licensed to serve the public interest. Perhaps society's interest in assuring that broadcast licensees do not dominate the electoral process compels some regulation, some obligation to provide candidate access to the airwaves. Unfortunately, the current application of FCC regulations stifles the airing of political opinion.

## Issue Advertising

While the FCC has moved to protect those subjected to personal attacks or opposed in political editorials, the treatment of issues raised in advertisements has proven much more ambivalent. For a while it seemed that organizations objecting to commercials for controversial products might gain access rights similar to those under the Personal Attack Rule and the Political Editorializing Rule. Instead, the commission pulled back when the consequences to the economic base of commercial broadcasting became clear. Still, a myriad of case law and regulatory edict has grown up, subjecting broadcasters to somewhat more rigorous standards than imposed by the general Fairness Doctrine. As we saw in the evaluation of the workings of the FCC in Chapters 3 and 4, one of the most frequent type of case handled by the FCC is a demand for time to counter paid issue advertising. Chapter 8 looks at how best to provide maximum access of individuals and groups to the airwaves, with special attention to providing commercial time to those willing to use it to express opinions on issues.

It is that type of commercial, the atypical advertisement that addresses a controversial issue of public importance, that can trigger the Fairness Doctrine. Much of the adjudication in this area has involved claims that standard product commercials have raised such issues, for example, that cigarette advertisements inherently raise the controversial issue of the health hazards of cigarettes.[76] But commission policy for the past decade has been to restrict use of the Fairness Doctrine to commercials that obviously address an issue or have an obvious and substantial relationship to such an issue.

Needless to say, if a broadcaster has a choice between carrying a standard product ad that does not cause Fairness Doctrine problems or an issue advertisement that might prompt demands for free reply time, he is likely to opt for the one that provides the safest revenue. So viewers are more likely to see commercials featuring cars, detergents, deodorants, and the like, than ones addressing the relative merits of federal budgetary choices. Some would say that's fine because, when ads about complex issues are carried, they often use the same techniques as the deodorant spots. But the effect of the Fairness Doctrine is to deprive the public of even that type of discourse.

As we have seen, many stations avoid grappling with the complex rules by not accepting ads that trigger the Fairness Doctrine. Others accept some, but when they do, they quickly negotiate with groups demanding access for reply time and give away time rather than fight a complaint. Of these two ways of avoiding trouble, the first is easier. But does it promote a robust debate? The silencing of editorial viewpoints proferred by advertisers can result from the broadcasters' efforts to cope with the regulations.

Thus the effect of all three special cases, the personal attack, political editorializing, and issue advertising rules, has been to limit the expression of views. Does that serve the First Amendment rights of the viewers and listeners?

## *References*

1. *Avery D. Post et al.* v. *CBS,* FCC mimeo 5565, released July 29, 1983.
2. *Cullman Broadcasting Co.,* 40 FCC 576 (1963).
3. *Sam Morris,* 11 FCC 197 (1946).
4. Id. at 199.
5. *Report on Editorializing by Broadcast Licensees,* 13 FCC 1246, 1252 (1949).
6. *Clayton W. Mapolies,* Pike & Fischer, 23 *Radio Regulation* 586 (1962).
7. Id. at 591.
8. *Billings Broadcasting Co.,* Pike & Fischer, 23 *Radio Regulation* 951, 953 (1962).
9. *Times-Mirror Broadcasting Co.,* Pike & Fischer, 24 *Radio Regulation* 404 (1962).
10. Id. at 408.
11. Id. at 406.
12. Id.
13. FCC letter of September 18, 1963, to Douglas A. Anello.
14. *Station's Responsibilities under Fairness Doctrine as to Controversial Issue Programming,* 40 FCC 571, 572 (1963).
15. Id.
16. *Cullman Broadcasting Co.,* 40 FCC 576 (1963).
17. *Applicability of the Fairness Doctrine in the Handling of Controversial Issues of Public Importance,* 29 Fed. Reg. 10415 (1964). [Hereafter *Fairness Report.*]
18. 32 Fed. Reg. 10305–06 (1967).
19. Under Section 315 of the Communications Act.

20. *Capitol Cities Broadcasting,* 13 FCC 2d 869 (1968).
21. *John H. Norris,* 1 FCC 2d 1587 (1965), *aff'd sub nom., Red Lion Broadcasting Co.* v. *FCC,* 395 U.S. 367 (1969).
22. 32 Fed. Reg. 11551 (1967).
23. See Fred W. Friendly, *The Good Guys, the Bad Guys, and the First Amendment* (New York, Vintage, 1976), pp. 50–60.
24. Id. p. 53.
25. Id. pp. 54–55.
26. 33 Fed. Reg. 5362, 5364 (1968).
27. The exemptions to the Personal Attack Rule are similar to the exemptions to the Equal Opportunities Rule. 33 Fed. Reg. 5362, 5363.
28. Id.
29. Id.
30. See *Rev. Paul E. Driscoll,* 40 FCC 2d 448 (1973).
31. Steven J. Simmons, *The Fairness Doctrine and the Media* (Berkeley, University of California Press, 1978), p. 79.
32. *John Birch Society,* 11 FCC 2d 790, 791–792 (1968).
33. *Lee H. Cherry,* 25 FCC 2d 887, 888 (1970).
34. *Freedom of the Press* v. *Public Access* (New York, Praeger, 1976), p. 171.
35. *John B. Walsh,* 31 FCC 2d 726 (1971).
36. *Mrs. Frank Diesz,* 27 FCC 2d 859 (1971).
37. *Port Jervis Broadcasting Co.,* 56 FCC 2d 1050 (1976).
38. Simmons, op. cit., pp. 81–85.
39. *Senator Florian W. Chmielewski,* 41 FCC 2d 201 (1973).
40. *Richard S. Manne,* 26 FCC 2d 583 (1970).
41. *John J. Salchert,* 48 FCC 2d 346 (1974).
42. *Francis X. Bellotti,* 40 FCC 2d 328 (1967).
43. *Rome Hospital,* 40 FCC 2d 452 (1973).
44. *Charlotte Observer,* 38 FCC 2d 522 (1972).
45. *Columbia Broadcasting System, Inc.,* Pike & Fischer, 21 *Radio Regulation* 2d 497 (1971).
46. *WIYN Radio, Inc.,* 35 FCC 2d 175 (1972).
47. Simmons, op. cit., p. 82.
48. *Straus Communications, Inc.,* 51 FCC 2d 385 (1975).
49. Id.
50. *Straus Communications, Inc.* v. *FCC,* 530 F.2d 1001, 1011 (D.C. Cir. 1976).
51. Id.
52. *Howard Lockwood,* Pike & Fischer, 39 *Radio Regulation* 2d 1501 (1977).
53. *Red Lion Broadcasting* v. *FCC,* 395 U.S. 367, 390 (1969).
54. Simmons, op. cit., p. 87.
55. 24 FCC 2d 18 (1970).
56. *Brandywine-Main Line Radio* v. *FCC,* 473 F.2d 16 (D.C. Cir. 1972).
57. Id. at 63–64.
58. FCC, *Sixth Annual Report,* 55 (1940).
59. *Mayflower Broadcasting Corp.,* 8 FCC 333 (1941).
60. Id. at 339.
61. Id.

62. See infra note 74 and accompanying text.

63. 13 FCC 1246 (1949).

64. Id. at 1258 (additional views of Commissioner E.M. Webster).

65. 32 Fed. Reg. 10305-06 (1967).

66. Id.

67. Id. at 10305.

68. Id.

69. *Bill Bishop,* 30 FCC 2d 829 (1971).

70. *George E. Cooley,* 10 FCC 2d 969 (1967).

71. *Taft Broadcasting Co.,* Pike & Fischer, 33 *Radio Regulation* 2d 1260, 1268 (1975).

72. Hearings on H.R. 3333 before the Subcommittee on Communications of the Committee on Interstate and Foreign Commerce, House of Representatives, 96th Cong., 1st Sess. (1979), Vol. II, Pt. 1, p. 555, as quoted in Peter Kokalis, "Updating the Communications Act; New Electronics, Old Economics, and the Demise of the Public Interest," 3 *COMM/ENT Law Journal* 455, 495-496, fn. 250.

73. NAB, *Motion for Leave to File Supplemental Comments in Petition for Rulemaking to Repeal and/or Modify the Personal Attack and Political Editorializing Rules,* RM-3739, January 10, 1983.

74. Id.

75. Simmons, op. cit., p. 90.

76. *WCBS-TV,* 8 FCC 2d 381 (1967); *aff'd on reconsideration,* 9 FCC 2d 921 (1967) (referred to as the *Banzhaf* case); sustained, *Banzhaf* v. *FCC,* 405 F.2d 1082 (D.C. Cir. 1968), *certiorari denied,* 396 U.S. 842 (1969).

# EIGHT

# The Marketplace
# of Ideas

"ONCE UPON A TIME in a far-off jungle, a variety of animals lived in perfect harmony."

That's the way a Mobil Corporation commercial begins, mixing animation, dancers, and clever advertising copy to create a "fable" that unless the oil industry reaps a profit proportionate to its size, it won't find future energy supplies. Many television stations refused to air the advertisements, fearing that it would prompt Fairness Doctrine requests for reply time. Mobil's Herbert Schmertz condemned the refusal of the three big networks to carry Mobil's issue ads. "The commercials make a contribution to the dialogue on an important issue," he said. "If we believe in a pluralistic society that depends on a robust marketplace of ideas, then the networks and stations are really shortchanging the American people."[1] Mobil has even offered to pay twice the going rate for airtime to compensate the broadcaster if he's hit with a demand for free reply time. Not many advertisers would underwrite their opponents in this way.

On the other side of the political spectrum, groups such as the National Citizens Committee for Broadcasting, the Committee for Open Media, and the Media Access Project have pushed to get their viewpoints on the airwaves. In an article in a newspaper called *access,* Samuel Simon asserted that the audience has a First Amendment right to the airwaves:

> The Constitution gives two rights to a broadcaster's audience:
>
> (1) a fair chance to contribute to the marketplace of ideas, and
> (2) receipt of an uncensored and diverse sampling of views.

The broadcaster, as a single citizen, also has these rights, but the broadcaster does not have the *sole* right of expression, and most assuredly does not have a constitutional power to silence any speaker or idea that [s]he may personally find objectionable.[2]

Here we have two spokesmen for two very different constituencies, one for a major corporation, the other for a group that says it represents the public interest. Yet each asserts the need for greater access to get additional viewpoints on the air and each complains that broadcasters have failed to provide adequate news coverage and have suppressed views. At times their complaints seem interchangeable. At a Washington conference sponsored by the American Enterprise Institute in March 1983, where both Schmertz and Simon appeared, one of them said:

(1) The press says it's the surrogate of the public, and in my mind it's really failing in that capacity. It's abandoned its responsibilities in search of some awesome power and sometimes unbridled power to act without any accountability.

The other responded:

(2) If business doesn't get a fair shake, what are you going to do about it? In many ways that's the most important question. If labor doesn't get a fair shake, what are they going to do about it? . . . What happens when the system of fairness or access breaks down. . . . what are the options available to remedy the situation?

An additional view was offered:

(3) I really can't take the claim of surrogateship seriously when I look at these abuses and how the public is being shortchanged.

To which this reply was offered:

(4) I think it's awfully difficult to see ourselves and what we do portrayed on television or in radio because they will never or almost never meet our expectations.

What both Mobil's Schmertz and Simon, director of the Telecommunications Research and Action Center (TRAC), were saying is that they want direct access to espouse viewpoints without editing by broadcasters. In reading a transcript of the meeting it's hard to tell who said what. Schmertz uttered Quotations 1 and 3, and Simon offered the views numbered 2 and 4. Although Schmertz and Simon agree on little else, both distrust broadcasters.

Some stations simply refuse to accept advertisements that editorialize on public issues, so-called "advertorials." Stations that do accept such ads usually require the advertisers to prove the factual assertions in the spots. One station executive, who asked not to be identified, said seven station employees plus a lawyer are needed to screen each issue ad. Such manpower costs wipe out the profit potential of such ads.

Some stations that accept issue ads regularly charge more for the time. Then they are willing to agree to demands for free spots to reply to the advertorials. Capitulation usually costs less than the legal fees to fight fairness complaints. Sometimes the stations attempt to relegate the free countercommercials to periods outside of prime time, despite FCC policy against airing only one side during more attractive time periods.

The three networks have an aversion to issue ads, according to a telephone survey. CBS and its affiliate stations do not accept issue ads, except for spots on ballot propositions. The network feels public controversies are better discussed on news and public affairs programs and that issue ads only showcase the ideas of those with money to spend.

The CBS policy of permitting issue ads about ballot propositions still restricts expression on controversies, as shown in an excerpt from a letter the network sent the FCC regarding a complaint against the CBS-owned and operated station in Los Angeles:

> KNXT and CBS believe it is in the public interest to provide paid access to supporters and opponents of ballot propositions. At the same time, CBS and KNXT recognize that disparities in financial resources may raise questions of fairness in this area and accordingly limit the extent of such purchases where only one side has indicated an interest in buying time. . . . Thus, on March 6, 1980, the anti-Proposition 11 group sought to purchase a total of 44 prime time announcements (22 minutes) on KNXT, commencing on March 11 and continuing through June 22. *The station, cognizant of possible fairness concerns, limited the opponents of Proposition 11 to only 3½ prime time minutes over the course of the campaign.* (Emphasis added.)

Proposition 11 was a California ballot initiative that would have levied a surtax on profits of oil companies. The letter was written in the context of a Fairness Doctrine complaint by supporters of the measure, Citizens to Tax Big Oil, requesting free airtime on KNXT in Los Angeles. The FCC found the complaint without merit on the basis that KNXT's overall programming had been balanced. The significant point is that another group that opposed the proposition, that wanted to address the public, and that was willing to pay for 22 minutes was kept to only 3½ minutes because CBS and KNXT wanted to avoid Fairness Doctrine problems.

NBC also bans most issue ads. Only spots about ballot referendum issues are accepted. NBC, too, justifies the policy by asserting that groups with the most money would end up dominating debate on the topic, and fairness obligations would be triggered.

ABC accepts issue advertisements on the network only under very limited conditions. In 1982 its policy was to accept such ads only late in the broadcast day between midnight and 7 a.m. This policy, dubbed the "Pumpkin Theory of Advertising," relegated such messages to times when viewership was low. Perhaps that helps explain why no one placed an issue ad on ABC during the first 15 months the policy was in effect.

All three networks easily sell most of their commercial time for standard product ads, so why bother with controversial ads?

Newspapers do not share this reluctance. In 1981, for example, W.R. Grace and Company ran a series of ads in major papers promoting the Reagan tax-cut plan. One ad that appeared in the *Washington Post* criticized a *Post* editorial on the subject. In a series of Grace ads and *Post* editorials over the next few weeks, the company and the paper debated the tax cut, trading jabs at each other's facts and logic. After several ads had appeared, the *Post* commented on April 9, "Thanks to W.R. Grace, the newspapers running these ads are the only business in the country that can rest assured of benefitting from the administration's supply-side economics." The paper jokingly denied that editorial page writers were getting commissions from the advertising department for the Grace ads. The ads cost Grace about $22,000 each.

Finally, on April 30, 1981, the *Post* gave Grace's president, J. Peter Grace, free space on the op-ed page to present his views at length. Mr. Grace wrote that the *Post*'s advertising department "can stop salivating as of now." He called off the dialogue because of the cost of the ads. In an accompanying editorial the *Post* concluded that neither side had changed the other's mind "but we trust the readers will have found these exchanges useful."

Of course the unregulated newspaper is free to accept or reject such ads. It could, if it wished, let well-heeled advertisers dominate the debate without challenge. Newspapers have no obligation to present contrasting views. Unlike the *Post,* many newspapers fall short of providing the kind of dialogue the Grace ads spurred. But the exchange was balanced and robust. It was as the editorial said, "useful" to the public.

What can be done to facilitate the exchange of views on radio and television? To encourage a robust debate? To make certain that the views of some of the activist, reform groups supported by TRAC are aired? To assure that corporations can make their case? Is the system inadequate now, as the men from Mobil and TRAC suggest? Before looking at this, it is necessary to look back—at the origins of the tug-of-war over advertising and free response time.

## Smoking: A Burning Issue

A firestorm that swept the nation was directed against cigarette advertisements. It singed its target; it prompted a new regulatory zeal. Fairness Doctrine cases began cropping up all over as the debate about advertising—and its impact on public debate of significant issues—heated up. The history of how the federal government and broadcast industry handled the smoking issue and its aftermath contains lessons for those pondering how to make broadcast regulations work to promote wide-ranging, diverse discussion of public issues.

The FCC became involved in requiring stations to provide airtime for groups opposed to commercial messages in 1967 when it ruled that cigarette advertising needed to be balanced with health warnings.[3] The commission acted on a Fairness Doctrine complaint filed by John Banzhaf III requesting that stations carry anti-smoking announcements. Although the cigarette ads made no claim that smoking was healthy, the FCC noted that the government had issued warnings of the danger of smoking. Banzhaf and other crusaders against tobacco wanted to counter an issue that the cigarette manufacturers had never directly raised in their ads, but which, it was claimed, was implicit in the commercial message about the desirability of smoking.

The FCC called cigarette advertising a "unique situation" and asserted that no other product had received such government criticism as a health hazard.[4] The commission stressed that its ruling applied only to cigarette ads and did not extend to other product advertising.[5] It said that extending Fairness Doctrine obligations to other products would be rare, "if indeed they ever occurred."[6] But soon other complainants demanded airtime to respond to other product advertisements, asserting that the products endangered the environment, and thus raised a controversial issue of public importance.

The threshold problem in dealing with commercials is that few of them seek to be controversial. Most ads, after all, try to persuade or motivate people to purchase a product or service. Controversy rarely helps the sales pitch, and standard product advertisements make waves only when they suggest that Brand X is better than Brand Y. That clearly is not the kind of controversy the Fairness Doctrine was designed to regulate.

Some commercials, a minority, seek to do more than sell a product. Institutional or image advertising attempts to promote a company in the public's eye. Sometimes while bragging about its virtues, an advertiser may implicitly refer to a matter of public concern affecting the environment, the economy, energy policy, or a host of other issues. But it is not always clear if an issue has even been raised, much less squarely addressed. So it is hard to tell if fairness requirements have been triggered.

Easier to handle are the smaller number of commercials in which companies take a stand on a major public issue. For example, if a telephone company advertises about the need for a change in local regulations to permit a new rate structure for billing customers, the station must provide balance in its coverage of the issue if the rate proposal is controversial and has organized opponents. Likewise, if an association of retired public employees advertises against pending proposals in Congress to alter the Social Security system, the station must present an opportunity for opposing views to air. But even commercials of this type sometimes fall into a hazy area if it is unclear whether the issue they address is truly controversial and of public (as contrasted to private) importance.

Easiest of all to fit into the regulatory framework are ads urging voters to pass or defeat ballot referendum proposals. These are automatically regarded as addressing controversial issues of public importance because the public is asked to vote on them.[7]

Stations prefer product advertisements because these commercials raise the fewest Fairness Doctrine problems. When a station elects to sell time for image advertising or a message designed to sway opinion on a political question, under the Cullman Principle it might be required to give away time for opponents to express other views. Consequently, the airwaves are filled with spots hawking the virtues of this soap or that beer, this tampon or that hemorrhoidal ointment, and only occasionally with an ad urging changes in the tax laws or one on military spending. Most stations shy from controversial ads and one reason is the Fairness Doctrine. That's somewhat ironic, because the rule is designed to promote the airing of major issues.

Under the system of regulation that has evolved, it is easier—and safer—for a station to refuse to accept advertising that raises a controversial issue of public importance than it is for the station to avoid giving away time to counter such an ad after it has aired. The Supreme Court has held that groups do not have a constitutional or statutory right to purchase airtime for commercials supporting their views on major public controversies.[8] The FCC has upheld a station's refusal to sell commercial time to an antiwar group to run spots opposing U.S. involvement in Vietnam.[9] Leeway has been accorded stations in deciding which format to use to present controversial issues, but if they sell time for issue ads, they will find their discretion limited in providing contrasting viewpoints.

This reluctance to sell time for issue advertising stems in part from the *Banzhaf* ruling and the confusion it engendered over fairness in advertising. Despite the FCC's effort to limit the impact of *Banzhaf,* the commission almost opened a Pandora's Box of countercommercials. One scholar stated that *Banzhaf* "haunted the Commission." [10]

It wasn't long before broadcasters, and the FCC, were besieged with requests for time for counteradvertisements. One complaint, by Anthony R. Martin Trigora, was directed at self-promotion by the television industry.[11] He complained about ABC network promos and ads sponsored by the National Association of Broadcasters that ran during the dispute over pay television proposals. The ads made no clear criticism of pay-TV and the FCC rejected his assertion that they raised Fairness Doctrine issues. "Were we to rule otherwise," the FCC stated, "the institutional or promotional advertisements of many companies would be regarded as stating one side of a controversial issue." [12]

But the first indication that the FCC would not limit its *Banzhaf* ruling involved advertisements aired during a labor dispute. A station had stopped running ads supporting a union boycott of a department store, but had continued to air the store's regular product commercials. Although the FCC did not want to hold hearings, the U.S. Circuit Court of Appeals said that the store's product advertisements inherently raised one side of the boycott issue.[13] Like the cigarette ads, the store's commercials carried an implicit rather than explicit comment on a controversial issue—in this case, the labor dispute. The court said the FCC had to consider whether the station's unwillingness to carry the pro-union ads while running the store's commercials violated the Fairness Doctrine.[14]

Other complaints flowed in to the FCC, seeking to apply *Banzhaf* to commercials for soap,[15] trash compactors,[16] airbags,[17] leaded gasoline and big automobiles.[18] The early 1970s were years of heightened environmental awareness, consumerism, and protest against the war in Vietnam. The FCC seemed to be dangling a new tool for activists to get their messages to the public. One early challenge involved announcements urging young men to volunteer for the Marine Corps.[19] One spot stated:

> This is Frank Blair speaking to the young men facing a military obligation. As a father, I was pleased when my sons Thomas and John told me they wanted to become Marines. They told me that there was more than one way to look at an obligation: to consider it something you have to do, or as an opportunity to grow as an individual. How about you? Are you ready to develop in body, mind and spirit? Find out details from your Marine Corps representative today.[20]

It was alleged that this spot raised the war issue and the controversy over young men fleeing from the country to escape the draft. But the FCC found otherwise. It upheld a station's determination that the spots did not raise the issues of the Vietnam war or the draft, but only the noncontroversial issues of whether armed forces should be maintained through voluntary recruitment.[21]

While rejecting the idea that Marine Corps commercials inherently raised the war issue, the commission was willing to find that more mundane controversies attached to seemingly innocuous public service messages about charitable fund raising. In the *United People* case, a group by that name objected to public service announcements touting the United Appeal charity.[22] United People claimed that the United Appeal was controlled by businessmen and did not funnel money into community projects. Although the commercial did not explicitly raise any controversial issue, the charitable organization itself was controversial. The FCC ruled in favor of the United People complaint.[23]

But the FCC turned down a fairness complaint that said detergent commercials raised the issue of dangerous phosphate in the environment.[24] Although, like cigarettes, phosphate-based detergents had been criticized in government studies, the commission ruled there was no evidence that the product ads dealt directly with controversial issues of public importance.[25]

And when a complaint was submitted objecting that ads for trash compactors touted a product that hindered recycling, the FCC was not moved by language in the National Environmental Policy Act of 1969 urging recycling.[26] The commission rejected the fairness complaint because it involved ordinary product commercials.

But when a 2-minute advertisement urging use of seat belts included a 12-second reference to the alternative air bag devices, referring to them as costly and unreliable, the FCC ruled that a Fairness Doctrine obligation had been triggered.[27] In view of the dispute over air bags, the FCC held that a controversial issue of public importance had been raised.[28]

When environmentalists filed a complaint against NBC for airing Esso commercials about Alaskan oil and the proposed pipeline, the commission scrutinized the oil company's institutional message.[29] One commercial concluded, "If America's energy supply is to be assured in this unpredictable world, the search for domestic oil must go on and fast." Another spot mentioned preserving "the ecology" and stated, "By balancing demands of energy with the needs of nature, they're making sure that when wells are drilled or pipelines built, the life that comes back each year will have a home to come back to." The complaint in the *National Broadcasting* case alleged that these commercials raised the issue of the need for rapid oil development in Alaska, and inherently raised the issue of the need for a new pipeline. While discussion of the pipeline proposal was not explicit, the FCC rejected NBC's contention that the ads were merely institutional advertising. The FCC told the network it had to provide contrasting views, but agreed that NBC had already done so.[30]

Another complaint was filed involving an ad for a gasoline additive named F-310. The spot claimed that "Chevron with F-310 turns dirty smoke into good, clean mileage."[31] In the *Neckritz* case the FCC found that this ad did not deal directly with a major public issue and hence, did not trigger fairness obligations.[32]

The FCC reached a similar conclusion regarding advertisements for large automobiles and leaded gasoline in a complaint brought by Friends of the Earth.[33] One ad urged motorists to consider "moving up" to a bigger car; another promoted high octane gasoline.[34] The FCC rejected the idea that these ads raised the issue of air pollution, although it acknowledged that the Fairness Doctrine would fully apply had the ad dealt directly with the issue.[35] The commission's refusal to extend the Fairness Doctrine to general product advertisements was rejected in this case by the Court of Appeals.[36] The court noted that there was government concern about the health problems caused by auto pollution. While these spots did not address those issues, neither had the cigarette ads covered by the *Banzhaf* ruling. Like cigarette advertising, the automobile and gasoline ads were for products that aggravate health hazards, and the court found the *Banzhaf* precedent relevant.[37]

The commission's effort to limit the Fairness Doctrine only to product advertisements about cigarettes was rejected by the appeals court. And the scope of fairness seemed to be expanding over institutional advertising, as well. In the *Media Access Project* case in 1973, the FCC confronted a complaint filed by MAP about ads for the Georgia Power Company.[38] The ads aired during a controversy over utility rate increases. While the ads did not explicitly mention rate proceedings, one did state:

> . . . to continue providing the power needed by Georgia homes and industries, we must be able to build. Which means borrowing money. Lots of it. An increase in price will help us borrow the money that's needed and keep power flowing. To your home and your job. Electricity. What would you do without it?[39]

The FCC rejected the idea that the ads were simply "institutional in nature" and ruled that some raised one side of the issue and required airing of contrasting views.[40] The Fairness Doctrine applied where an ad "clearly" presented a position on an issue.[41]

These cases are a "crazy quilt," according to Professor Simmons.[42] The cases came to inconsistent conclusions where advertisements touched on controversial subjects explicitly, implicitly, suggestively, or indirectly.[43]

> *Neckritz* states the advertisement must deal "directly" with the issue; *National Broadcasting* speaks of advertisements "inherently" raising and having

a "cognizable bearing" on the issue; and *Media Access* focuses on an advertisement that "clearly presents" the issue. But what do these terms mean? [44]

How could broadcasters be expected to know how to behave if the commission handed down inconsistent rulings? In 1974 the FCC pulled back and tried to impose order. It issued the *Fairness Report*, [45] which categorized commercials as to their type: commercials to sell products, advertisements about the efficacy of products, and advertisements about public issues.

In the 1974 *Fairness Report* the FCC tried to slam the lid of the Pandora's Box it had opened with *Banzhaf*. While noting that the decision in the cigarette matter may have represented the proper policy in light of the health hazards, the FCC said the *Banzhaf* precedent "is not at all in keeping with the basic purposes of the fairness doctrine. . . ." [46] Moreover, the FCC repudiated the *Banzhaf* case, stating that "standard product commercials, such as the old cigarette ads, make no meaningful contribution toward informing the public on any side of any issue." [47]

Advocacy of a product and claims about a product's efficacy were deemed not to raise fairness issues, absent explicit discussion of a specific issue of public controversy. The Fairness Doctrine continued, however, to apply to institutional advertising and issue-oriented commercials. Advertisements which are "overt editorials" will bring the Fairness Doctrine to bear. But the line between editorializing and image making is often unclear. When an institutional ad raises an issue of public controversy, even implicitly, the fairness rules may apply. [48] Broadcasters are supposed to judge whether the commercial "obviously addresses" and "advocates" a position on such an issue. While a "tenuous relationship" between the ad and the issue would not trigger the Fairness Doctrine, a "substantial" and "obvious" relationship would. [49]

In trying to clarify the impact of the Fairness Doctrine on advertising, the commission made it harder for groups seeking access to prevail. But the FCC continued to impose the regulation on advertisements that explicitly discussed a controversial issue, and on image advertisements that implicitly raised such an issue in an obvious and meaningful way. It is not an easy task to decide which institutional commercials fall under the rule.

The difficulty of applying consistent standards to commercials was demonstrated in a complaint against 13 radio stations that ran a series of 1-minute spots on nuclear power produced by a utility company. [50] Most of the stations denied that the commercials raised a constitutional issue of public importance, but the FCC decided the issue did fall under the Fairness Doctrine and evaluated station compliance. While it asserted the absence of a "mathematical formula or mechanical requirement for achieving fairness," it found eight stations had acted unreasonably, including one violation based on the frequency of presentation, and a 3-to-1 ratio. The FCC ruled, however, that one of the other stations had met its responsibility with a 60-to-27 ratio without any frequency data. The Court of Appeals ruled that such findings were inconsistent, and remanded with instructions that the FCC explicitly state its standards.[51] The court said:

> While [FCC] decisions are in accord with this court's general command that "the essential basis for any fairness doctrine . . . is that the American public must not be left uninformed," the Commission has used differing factors to define a reasonable opportunity. Its decisions have relied upon the amount of time allotted each point of view, the frequency with which points of view are aired, the repetitive, continuous nature of programming, the amount of programming broadcast during prime time, and on occasion, the Commission has acted without explicit reference to any of these factors.[52]

The Appeals Court went on to quote an especially cutting comment about the Fairness Doctrine from former FCC Chairman Dean Burch:

> . . . in the fairness area, the bond of theory and implementation has come unstuck and all the principal actors—licensees, public interest advocates, the Commission itself—are in limbo, left to fend for themselves.[53]

## A Right of Access?

Aside from the regulatory quagmire the FCC created by its *Banzhaf* ruling, some very large questions have been raised by the use of advertising and counteradvertising to debate public issues. Stations that reject issue advertisements usually justify their refusal to air such spots on the grounds that controversial issues are better handled in news and public affairs programs. As we have seen, critics on both the left and the right have objected to lodging sole discretion with the broadcaster to determine which issues to present and which spokespersons to feature. Some go so far as to suggest that press freedom has become an excuse for owners of mass media to exercise the censorship role the First Amendment denied the government.

In a 1967 article in the *Harvard Law Review,* Jerome A. Barron articulated the need for a right of access to the media. He said the notion that a marketplace of ideas exists is a romantic one and that "if ever there were a self-operating marketplace of ideas, it has long ceased to exist."[54]

> The mass media's development of an antipathy to ideas requires legal intervention if novel and unpopular ideas are to be assured a forum—unorthodox points of view which have no claim on broadcast time and newspaper

space as a matter of right are in a poor position to compete with those aired as a matter of grace.[55]

Barron suggested that publishers and broadcasters ignored novel ideas for an odd reason. "The controllers of the media have no ideology. Since in the main they espouse no particular ideas, their antipathy to all ideas has passed unnoticed."[56] It wasn't that the media pushed certain points of view and rejected others, Barron wrote, but that they avoided ideas and failed to act as a sounding board, with the result being that

> the opinion vacuum is filled with the least controversial and bland ideas. Whatever is stale and accepted in the status quo is readily discussed and thereby reinforced and revitalized.[57]

There is validity in Barron's diagnosis, even if one rejects the cure he proposed. He suggested that a right of access be created so individuals and groups could purchase editorial advertisements in newspapers and on broadcast stations.

That suggestion was tested and rejected by the Supreme Court as regards broadcasting in the *CBS* v. *DNC* case.[58] The case, however, did not slam the door on the FCC's establishing access mechanisms. One of the issues was whether broadcasters—because of their role as trustees of the public airwaves—in effect were performing governmental actions in denying access to those seeking to purchase advertising time. If broadcaster decisions could be characterized as governmental action, then denying the right to express political views would be an unconstitutional infringement against those seeking airtime. Two members of the Supreme Court indicated that the "public nature of the airwaves, the governmentally created preferred status of broadcasters, the extensive governmental regulation of broadcast programming, and the specific governmental [FCC] approval of the challenged policy" turned the licensee's conduct into governmental action.[59] Three members of the Court believed that the broadcasters' denial of access was not governmental action, but that the question was not definitively resolved.[60]

The Court, however, upheld the FCC's policy of not requiring stations to accept issue advertisements, giving the agency great deference in determining what the public interest demands of broadcasting.[61] Neither the public interest standard nor the First Amendment requires stations to accept paid spot announcements that discuss controversial issues.

After the Supreme Court ruled that advertisers have no statutory or constitutional right to place their commercials on television and radio, the Appeals Court in the District of Columbia turned its attention to the other side of the coin: toward those demanding reply time to answer commercials touting products. While it was clear that issue advertisements that stations did elect to air could trigger fairness obligations, the FCC had

ruled in 1974 that no such obligation attached to standard product advertisements.[62] Groups that had hailed the cigarette ad decision in *Banzhaf*
fought back. The National Citizens Committee for Broadcasting, Friends
of the Earth, and the Council for Economic Priorities sought judicial
review. They argued that the public's First Amendment right to receive information required a broadcaster to air countercommercials, and that the
FCC's decision was arbitrary, capricious, and an abuse of discretion.[63]

The *National Citizens* petitioners argued that since the First Amendment protects advertisements, opposing information is also constitutionally protected. Acceptance of this argument would have indicated
that the Fairness Doctrine is coextensive with the First Amendment.[64] But
the appeals court held that neither the First Amendment nor the Communications Act require application of the Fairness Doctrine to standard
product commercials that do not obviously and meaningfully raise a controversial issue of public importance. The Fairness Doctrine was viewed
as an administrative compromise for the FCC to strike. As David L.
Sinak has stated, the court's refusal to base a public right of access on the
First Amendment's protection of commercial speech "has diminished the
hope for a constitutionally-based public right of access on any issue." [65]
The court did, however, order the FCC to consider alternate access proposals suggested by both the Committee for an Open Media (COM) and
Henry Geller.

COM had suggested an access mechanism that licensees could voluntarily adopt and that would be deemed presumptive compliance with the
Fairness Doctrine. It has some attractive features, not the least of which is
that stations providing access under the scheme would have been freed
from other Fairness Doctrine obligations. The COM proposal has been
summarized as follows:

(1) A licensee would set aside one hour per week for spot announcements and
lengthier programming which would be available for presentation of
messages by members of the public.

(2) Half of this time would be allocated on a "first-come, first-served" basis
on any topic whatsoever; the other half would be apportioned on a
"representative spokesperson system."

(3) Both parts of the allocation scheme would be "nondiscretionary as to
content with the licensee."

(4) However, the broadcaster would still be required to ensure that spot
messages or other forms of response to "editorial advertisements" are
broadcast.[66]

Henry Geller, in his capacity as head of President Carter's National
Telecommunications and Information Administration (and, after the
change of administrations, as a private listener), urged a different solution on access. Geller proposed a "Ten Issue" approach as part of an

overall modification of the Fairness Doctrine. He suggested that stations be required to keep annual records of their coverage of the 10 most important controversial issues they had chosen to cover. The records, which would be public and would be considered at license renewal time, would include offers of responses made and programs aired, including the partisan spokespersons afforded access. News programming would be exempt from the reporting requirements.

The Geller proposal called for the FCC to stop evaluating fairness complaints on a case-by-case basis, except for election issues and personal attacks. Rather, the FCC would merely forward nonpolitical complaints to the licensees. At renewal, the commission would simply evaluate the file to see if the broadcaster had a flagrant pattern of violating the Fairness Doctrine. If that appeared to be the case, a license renewal hearing would be held.

Like the COM plan, the Geller approach had the virtue of simplifying the enforcement of the Fairness Doctrine. But both were a far cry from eliminating the doctrine entirely. Geller would keep much of it intact, but stop most case-by-case adjudication. COM would remove most adjudication, but keep it for one of the thorniest areas: issue ads and counter-commercials.

The FCC rejected both approaches.[67]

The commission said access would not be an adequate substitute for fairness, and rejected the "Ten Issue" approach as burdensome and lacking any guarantee that it would enhance coverage of important public controversies. The FCC also rejected the idea of reviewing fairness complaints only at license renewal, by restating a policy choice made in 1974:

> [A] review only at renewal time would remove a major incentive for interested citizens to file fairness complaints—that is, the chance to have an opposing view aired over the station before the issue has become stale with the passage of time. At present, citizen complaints provide the principal means of ensuring compliance with the Fairness Doctrine. If we were to remove the possibility that these complaints might result in broadcast time for a neglected point of view, we might as well have to rely on government monitoring to carry out our investigative role. Such monitoring, of course, would represent an unfortunate step in the direction of deeper government involvement in the day-to-day operation of broadcast journalism.[68]

### Access Evaluated

Proposals to mandate some form of public access to the airwaves—whether by according a right to purchase time for issue advertising or by requiring stations to provide free time—have some virtue. They would shift the regulatory focus away from the Fairness Doctrine concern with content and the attendant problems noted above. Phil Jacklin has suggested that the goal should be "to ensure fairness about who is heard rather than fairness in what is said." [69]

Under current regulations, the FCC responds to complaints about content. Except in special circumstances, such as a personal attack or political editorial, the focus is not on who should be allowed to appear on the air but whether a point of view must be broadcast. The distinction is important. Under the general application of the Fairness Doctrine, personnel of the station itself can state the viewpoint, and except in special cases, need not provide access to a particular spokesperson.

Proponents of access, like Jacklin and COM, criticize the media for failing to provide the kind of journalism that maximizes discussion of ideas. Because newspapers and television depend upon advertisers, circulation and ratings are essential to the success of the enterprise. Jacklin believes this affects editorial choices, and makes the news media more docile, thereby snuffing out discussion of new ideas.

The problem of deciding how access will work and who will decide who gets on the air is a difficult one, however, if one rescinds the editorial discretion of the broadcaster. Several ways of distributing free airtime have been suggested:

1.  The first-come, first-served method is the simplest. It has been tried on public access channels on some cable systems, and has led to some unorthodox programming, including shows featuring nude people discussing sex hangups. Is that what the First Amendment is designed to promote? The first-come, first-served idea fails to assure that significant issues will be discussed or that contrasting views will be aired. One can imagine situations where those first in line for access all agree on a proposition. Suppose the people who sign up for free time prefer to read poetry, lift weights, or chant. The National Association of Broadcasters said access could turn into "A Gong Show with no gong." [70]

2.  The "representative spokesman" concept is an alternative method of access that would avoid some of the uncertainties of letting anyone appear. However, establishing criteria for selecting spokespersons is no simple matter. Rather than rely on the journalist's notion of who speaks for a group, those favoring mandatory-access provisions have suggested some new mechanisms, including what Jacklin calls "access contributions." [71] Under his idea, citizens can pool their individual access rights and contribute them to a designated spokesperson. Airtime would be granted to those who had gathered what would be, in effect, votes. This is an interesting idea, for it could increase the grass roots endeavors of many organizations. But it has drawbacks as well. Could not the majority, by pooling its access rights, dominate the airtime devoted to public

access under such a scheme? It's difficult to structure priority of access.[72] In any event, access mechanisms are unlikely to assure balance.

Provision of free access might provide some with a new platform, but it does not assure that anyone will watch. Public access on cable systems has turned into "vanity video," satisfying the egos of those who appear, but generating a very small audience. Access proposals for television and radio similarly risk that public apathy will render such programming useless.

The broadcast industry opposed the COM proposal, naturally. No merchant likes to give away goods, and time is the broadcaster's inventory. Groups such as the NAB contended that while access might reduce regulation, it might also involve the FCC deeply in disputes between access seekers and stations over who should get on and—especially in the case of indecent language—what should get on the air. By removing the broadcaster's editorial control over such programming, television and radio would be partly turned into common carriers, which violates the Communications Act.[73] On the issue of access, the Supreme Court has sided with the journalists rather than "self-appointed" commentators:

> . . . Congress and the commission could appropriately conclude that the allocation of journalistic priorities should be concentrated in the licensee rather than diffused among many. This policy gives the public some assurance that the broadcaster will be answerable if he fails to meet its legitimate needs. No such accountability attaches to the private individual. . . . To agree that debate on public issues should be "robust, and wide open" does not mean that we should exchange "public trustee" broadcasting, with all its limitations, for a system of self-appointed editorial commentators.[74]

The motivating concern behind the access proposals—a distrust of the broadcaster's editorial judgment—thus creates the main stumbling block to its implementation. No one denies that *voluntary* action by broadcasters to grant citizens more airtime would be a worthwhile step. The proponents of *mandatory* access go a step further and want to remove the stations' discretion to select topics and spokespersons. But suspending editorial discretion would raise a host of practical, legal, and constitutional problems.

Under current law, for better or for worse, broadcast journalists are gatekeepers. They decide what and who gets on the air. Part of the reason for complaints about unfairness from both the left and the right is the feeling the electronic press has not done its job well enough, qualitatively or quantitatively. Not enough programming on public issues is aired; not enough citizens are invited to participate in discussions that do air.

The hope of voluntary improvements rarely satisfies those striving for change. But if the broadcast industry did more on its own to enhance access within the current system of news and public affairs programming, it would go a long way toward reducing the clamor for mandatory access, and eliminating complaints of unfairness.

## The Future of Access

In considering why broadcasters fail to afford as much time—paid or free—for expression of viewpoints as demanded by politically active groups, it is important to review the different access possibilities:

*Issue Advertising:* Provision of time for purchase by individuals, companies, and groups to air "advertorials."

*Countercommercials:* Provision of free time to groups opposing views expressed in issue advertisements.

*News Programs:* Coverage of various spokespersons and viewpoints as selected and edited by journalists.

*Public Affairs Programs:* Provision of time to various spokespersons, either in an interview format or an unedited appearance, as selected by the licensee.

*Special Access Programs:* Provision of unedited time to various groups under some mechanism that is not under the control of the licensee.

Because broadcasters face Fairness Doctrine obligations if they accept issue ads, and thus may have countercommercials, they are hesitant to accept such ads because they face loss of revenue if they must air free spots.

Broadcasters regularly provide edited access on newscasts and public affairs programs, but recognize that under the Fairness Doctrine they must provide contrasting points of view on significant public controversies. While most news departments cover the top stories, the regulation may restrain their zeal in covering issues that do not dominate the headlines. There's just so much most stations can cover. And if by choosing to cover an important but overlooked issue they simply trigger demands for more time from additional groups, the tendency may be to avoid the headaches.

Special access programs that would reduce the broadcasters' discretion in choosing spokespersons have been rejected by the FCC as a substitute for Fairness Doctrine compliance. Thus a station that undertakes a special access program would still have to abide by the fairness rules, meaning it could inherit all the potential for complaints and demands for free time that it now faces under other types of access.

Thus the major impediment to greater access to the airwaves is how the Fairness Doctrine collides with broadcaster's desire to control their airtime, maximize profits, and serve the community as the FCC requires. If, for example, a station did not have to fear that accepting an issue ad would require a free countercommercial, it might be much more willing to accept the issue ad.

If, for example, a station need not fear that coverage of less newsworthy issues on news and public affairs programs could stimulate demands for coverage by additional groups, it might undertake additional coverage. Of course, it might not. And there's the rub. Eliminating the Fairness Doctrine would remove the small protection possessed by individuals and groups dissatisfied with the fairness of broadcasters.

Moreover, abolition of the Cullman Principle, which requires free countercommercials, would permit those with economic resources to dominate debate on some issues. This could result in the public accepting or rejecting ideas not on their merit but because of the size of the advocate's pocketbook.[75] In testimony to a House Task Force on Elections, former FCC Chairman Charles Ferris asked, "In a situation where only money can buy access, who will pay to speak on behalf of welfare mothers who are accused of being cheats or for their children whose lunches are said to be a drain on the federal economy? Who can afford to present the views for the unemployed in a system where only money speaks?"

Current FCC Chairman Mark Fowler took a different tack in a speech to a First Amendment Congress in 1982:

> This country has long relied on the marketplace to determine what goods and services reach the people. . . . The marketplace of ideas is part of the general freedom that exists in society to buy or not buy, to consider or not consider."

It should be noted that under the current system, the Fairness Doctrine only gives groups without funds the power to *respond* to the initiative taken by those who successfully place issue ads on the air. Thus, even with countercommercials, those who pay for the issue ads have considerably greater power to frame the issue, structure the debate, and set the agenda.

There are several options for public policy in this difficult field:

1. *Prohibit all issue ads* on radio and TV to prevent the wealthy from dominating the debate. This, however, would stifle debate, restrict those who wish to organize to express their views, and violate the spirit and probably the letter of the First Amendment.

2. *Permit issue ads with no right of reply* under the Fairness Doc-

trine. This would enhance the discretion and money-making power of the broadcaster. It could silence the viewpoints of those with less money.

3. *Permit issue ads but require equal opportunities.* Stations would have to play fair; if ads were sold to express a viewpoint on an issue, opponents would be allowed to purchase similar airtime at identical rates to express a contrary view. This would handicap poorer groups. But if they could raise the money, stations could not decline their advertisements.

4. *Require stations to air issue ads* on any subject but remove the Fairness Doctrine requirement to air free countercommercials. This would remove station discretion to accept or reject ads.

5. *Require stations to accept issue ads and free replies* but structure the reply opportunities so they fall outside of the commercial format, for instance, during a special weekly program devoted to the expression of viewpoints. This would spare broadcasters a major loss of revenue, but it would also relegate the unpaid viewpoints to the recesses of the broadcast schedule.

6. *Require stations to provide access time* on a special access program at no charge to all comers, regardless of wealth. This is virtually identical to the mandatory access proposals discussed above.

7. *Change nothing;* permit issue ads and require countercommercials when the Fairness Doctrine applies.

The schema on page 172 indicates how these various options would serve the following (sometimes inconsistent) goals of (a) enhancing expression of ideas, (b) enhancing the expression of contrasting views, (c) providing equal treatment for various spokespersons, (d) enhancing broadcasters' ability to make money, and (f) permitting the public debate to be structured by disinterested nonadvocates.

This schema, although much oversimplified, indicates some of the tradeoffs in adopting the differing policy approaches. If equal treatment of differing groups is desired, it is clear that the current policy is deficient. Yet the current policy has the virtue of offering some slight benefits in furthering the other goals while maximizing none of them. The point is not to dictate which option is best, only which goals are served or thwarted under each approach. Of course, the goals are value judgments. The purpose of this model is to illuminate the options.

The real battle over access probably will be fought over cable. Newer cable systems have a multitude of channels, and municipalities often require that cable franchises set some aside for public access. While an examination of cable regulation is beyond the scope of this study, it is important to note that expanded access opportunities on that medium may take some of the "heat" off radio and TV to provide access.

But given the role of broadcasting in the political debate, it is unlikely that demands for greater access will evaporate.

## IMPACT OF VARIOUS ACCESS RULES
## ON DIFFERENT POLICY GOALS

| | 1<br>Ban Issue<br>Ads | 2<br>Ads OK,<br>No Free<br>Reply | 3<br>Equal<br>Time | 4<br>Ads<br>Must<br>Air | 5<br>Ads &<br>Free<br>Replies | 6<br>Free<br>Access | 7<br>Current<br>Rule |
|---|---|---|---|---|---|---|---|
| A<br>Enhance<br>Expression | No | Some | Some | Some | Yes | Yes | Some |
| B<br>Encourage<br>Contrasting<br>Views | No | No | Some | Some | Yes | Yes | Some |
| C<br>Provide<br>Equal<br>Treatment | Yes | Yes | Yes | Yes | No | Yes | No |
| D<br>Permit<br>Station<br>Discretion | No | Yes | Some | No | Some | No | Some |
| E<br>Encourage<br>Profit<br>Motive | No | Yes | Yes | Yes | Some | No | Some |
| F<br>Promote<br>Nonadvocacy | Yes | Some | No | No | No | No | Some |

## References

1. Quoted in *Time* magazine, February 11, 1980, pp. 67–69.
2. *access,* May 18, 1981, p. 1.
3. *WCBS-TV,* 8 FCC 2d 381 (1967); *aff'd on reconsideration,* 9 FCC 2d 921 (1967) (referred to as the *Banzhaf* case); sustained, *Banzhaf* v. *FCC,* 405 F.2d 1082 (D.C. Cir. 1968), *certiorari denied,* 396 U.S. 842 (1969).
4. 9 FCC 921, 953 (1967).
5. Id.
6. Id.
7. *Public Media Center,* 59 FCC 2d 494 (1976), reconsideration denied, 64 FCC 2d 615 (1977), remanded on other grounds, 587 F.2d 1322 (D.C. Cir. 1978); on remand 72 FCC 2d 776 (1979).
8. *Columbia Broadcasting System, Inc.* v. *Democratic National Committee,* 412 U.S. 94 (1973).
9. *Business Executives' Move for Vietnam Peace,* 25 FCC 2d 242 (1971), reversed

on appeal, *Business Executives' Move for Vietnam Peace* v. *FCC,* 450 F.2d 642 (D.C. Cir. 1971) reversed and FCC decision upheld in *Columbia Broadcasting System, Inc.* v. *Democratic National Comittee,* 412 U.S. 94 (1973).

10. Louis L. Jaffe, "The Editorial Responsibility of the Broadcaster: Reflections on Fairness and Access," 85 *Harvard Law Review* 768, 775 (1972).
11. 19 FCC 2d 620 (1969).
12. Id. at 621.
13. *Retail Store Employees Local 880* v. *FCC,* 436 F.2d 248 (D.C. Cir. 1970).
14. Id. at 258–259.
15. *William H. Rodgers, Jr.,* 30 FCC 2d 640 (1971).
16. *John S. MacInnis, Consumers Arise Now,* 32 FCC 2d 837 (1971).
17. *Center for Auto Safety,* 32 FCC 2d 926 (1972).
18. *Friends of the Earth,* 24 FCC 2d 743 (1970), reversed 449 F.2d 1164 (D.C. Cir. 1971).
19. *David C. Green,* 24 FCC 2d 171 (1970), *Green* v. *FCC,* 447 F.2d 323 (D.C. Cir. 1971).
20. 447 F.2d at 324, 325.
21. 24 FCC 2d 171 (1970).
22. 32 FCC 2d 124 (1971).
23. Id.
24. *William H. Rodgers, Jr.,* 30 FCC 2d 640 (1971).
25. Id. at 642.
26. *John S. MacInnis, Consumers Arise Now,* 32 FCC 2d 837 (1971).
27. *Center for Auto Safety,* 32 FCC 2d 926 (1972).
28. Id.
29. *National Broadcast Co.,* 30 FCC 2d 643 (1971).
30. Id. at 644; *Wilderness Society,* 31 FCC 2d 729 (1971).
31. *Alan F. Neckritz,* 29 FCC 2d 807 (1971), reconsidered 37 FCC 2d 528 (1972), affirmed, 502 F.2d 411 (D.C. Cir. 1974).
32. 29 FCC 2d at 812.
33. 24 FCC 743 (1970).
34. 449 F.2d at 1165.
35. 24 FCC at 749.
36. *Friends of the Earth* v. *FCC,* 449 F.2d 164 (D.C. Cir. 1971).
37. Id. at 1169.
38. 44 FCC 2d 755 (1973).
39. Id. at 765.
40. Id. at 758.
41. Id. at 761.
42. Steven J. Simmons, *The Fairness Doctrine and the Media* (Berkeley, University of California Press, 1978), p. 106.
43. Id. at 109.
44. Id.
45. *Fairness Doctrine and Public Interest Standards, Fairness Report Regarding Handling of Public Issues,* 39 FED. REG. 26372 (1974) (*Fairness Report*).
46. Id. at 26381.
47. Id.

48. Id. at 26380.
49. Id.
50. *Public Media Center,* 59 FCC 2d 494 (1976), *remanded,* 587 F.2d 1322 (D.C. Cir. 1978), on *remand,* 72 FCC 2d 776 (1979).
51. 587 F.2d at 1331.
52. Id. at 1328-1329 (quoting from *Wilderness Society,* 31 FCC 2d 729, 734 (1971); see 30 *Cleveland State Law Review,* 485, 513 (1981).
53. Id.
54. Jerome A. Barron, "Access to the Press: A New First Amendment Right," 80 *Harvard Law Review* 1641 (1967).
55. Id.
56. Id. at 1646.
57. Id. at 1646-1647.
58. 412 U.S. 94 (1973).
59. Id. at 180-181 (dissenting opinion of Brennan, with whom Marshall concurred).
60. Id. at 114-121; see Roscoe L. Barrow, "The Equal Opportunities and Fairness Doctrines in Broadcasting: Should They Be Retained?" 1 *COMM/ENT Law Journal* 65, 77-78 (1979).
61. Id. at 102.
62. 1974 *Fairness Report,* 39 FED. REG. 26372.
63. *National Citizens Committee for Broadcasting* v. *FCC,* 567 F.2d 1095 (D.C. Cir. 1977), *cert. denied,* 98 S.Ct. 2820 (1978).
64. See David L. Sinak, "Application of the Fairness Doctrine to Ordinary Product Advertisements: National Citizens Committee for Broadcasting v. FCC," 20 *Boston College Law Review* 225 (1979); reprinted in Brenner and Rivers (Eds.), *Free but Regulated* (Ames, Iowa State University Press, 1982), p. 200.
65. Id. at 202.
66. FCC, *The Handling of Public Issues under the Fairness Doctrine and the Public Interest Standards of the Communications Act* (FCC 79-706, November 9, 1979), p. 2.
67. Id., reconsideration denied (FCC 82-185, April 21, 1982).
68. 1974 *Fairness Report,* 48 FCC 2d 1, 18.
69. Phil Jacklin, "A New Fairness Doctrine—Access to the Media," 8 *The Center Magazine* (May/June 1975), pp. 46-47.
70. NAB, Comments in BC Docket No. 78-60, September 5, 1978, p. 34.
71. Jacklin, op. cit., p. 50.
72. See Louis H. Mayo, "The Limited Forum," 22 *George Washington Law Review* 261, 387 (1954).
73. *FCC* v. *Midwest Video Corp.,* 47 U.S.L.W. 4335 (Supreme Court, April 2, 1979).
74. *CBS* v. DNC, 412 U.S. 94, 125 (1973).
75. For an examination of this point of view, see Randy M. Mastro, Deborah C. Costlow, and Heidi P. Sanchez, "Taking the Initiative: Corporate Control of the Referendum Process through Media Spending and What to Do about It," 32 *Federal Communications Law Journal* 315 (1980).

# NINE

# The Magic Elixir

NINETEEN EIGHTY-TWO was a typical election year in one respect. The nation couldn't get through the campaign without a major dispute over the political use of the nation's airwaves.

It started when the Republican party was rebuffed in its effort to purchase a half-hour of network time for a campaign program. Then the White House came up with an even better idea—from the Republican point of view. It asked the networks to carry an address by President Reagan—for free.

The address was billed as a speech on the economy, but the Democratic Party assailed Reagan for "partisan campaigning" and urged the three networks not to air the address.

ABC decided the speech was not newsworthy and declined to carry it live or in its entirety. Excerpts were, of course, carried on ABC's regular newscasts. CBS and NBC decided to air the Reagan address. The Democratic National Committee (DNC) demanded equal time from CBS and NBC to reply to the presidential speech.

The case that resulted is a textbook example of the interaction between the Fairness Doctrine, Equal Opportunities Rule, and the Reasonable Access Provision. It speaks volumes about the complexity of regulating political broadcasting, and of the inadequacy of the present system in assuring fairness and equal treatment to candidates.

The Democratic National Committee worked out a deal with NBC whereby the Democrats would have a chance to reply immediately after the president spoke at 7:30 p.m. on October 13. NBC had initially offered the DNC an equal amount of time on the following night, but the DNC opted for a shorter amount of time (approximately 10 minutes versus the president's 20 minutes) in order to appear right after Reagan spoke (and just before the start of a World Series game).

CBS declined to give the DNC time immediately after Reagan, or a similar time slot the following night. Instead, CBS broadcast a news special later the same evening after the Reagan address. The 11:30 p.m. news program featured interviews with various Democrats and a brief excerpt from the Democratic reply, delivered by Senator Donald Riegle.

Riegle was the choice of the Democratic party to make the reply that aired on NBC. CBS chose instead to produce its own news program, partly out of concern that Riegle's appearance could trigger equal time requests from the Republicans. After all, Riegle was running for reelection in Michigan, and his use of airtime could prompt his opponent to ask the network for similar exposure. Thus there was fear that affording the Democrats time to reply to Reagan might result in additional requests for reply time from Republicans. No wonder CBS felt it wiser to produce its own news show, which would be immune from this type of equal opportunity treatment.

The DNC did not feel that CBS had treated the Democratic reply fairly. It filed a complaint with the FCC alleging that CBS had relegated the reply to the "deepest recesses of its schedule" and demanding prime time for a spokesperson of the Democrats' choice.[1]

The first hurdle the DNC faced involved the Equal Opportunities Rule, which applies only to candidates during a campaign. Reagan was not running for reelection in 1982, so he was not a candidate. Therefore, his appearance would not automatically require the network to afford equal time to the Democrats. Moreover, the equal time provisions do not apply to bona fide newscasts, news interview programs, news documentaries (except those that are about the campaign or a candidate), and on the spot coverage of bona fide news events. The presidential speech qualified as a bona fide news event.

Of course, the Fairness Doctrine does apply to news coverage, and the DNC based its complaint on the fairness regulations. Unlike the Equal Opportunities Rule, the Fairness Doctrine does not require *equal* treatment of opposing sides. As we have seen, broadcasters need only provide contrasting views in their *overall* programming. The equal time regulations are much less flexible. Under the Fairness Doctrine, the broadcasters retain discretion as to when to air a viewpoint and whom to choose to state the view.

CBS had given broad coverage to the state of the economy, had regularly programmed news items about Reagan's policy and the opposition to it, and had featured Democrats criticizing the Reagan speech.

There was no claim that CBS had failed to provide contrasting views in its overall coverage.

How then could the Democrats hope to prevail in a Fairness Doctrine complaint?

The law on political broadcasting is neither simple nor clear. The DNC, led by its lawyer, former FCC Chairman Charles Ferris, pressed its claim under a 1970 ruling called the Zapple Doctrine.[2] The *Zapple* case attached some of the equal time provisions to the Fairness Doctrine in instances when a spokesperson for a candidate appears on television or radio.

Unlike the Equal Opportunities Rule, which only involves candidates, and the Fairness Doctrine, which affects issues, the Zapple Doctrine requires "quasi equal opportunities" for spokespersons for candidates.

Consider the hybrid nature of this beast. Two fundamentally different rules intersect. One rule is inflexible and mandates equal treatment. The other rule vests broad discretion with broadcasters and requires only overall balance. One is triggered by an appearance by a particular class of person (a legally qualified candidate for public office) while the other is concerned with a more amorphous concept (significant issues of public importance).

What is clear is that disputes involving spokespersons for candidates fell through the cracks, so to speak, avoiding the operation of either the equal time or fairness provisions. Until *Zapple*.

The Zapple Doctrine applies to the sale or furnishing of time to the supporters of candidates. If supporters of Candidate A are sold or given airtime, Candidate B's supporters must be sold or given comparable amounts of time in a similar time slot.[3]

The DNC complained that the president's "clearly partisan address" had been aired "so close to a national election that it was by its nature, time and content a program supporting the candidacies of Republican candidates for public office, [and that CBS] failed to provide free to a spokesperson from the Democratic party an amount of time equal in length and placement."[4]

The DNC claimed that CBS violated the Zapple Doctrine in several ways: (1) by not providing a reply at a comparable time that would reach an equivalent audience, (2) by not letting the Democratic party select the spokesperson or coordinate the program's format, and (3) by not providing an equivalent amount of time for the reply.

CBS responded by pointing out that the Zapple Doctrine had never been extended to apply to presidential appearances, "even if they are alleged to be motivated by partisan purposes."[5]

Under the Equal Opportunities Rule, coverage of a newsworthy presidential address would not trigger a requirement for equal time for opponents because news coverage is exempt from the rule. News coverage is not exempt under the Fairness Doctrine, of which the Zapple Doctrine is a subpart.

The DNC argued that *Zapple* should apply to a presidential speech like Reagan's, which it said "cannot be likened to a bona fide, nonpartisan news event." Previous cases had simply declined to apply the Zapple Doctrine to *all* presidential addresses, the DNC said.

The FCC turned the Democrats down. It held that *Zapple* was not designed to apply to news coverage of events the broadcaster reasonably felt were newsworthy. Although *Zapple* is part of the Fairness Doctrine, the idea of "quasi equal opportunities" requires that it not be applied to the types of news programming exempted from the Equal Opportunities Rule.[6]

The case raises several points, not the least of which is that the rules are complicated. During the 1982 campaign, the FCC had staffers manning phones 24 hours a day, fielding about 3,000 calls a month. The inquiries from candidates, campaign managers, and stations were about fairness, equal time, *Zapple* and *Cullman* obligations. The rules are complex, and, naturally, politicians try to use them to gain some advantage over opponents.

What is significant is that in determining the DNC's case against CBS, the FCC had to second-guess the news judgment of the network. Rather than looking at what the DNC said was important—Reagan's political use of the media—the FCC tried to peer into the mind of the broadcaster:

> It is not the partisan political purpose of the speaker [Reagan] that is controlling; rather it is the intent of the broadcaster in making a judgment whether to carry specific news programming. In short, it is recognized that political discussion is inherently partisan. To place the broadcaster and ultimately the Commission in the role of assessing the content of speech contained in news programming to determine whether it was partisan would be an inappropriate and impracticable intrusion. . . . If the broadcaster intends to further a candidacy rather than affording coverage solely because of its newsworthiness, then and only then did Congress indicate an intention to remove the bona fides of particular news programming.[7]

To its credit, the FCC refused to assess "the content of speech contained in news programming," but it continued the practice—equally intrusive—of trying to judge the "intent of the broadcaster" in deciding whether to carry a specific news item.

The record of regulation is replete with examples of regulators restricting or overruling the judgments of broadcasters through interpretation of these complex regulations.

No one can blame politicians for trying to maximize their exposure on the air; it's another form of political contest. But to mask the use—and occasional abuse—of the regulatory framework with concepts of fairness, equality, and "reasonable" access is to disguise what the rules really are: a tool of the powerful.

Politicians need television and radio exposure and broadcasters need licenses. Politicians want to get on the news, and they want favorable coverage. They want the right to buy commercial time during campaigns. During noncampaign periods they would like to get free time to "report to constituents." It has been estimated that about 70 percent of the U.S. senators and 60 percent of the U.S. representatives regularly are given free time to report on radio and television.[8] That's in addition to any news coverage the station might voluntarily provide.

Broadcasters control a valuable commodity for politicians: media exposure.[9]

The relationship between broadcasters and politicians has been correctly described by Robert MacNeil as a "tense mutual interdependence":

> Imagine the situation of a street peddler who sells old-fashioned patent medicines. He needs a license to stay in business, and the city official who issued them is dubious about most of the peddler's wares. Yet it just happens that one product, a magic elixir, is the only thing that will cure the official's rheumatism and keep him in health. So the two coexist in a tense mutual interdependence, the peddler getting his license, the official his magic elixir.[10]

The politicians' addiction to this "magic elixir" is not altogether healthy for society. Our political system has changed as officials have become hooked on the media. Short campaign spots predominate; thoughtful political discourse seems in short supply. News coverage centers on the exciting, the visual, the confrontational; issues seem overlooked in the wild rush to report who is up and who is down in the latest opinion poll.

The political season poses special problems for broadcasters who must comply with the Fairness Doctrine and assorted regulations.

## Independent Political Expressions

Nowhere are the problems of regulation more apparent than when a noncandidate seeks to express a political view on a broadcast station. Candidates, as noted, have special access rights. But what of the advocate who desires to use the media to espouse a political cause, particularly a new or unique movement?

The following fictional example may help describe the barriers. Leif N. Branch organizes a group dedicated to vegetable rights. It is called Citizens Advocating Rights for Plants (CARP). CARP has few members at first, but Branch is a dynamic personality and some converts are won over. Soon he decides the group needs publicity to promote its view that "plants don't eat you, you shouldn't eat them." So he visits the local newspaper city room, armed with a press release he's written denouncing plant eaters and touting the health benefits of eating only meat. The editor laughs in his face. On his way out, Branch stops at the advertising department to inquire about rates for full-page ads. "I want to inform people about the immorality of slaughtering helpless plants," he says. The paper's advertising salesman says: "If it's not libelous, obscene, or subversive, we'll print it—but bring cash, please."

Branch next stops at WORM-TV, the local station. The WORM news director listens to his pitch about the kickoff of "Spare an Asparagus Week," but—choking back laughter—tells Branch to get lost.

Upset, and recalling that there's something called a Fairness Doctrine, Branch seeks an attorney. What are the possibilities?

*Situation A.* Branch files a Fairness Doctrine complaint against WORM-TV for failing to cover what CARP deems an important controversial issue, vegetable rights.

*Situation B.* Unable to get WORM News to cover CARP voluntarily, Branch raises several thousand dollars and asks to buy commercial time. The station turns him down. CARP files a fairness complaint.

*Situation C.* Outraged that his ad was rejected, Branch notes the frequency with which the station runs commercials for products produced by the Jolly Green Giant, Del Monte, and others who sell vegetables. He demands time under the Fairness Doctrine to respond to the issues raised in the food commercials. By now he's spent the money he had raised earlier to pay for ads, so he demands free time.

*Situation D.* At last Branch has attracted the attention of station management, which alerts the news department. They send their crack feature reporter out to interview Branch. But to Branch's chagrin, the short "kicker" story that later appears at the close of a newscast refers to him as a "weirdo, a kook, someone who's probably out to make a fast buck." In a fit of anger, Branch files a complaint under the Personal Attack Rule.

*Situation E.* The network affiliated with WORM runs a morning news report about "the growing controversy over animal rights," which features interviews with people who advocate vegetarianism. Branch files a fairness complaint against both the network and WORM, alleging that a controversial issue has been raised and that they must air a contrasting viewpoint, namely CARP's pro-vegetable, anti-animal views.

*Situation F.* The station airs an editorial several weeks later endorsing a nutrition study recommending balanced diets for school children. The hard-hitting editorial calls for everyone to eat meat, milk, eggs, cereal, and vegetables. The editorial ends with an announcement that "replies from responsible spokespersons are welcome." Branch, as president of CARP, demands airtime to denounce the slaughter of vegetables.

*Situation G.* Perturbed at the slowness with which his complaints are being processed at the FCC, Branch goes to the station manager and offers a compromise. "If you let me appear on the "Coffee Break" interview program one weekday morning, I'll call it all off." What do you think the station manager would do?

The issue of vegetable rights is trivial, but if the scenario sketched above had actually happened, the station would be facing legal bills approaching $5,000, by one practitioner's estimate. How would the station fare if it chose to fight?

WORM would win the complaint in Situation A. Vegetable rights is not a controversial issue of public importance, much less the burning issue needed to fit this part of the rule. But suppose Branch was advocating an end to strip mining? The result could be different.

WORM wins in its rejection of Branch's request to purchase commercial time (Situation B); that's within station discretion.

WORM would almost certainly win in Situation C, where Branch demanded time to respond to a standard product advertisement. But what if CARP had demanded to respond to cigarette commercials? That case would come out differently.

In Situation D, where Branch alleged a personal attack was broadcast on a news program, the station would win because newscasts are exempt from the Personal Attack Rule. But what if the comment was made on a news documentary or a talk show? The result likely would be different.

After the network ran a story about "the growing controversy over animal rights" (Situation E), it—and the station—would answer the complaint by asserting that animal rights was not a controversial issue of public importance. The assertion is reasonable, and the broadcasters would probably win. But what if the issue was described as whether too much fat in the diet causes cancer?

The station would also probably win the case involving its editorial on nutrition (Situation F). Despite its invitation for responsible spokespersons to reply, the station need only furnish time to those individuals it deems responsible. Stations need not provide an opportunity for presentation of every view on an issue.[11] Moreover, it need present contrasting views only on controversial issues of public importance. It's that point, the definition of issue, that dooms Branch's complaints. He might prevail if he had a more traditional gripe, more attuned to the mainstream. On the other hand, what is more important than what we eat? We *are* what we eat. Why shouldn't the issue be treated fairly?

Encouraged by the capitulation of the station manager (who was glad to be rid of the legal headaches) in Situation G, Branch appears for four minutes on the "Coffee Break" show. It's a heady experience and Branch decides to enter politics. He's tasted the magic elixir.

*Situation H.* Branch sends out a press release announcing the kickoff of his congressional campaign. When no reporters show up, he files a new complaint against WORM-TV, this time alleging that since the station covered the campaign kickoff of his opponent, the incumbent, Branch is entitled to equal time.

*Situation I.* Branch has become a legally qualified independent candidate for Congress, supporting "Plants' Right to Life." WORM stages a debate between all the candidates running in the Democratic party primary, which is six weeks away. Branch, who was excluded, demands equal time.

*Situation J.* With the primary finally over, Branch faces two main opponents, the Democratic and Republican nominees, plus assorted other candidates from the Animal Rights and Mineral Rights parties. The station schedules interviews with the Democrat and the Republican on "Meet the Media," its regular Sunday news interview show. Branch demands to be included.

*Situation K.* Branch has now converted more disciples to vegetable rights. Contributions have flowed in and Branch goes to WORM demanding to purchase time for campaign commercials. Will he be allowed to purchase it this time?

*Situation L.* WORM runs an editorial that does not endorse any of the candidates, but which urges voters to go to the polls. It also admonishes the public, "Don't throw away your vote on frivolous fringe candidates who are only running to publicize their zany causes." Branch demands time to reply.

*Situation M.* The station runs a prime time news special on the campaign, and—to avoid equal time problems—does not present the candidates themselves, but runs interviews only with supporters of the various candidates. None of Branch's supporters are included, and he complains.

*Situation N.* A massive flood hits the community and the president flies in to inspect the damage. WORM-TV cancels regular programming to cover the presidential visit. The live coverage of the tour also features the incumbent congressman. Branch demands equal time.

The Equal Opportunities Rule does not apply to newscasts, regularly scheduled news interview shows, or on-the-spot coverage of a bona fide news event. So Branch cannot win equal time because of news coverage of opponents (Situation H), exclusion from "Meet the Media" (Situation J), or flood coverage (Situation N). But a news special about the campaign (Situation M) is not exempt from the "quasi equal opportunities" provision of the Zapple Doctrine; however, *Zapple* does not protect fringe candidates and Branch would lose again.

Debates controlled by the station (Situation I) were not exempt from the equal time provision, but in this case the WORM debate included all contenders in a primary contest. Since Branch is not a candidate in the Democratic primary, he cannot assert a successful equal time claim.

However, Branch has a much stronger claim in Situation K, where he's offering to buy time for a campaign commercial. Under the Reasonable Access Provision, the station must afford access to Branch.

Moreover, in Situation L, where the station editorializes against wasting votes on fringe candidates, it's a close call whether the label applies to Branch. If it does (and a strong case could be made that it does), then he's entitled to have a spokesperson respond under the Political Editorializing Rule of the Fairness Doctrine. It affords access to supporters of candidates who are opposed, as well as to those whose opponents are endorsed.

If all this seems complicated, that's precisely the point. The rules saddle both candidates and broadcasters with a myriad of seemingly contradictory provisions. The above hypothetical case, it should be noted, must not be used as a predictive guide in other real cases. The factual context often determines the outcome of complaints.

If the vegetable rights scenario sounds farfetched, consider the real case of a candidate for public office who, before becoming a candidate, appeared with 120 other people in a public service announcement for a charity group. All the people in the spot sang the song "Let the Sunshine In." The charity wanted to continue using the zippy spot but broadcasters were concerned that the very brief appearance of a legally qualified candidate would oblige them to provide free equal time to his opponents. The candidate, incidentally, appeared in only two shots, for about four seconds in a wideshot of 100 people, and for almost three seconds in a medium shot of about six people in which only the lower half of his face was seen. FCC precedent required stations to provide equal time in similar situations involving public service, noncampaign appearances. But this time the FCC relented, ruling that the wideshot provided such a fleeting glimpse and that the medium shot caught such a partial view that the candidate was not readily identifiable.[12]

Daniel L. Brenner, who has served in various staff capacities at the FCC, recalls the thousands of calls to the agency seeking guidance on equal time and fairness rules:

> It is surely a messy business. One hypothetical example should suffice. Say a committee opposed to the election of one candidate, John Jones, but not favoring any other, buys a media spot. Does this entitle Jones to a reply opportunity? What if Jones has a sole opponent, Tom Smith? Would it matter if Smith's picture is used in an advertisement, even though his name isn't mentioned? (It could.) What if Jones's picture is used; would Smith be entitled to a reply opportunity, even though Jones appears in a Smith ad urging Jones's own defeat? [13]

Brenner notes that the questions get even thornier under the Reasonable Access Provision. The effect of these rules is that access rights of candidates for federal office are far superior to those of the average citizen, no matter how politically active.

This was manifested in two examples during the 1982 campaign, one involving a conservative group seeking to defeat incumbents it believed were too liberal, the other involving a liberal group campaigning against incumbents it considered hostile to arms control.

## Negative Campaigns

During the 1980 election campaign and for months thereafter, one needed only to mention one name to provoke fear and anger from liberal Democrats: "Nick Pack." That's not the name of any candidate or political wizard. It's the pronunciation of NCPAC, the National Conservative Political Action Committee. NCPAC raised funds, effectively targeted liberal incumbents, and mounted media campaigns to defeat them.

In 1980, Senators Church of Idaho, McGovern of South Dakota, Bayh of Indiana, and Culver of Iowa all fell, partly because NCPAC's ads successfully stoked the public reaction against liberal spending programs.

NCPAC operated in an interesting way, using provisions of the Federal Elections Campaign Act that free independent political efforts from the limitations imposed on contributions to candidates. For the most part, NCPAC did not contribute to conservative Republican candidates, but maintained an independence from their campaign organizations. That freed NCPAC to pour money into negative commercials attacking the liberal Democrats.

It was a winning strategy in '80, but NCPAC had less success in 1982 when the public had a Republican president to blame for economic woes.

The lesson of 1980 wasn't lost on other politicians, who organized their own political action groups to operate independently, and to take aim at those they opposed. For instance, an anticonservative group named PROPAC was formed by liberals.

The use of negative campaigns—attacking rather than supporting someone—raises fundamental political questions beyond the scope of this study. Negative politics help distort the political process with slogans, and in some cases, smears. But there's little question that groups like NCPAC have a First Amendment right to speak out against officials they oppose and to petition for a redress of grievances. In fact, the Supreme Court gives First Amendment rights of independent groups greater protection from congressional regulation than it gives individuals who donate money to candidates.[14] The Court upheld limits on contributions to candidates to protect against influence peddling, but struck down limits on independent political activity.[15] After all, what could be more in the tradition of Tom Paine than to oppose the current power structure?

Broadcast regulation, however, accords more power to the establishment than to the Tom Paines of today. The right of candidates to the magic elixir of the airwaves is superior to that of independent groups affiliated with no candidate. Under the Reasonable Access Provision of Section 312(a) (7) of the Communications Act, commercial stations must sell airtime to candidates for federal office. Incumbents of both parties who usually can attract support and contributions from special interest groups and their political action committees can buy access to the airwaves.

Independent groups such as NCPAC and PROPAC can raise money and proffer it to stations for commercial time, but the broadcasters retain discretion to reject the ads. While Section 315 of the Communications Act forbids a station from censoring the message a candidate wishes to deliver in his or her paid commercial, stations may insist on changes in the language of independent commercials as a condition for their acceptance. This makes sense because the same section of the act that prohibits censorship of candidates also protects stations from libel suits based on what candidates say. The station has no such immunity from libel suits directed against what independent groups may say on the air. Hence, stations exercise reasonable care when they screen commercials of groups such as NCPAC before deciding whether to accept the ads for airing.

Unfortunately for NCPAC, several stations refused to run the group's negative ads during the 1982 political season. NCPAC even sued several broadcasters for conspiring with candidates to keep NCPAC ads off the air.[16]

NCPAC demonstrated one ingenious way it could counter blackballing by broadcasters in Nevada in the '82 race. NCPAC had targeted

Senator Howard Cannon for defeat, but it could get only one station in the state to air its anti-Cannon spots. So NCPAC worked with a Republican candidate for governor to win access to the airwaves. Most, if not all, stations had been airing various commercials on behalf of those running for governor, and thus, under the Equal Opportunities Rule, could neither reject nor censor ads by a legally qualified candidate. NCPAC found a candidate willing to incorporate the anti-Cannon spot within his own spot. It started something like this: "Hi, I'm Mike Moody. I'm running for governor and one thing that really burns me up is censorship. . . ." He turns to a TV set and the NCPAC ad, directed at the senatorial contest, appears on the screen. NCPAC paid for the commercial, of course. After the ad ran several times, a number of Nevada TV stations broke down and began accepting the NCPAC spot itself.

NCPAC is vigorous in its efforts to get its message on the air. But it avoids going to the FCC because a staff member said, "It takes so long, that the political cost is extraordinarily high." NCPAC's media director, Mike Murphy, described his technique for winning airtime:

> We try to go to the station and we coerce them by saying we'll sue you, we'll go to the FCC, or we'll send a letter to every right-wing nut within a thousand miles of the station and ask them to call the FCC and have your license revoked.[17]

Not only conservative groups such as NCPAC face problems getting their messages on the air. During the 1982 campaign, a group supporting the proposal to freeze the construction and deployment of nuclear weapons produced commercials that included the following words:

> People everywhere are worried about the continuing weapons buildup. . . . A computer error could trigger a nuclear war. How can we reduce this threat? With a nuclear freeze. . . . Most Americans now support a nuclear freeze. But not Peoria's Congressman Robert Michel. He voted against the nuclear freeze. . . .

This commercial and others like it targeting other incumbent members of Congress were devised by a group called Citizens for Common Sense in National Defense. CCSND, which was chaired by Philip M. Stern, opposed three senators and seven representatives, including Robert Michel, the House Republican leader. Viewers were asked to vote against those who had opposed the nuclear freeze plan.

But Stern later complained that of the ten contests, his group could only get messages on broadcast stations in three. Broadcasters declined to carry the CCSND commercials in seven of the races. Even though Stern's group had prepared a seven-page memo documenting the factual accuracy of the charges in the spots, stations cited the following reasons for not running the ads:

—They fell short of acceptable standards;
—They were too controversial;
—'I don't think this is the style that the people of Wyoming like. In my judgment it is not in the interest of the populace of Wyoming. They would not understand;'
—An incumbent's voting record did not constitute a controversial issue of public importance; and
—It is not in the best interest of the station to run them.[18]

Stern alleged that in Utah, Senator Orrin Hatch (one of those targeted by CCSND) had gotten together with his Democratic challenger, Ted Wilson, and decided there were certain issues neither candidate wanted to debate, including the nuclear freeze. A station executive allegedly said the station did not want to go against the wishes of the two candidates. Stern complained to the FCC about the refusal of KTVX to air the anti-Hatch ad, but the commission turned down the complaint.[19]

In states where CCSND was frozen out by broadcasters, Stern purchased full-page newspaper ads headlined "The TV Ad They Don't Want You To See." But he said that one paper, the *Albuquerque Journal,* refused to carry the ad because it contained libelous innuendos against the TV station.

As for the television stations that refused to run his group's advertisements, Stern said it was

incongruous that in the name of protecting the First Amendment rights of broadcasters, they are empowered to *curb* speech and deny viewers and listeners their right to see and hear.[20]

Several weeks after Stern vented his frustration in a guest column in the *Washington Post's* op-ed section, the *Post* printed a reply column authored by Henry Geller. The former FCC general counsel noted that while stations do not have complete discretion to reject ads promoting views with which they disagree, they have "complete practical control" over the ads they are offered. While there was "no hope for the Sterns of this world seeking fast media reform," Geller offered a hint: Run for president.[21]

Geller noted that candidates for federal office (including for Congress, of course) are protected by laws requiring broadcasters to afford reasonable access and accept campaign ads at the lowest rate charged by each station. The broadcaster cannot censor the candidate and must provide an equal opportunity if the opposition uses the station facilities.

Nineteen eighty-two was not a presidential election year, so groups such as CCSND would have had to field candidates in congressional races to assure themselves of unedited paid access to the airwaves. In a presidential contest, a candidate would need enough signatures to get on the ballot in the states in which he sought to air his views.

Geller recognized that it could cause a mess if every group seeking to air a political viewpoint ran a candidate for office simply to get access to state its view. But he noted that Congress is unlikely to change the system anytime soon.

> [Stern's] cry is based on the underlying premise of the First Amendment—promotion of robust, wide-open debate. Congress has *no* interest in that. It is made up exclusively of incumbents, all passionately interested in political survival. They want no part of NCPAC or Stern PAC, and regard such independent committees, at best, as nuisances and, all too often, as interfering with the orderly process of *their* re-election.[22]

## *The Bias of Fairness*

The system of regulation has evolved to protect the political power of incumbents by giving them access to money and the airwaves. It permits broadcasters some discretion when dealing with independent activists, which licensees often exercise to deter strong challenges. For years politicians have used the rules to try to keep the mainstream from being polluted by ideological challenge, either radical or reactionary.

During the early 1960s, for instance, the Democratic party mounted a campaign to oppose right-wing commentary on hundreds of radio stations across the land. Fred Friendly relates how the plan was hatched in the Kennedy White House when appointment secretary Kenneth O'Donnell met with Wayne Phillips, a former reporter who would later join the staff of the DNC.[23] Phillips was instructed to meet with Nicholas Zapple, the counsel to the Senate Communications Subcommittee, to see how the fairness rules could be used to protect Kennedy and Johnson from attacks from the right. Zapple said the Democrats wanted to use the Fairness Doctrine to "counter the radical right."[24] The Democratic party began monitoring radio broadcasts, and developed a kit explaining "How to Demand Time under the Fairness Doctrine."[25] As Friendly states:

> The idea was simply to harass radio stations by getting officials and organizations that had been attacked by extremist radio commentators to request reply time, citing the Fairness Doctrine. . . . "All told," [Phillips] recalls, "this volunteer effort resulted in rebuttals on over five hundred radio programs."[26]

In the campaign year of 1964, the Democrats decided not simply to respond to attacks but to go on the offensive. Phillips expanded his staff, adding a former staff member of the FCC, Martin Firestone, an attorney familiar with the rule. He inundated stations with complaints in an effort to persuade broadcasters that it was too expensive to carry the ultraconservative commentators. Firestone reported that

> the constant flow of letters from the Committee to the stations may have inhibited the stations in their broadcast of more radical and politically partisan programs.[27]

Some 1,035 letters to the stations produced a total of 1,678 hours of free time for the Democrats. Phillips concluded that "Even more important than the free radio time was the effectiveness of this operation in inhibiting the political activity of these right-wing broadcasts." [28]

In a 1982 interview for this book, Firestone conceded that there may have been an "anticonstitutional" element to using the Fairness Doctrine to suppress viewpoints. But he observed that if free response time was eliminated, then the political debate could be dominated by the faction with the most money. He notes that traditionally Republicans have had greater access to funds. Equal time regulations wouldn't protect the Democrats, because an equal right to purchase time is only meaningful when one has comparable funds to expend.

The current complexity of the rules allows free time only in some cases. A 1982 report by a group known as the Democracy Project urged that broadcasters be required to provide free time to candidates who are attacked by independent political groups, such as NCPAC. The study, "Independent Expenditures in Congressional Campaigns: The Electronic Solution," recommends that fairness regulations be expanded to allow criticized candidates to reply. Currently, *during campaigns,* candidates themselves have no such recourse under the Fairness Doctrine; they must rely on equal time provisions. Their supporters, of course, can demand— and sometimes get—free time if the independent group's ad raises a controversial issue of public importance.

The Democracy Project's report also recommended that in the last weeks before an election, the major party candidates for the House and Senate be provided free time on broadcast stations.[29] The provision of free time would alleviate the pressure on candidates to raise funds from political action committees, according to Mark Green, the former Ralph Nader aide who heads Democracy Project. "Candidate access to the electronic media is a constitutionally permissible, politically appealing and inexpensive solution" to the growing influence of PACs, Green said.

The proposal would put the cost of the "free" time on the taxpayers and television stations. The broadcast industry is likely to lobby hard to defeat such a measure, teaming up with the many members of Congress who resist any form of public funding for congressional races.

If enacted, the Democracy Project plan would have several results. First, it would enhance the power of incumbents. Second, it would enhance the power of the two major political parties. Third, it would weaken the influence of independent political groups. Fourth, it would provide an added incentive to broadcast stations to accept no advertisements critical of incumbents.

Perhaps it would be wise public policy to require broadcast stations—as a price for their exclusive licenses—to give time to candidates for discussion of campaign issues. But would it only be more spot commercial time for the quickie announcements that hardly contribute to the public debate of issues? Would anyone watch those boring half-hour political harangues that used to characterize political broadcasts? Would candidates not opt to produce slick "informercials"—those political documentaries that skirt issues and promote images?

Or how about mandating that stations air debates between all the contenders? Should they include fringe candidates with no real chance of winning? Would major contenders appear if the fringe contestants were present? If a candidate declined to appear on a station-sponsored debate, later he or she might demand free, equal time under previous applications of the rule.

As important as improving the quality and quantity of political debate in this country may be, much more thought needs to be given to how to accomplish that goal. It might not burden a station as much in a small market with only one congressional district. It would have to cover only one congressional and one senatorial race at most. But what of a station in New York City, facing the prospect of giving time to dozens of congressional candidates from New York, New Jersey, and Connecticut?

The bottom line on evaluating proposals for change is that Congress is reasonably comfortable with the current mix of rules. It benefits from them, and as long as that remains the case there will be resistance to change.

As long as broadcasting is perceived as dispensing the magic elixir for politicians, it is unlikely Congress will permit the elixir to become a generic drug, available without prescription.

### Regulatory Schizophrenia

Consider the effect of the following two rules, for it merits closer examination.

The Zapple Doctrine requires that when a station gives or sells time to a supporter of a candidate during a campaign, it must afford a "quasi equal opportunity" to supporters of the candidate's opponents.[30] This means if free time is given to one candidate's supporters, it must be given to the other candidates' supporters. If paid time is sold to one supporter, it must be available for sale to the others' supporters.

The Cullman Principle requires a licensee that has chosen to broadcast a sponsored program or issue advertisement that raises a controversial issue of public importance to air opposing views, even if it cannot find sponsorship for the contrasting viewpoints.[31] Thus if one side of an issue is presented in a paid ad, the station may have to give away time for the reply.

Both *Cullman* and *Zapple* are Fairness Doctrine cases, but they reflect very different perspectives. *Cullman* requires free response time for paid issue ads. *Zapple* requires equal treatment; a paid ad only need be rebutted if the other side can afford to pay for its message.

The Zapple Doctrine was devised to avoid unequal treatment of candidates; it does not seem fair to require one candidate to buy time then permit his opponent to plead poverty and receive free time under *Cullman*. But *Zapple* applies only during campaign seasons. The rest of the time *Cullman* applies. Usually.

The Zapple Doctrine has been extended in limited circumstances outside of the campaign season. In a 1970 FCC decision the Commission confronted a request for free response time that shows how complicated the interaction of these two conflicting doctrines can become. In the 1970 case, the RNC demanded time to respond to a half-hour program that CBS aired featuring a DNC response to an address by President Nixon. To summarize, Nixon spoke on TV free, the Democrats were given free response time, then the Republicans sought free response time to answer the Democrats. All this happened in a noncampaign period. The FCC ruled in favor of the RNC request, extending the Zapple Doctrine because "electioneering is a continual process."[32]

Later, the FCC tried to limit this extension of *Zapple* to noncampaign periods by saying that reply time need only be provided for "appearances by party spokesmen in response to presidential appearances when the licensee does not specify the issues to be treated as those which were discussed by the president."[33] In sum, if the broadcaster didn't make certain that the response stuck to the topic raised by the president, *Zapple* applied and the president's party would get a chance to respond to the response.

In 1981 the Democratic party complained about the refusal of CBS and NBC to give it free time to respond to the paid messages of the Republican National Committee and its affiliated senatorial and congressional committees. The RNC purchased time in 1981 to promote the

Reagan Administration's domestic policy. Had the RNC purchased the time during the campaign, *Zapple* would have applied and the DNC would have had to buy time to reply. Because 1981 was not a campaign year, the DNC demanded free time to respond to paid time under *Cullman*.

Unlike some of the earlier cases, the 1981 complaint was not a *Zapple* request for free time to respond to free time. In the 1981 case, if *Zapple* were applied the DNC would be entitled only to equal treatment and would lose its request for free time. The FCC ducked that issue. It ruled against the DNC's request for free time by noting that the party had not shown that the networks had failed to air contrasting viewpoints on the subjects discussed in the RNC ads. Because the networks had not violated the Fairness Doctrine, the Cullman Principle did not apply.[34]

If this seems confusing, it is because the rules are schizophrenic. Consider the plight of independent political committees. If they pay for time to attack an incumbent for his or her stand on the issues prior to the start of a campaign, the broadcaster may have to give away time to the incumbent under *Cullman*. But if the independent committee's attack comes during the campaign, *Zapple* applies and no free time need be given.

In 1981, NCPAC filed a complaint with the FCC against stations that refused to run NCPAC ads. NCPAC said it should have a "reasonable right of access." The FCC turned it down and warned that acceptance of NCPAC ads outside campaign periods by stations could trigger *Cullman* obligations.[35] The FCC reached this decision even though earlier cases had refused to extend *Cullman* into the "political arena." [36] Moreover, independent groups are treated differently than established political parties; when a party buys advertising time outside campaign periods, *Cullman* does *not* apply.[37]

And consider the inconsistent treatment of issue-oriented advertisements that do not express a preference for any candidate. They are subject to *Cullman,* even if they relate to ballot referendum issues. Thus if a group buys an ad to support a ballot proposition, the station running the ad may later have to give away time to an opposing group that asserts that it cannot pay for the airtime.

Is it fair to treat candidates, supporters of candidates, political parties, independent groups, and issue advocates in such an inconsistent and confusing way? If the above description leaves one muddled, this is because regulatory policy is muddled. The distinctions between candidate and issue, between campaign and noncampaign period, between established party and independent PAC are illogical. Candidates run on issues, even if not always comfortably. Issues are in the "political arena," even if not always in a partisan way. Ballot propositions stir political fervor just as candidate races do. Why treat them differently? If "electioneering is a continual process," why distinguish between campaign and noncampaign periods at all? Why grant access rights to candidates, but deny them to independent groups opposing the candidates?

There's no good answer to these questions. The FCC has played a sorcerer's role, waving the magician's wand, doling out doses of the magic elixir. The mesmerizing effect of words such as *fairness* and *equal time* is only dispelled if one focuses on who gets what, when, and how. The rules have been rigged to favor the powerful.

## References

1. *Democratic National Committee* (FCC 82–477, October 28, 1982).
2. *Nicholas Zapple,* 23 FCC 2d 707 (1970).
3. *The Law of Political Broadcasting and Cablecasting,* 69 FCC 2d 2209, 2302 (1978).
4. FCC 82–477 at pp. 1–2.
5. Id. at 2; CBS cited *Republican National Committee,* 25 FCC 2d 739 (1970), reversed on other grounds sub nom. *Columbia Broadcasting System, Inc.* v. *FCC,* 454 F.2d 1018 (D.C. Cir. 1971); *Democratic National Committee,* 31 FCC 2d 708 (1971), affirmed sub nom. *Democratic National Committee* v. *FCC,* 460 F.2d 891 (D.C. Cir. 1972), *cert. denied,* 409 U.S. 843 (1972).
6. FCC 82–477 at pp. 5–6, 9.
7. Id. at 7–8 (footnotes deleted).
8. Robert MacNeil, *The People Machine; The Influence of Television on American Politics* (New York, Harper & Row, 1968), p. 246.
9. Erwin G. Krasnow, Lawrence D. Longley, and Herbert A. Terry, *The Politics of Broadcast Regulation* (New York, St. Martin's Press, 1982), p. 90.
10. MacNeil, op. cit., p. 243.
11. *Horace P. Rowley III,* 39 FCC 2d 437, 441–442 (1973).
12. Public Notice: Political Broadcasts, Pike & Fischer, 19 *Radio Regulation 2d,* 1923 (1970); see Michael J. Petrick, " 'Equal Opportunities' and 'Fairness' in Broadcast Coverage of Politics," 427 *Annals of the American Academy of Political and Social Science* 73, 80 (September 1976).
13. David L. Brenner and William L. Rivers (Eds.), *Free but Regulated* (Ames, Iowa State University Press, 1982), p. 211.
14. *Buckley* v. *Valeo,* 424 U.S. 1 (1976).
15. Id. at 35, 45–48.
16. *NCPAC* v. *FCC,* D.C. Circuit No. 82–1579. Petition for review filed May 24, 1982.
17. Murphy was interviewed by Janissa Strabuk of the Medill News Service of Northwestern University for a report, "Issue Advertising," December 8, 1982, p. 5.
18. "How TV Gagged Our Freeze Ads," *Washington Post,* November 21, 1982, p. C1.
19. Id., p. C2.

20. Id.
21. "Avoid Censorship—Run for President," *Washington Post,* January 9, 1983, p. C5.
22. Id.
23. Fred W. Friendly, *The Good Guys, the Bad Guys, and the First Amendment* (New York, Vintage, 1976), p. 33.
24. Id. The Zapple Doctrine was promulgated in response to an inquiry from Nicholas Zapple to the FCC, 23 FCC 2d 707.
25. Friendly, op. cit., p. 35.
26. Id.
27. Id. at 32.
28. Id. at 42.
29. The recommendations are described in the *New York Times,* September 26, 1982, p. 30, and the *Washington Post,* September 26, 1982, p. A4.
30. *Nicholas Zapple,* 23 FCC 2d 707 (1970).
31. *Cullman Broadcasting Co.,* 40 FCC 576 (1963).
32. *Republican National Committee,* 25 FCC 2d 739 (1970), reversed on other grounds, *CBS* v. *FCC,* 454 F.2d 1018 (D.C. Cir. 1971).
33. *Democratic National Committee,* 31 FCC 2d 708, 713 (1971) affirmed on other grounds, *DNC* v. *FCC,* 460 F.2d 891 (D.C. Cir. 1972).
34. *Democratic National Committee,* FCC 82-248, June 4, 1982, pp. 13–14.
35. *National Conservative Political Action Committee,* FCC 82-167, April 6, 1982.
36. *Hon. Thomas F. Eagleton,* 81 FCC 2d 423 (1980).
37. *National Conservative Political Action Committee,* 89 FCC 2d 626 (1982).

# TEN

# *Assuming the Risk*

COMMUNICATIONS IS A FORCE for change, and a form of control. Its oldest manifestation has been a two-way flow of information. Face-to-face interaction historically characterized communication; it assured some safeguards. Leaders who spoke the most had the benefit of feedback, a corrective force that counterbalances coercive speech.

When speech was supplemented with the written word, the back-and-forth nature of communicating began to change. The isolation of those who transmit information from their audience has increased in the electronic age. Television and radio require passive audiences. Members of the media—print and broadcast—tell their stories while the readers, listeners, and viewers simply read, listen, and watch. Whether they *think* about what they have seen and heard is largely irrelevant to the communicator. Whether they *act* on the information they've received is of consequence mostly to advertisers and partisans—not to a press corps that considers itself objective, that believes it lets the chips fall where they may.

Broadcasters, especially, have little incentive to motivate their audiences. In its starkest economic terms, broadcasting does not try to sell soap, or cars, or aspirin, or candidates. The business of broadcasting works this way: Broadcasters sell audiences to advertisers. The production of big audiences is facilitated when the audience is docile rather than riled up. Viewer and listener passivity is essential to success in the current system.

However, one-way communication—I write, you read—is inferior to interactive communication. There's little or no feedback to assist the communicator to adjust the content of his or her statements. The isolation of the press from its public is a cause of lapses in the media's performance and of lapses in the public's trust of the media.

Technology has changed communication in several ways. In its first phase, the word as spoken could not be heard outside the immediate audience; proximity was essential. In its second phase, the word as written permitted communication over time—and a sense of history was reinforced.

In its third phase, the word as printed permitted easier communication over distance as well as time. The size of the audience increased dramatically. The leap into truly mass communicating accelerated in the fourth phase, the distribution of information by broadcasting.

Each step has reduced the need for proximity, increased the potential audience, and lowered the barriers of time. In sum, communicating has become more isolated, less individualized, and more disjointed. When media become mass media, this undercuts individualism and invites concentration of power.

The fifth phase in communication, one that is only beginning now, may not perpetuate all the trends of the recent past. We are entering an era where telecommunications technology is being married to computer technology, thus permitting interaction among those who gather, transmit, and store information, and those who use the data.

Two trends are now emerging that could, in time, blur the distinction between communicator and audience. One development is the growth of the concept of news on demand; the other is the emergence of information processing as a widely available tool.

## News on Demand

When I was a young child, we received a morning and an evening newspaper each day. The 15-minute radio newscast was an evening staple. When it ended the news stopped. Now listeners can get news on demand, and format changes are helping reshape the news that is transmitted.

Limitations of time and space will always force the compression of information that appears on the air and in newspapers. Meaningful stories often are oversimplified, sometimes compressed beyond comprehension.

The average story on the network evening news is about a minute-and-a-half long; "in-depth" stories run about five minutes. A lot more information can be put into five minutes, but time constraints still require the reporter to leave out many facts.

When "all-news" radio stations started airing news items around the clock, there was hope that the new format would permit more detailed reporting. But with a few exceptions that has not happened. Westinghouse broadcasting, which pioneered the concept with the slogan, "Give us 20 minutes and we'll give you the world," opted for a continuously updated headline service.

Other all-news stations and the main cable news service, Cable News Network featured 24-hour programming ranging from headlines to interviews. Most of the coverage consists of short stories strung together with sports, weather, and features. One wag once compared it with the background music service, dubbing the format "Newsak."

The exception, of course, is live coverage of a major event. But for every fascinating Watergate-style committee hearing, there are 100 boring ones, begging for the kind of excerpting reporters mercifully give us. Still, cable has found room for C-SPAN, a service bringing unedited coverage of the House of Representatives for those interested in watching the uninterrupted debate. It's a valuable service for a limited audience.

The success of these endeavors on cable stems from a new fact of life: There are more options for the viewers now than ever before. No longer are people subject to the tyranny of the network schedule. The mass audience is shared by more communicators. While getting the highest rating is still important, specialty communicators are cropping up looking for a more precise niche.

This happened with magazines, when television stole much of the audience of the general circulation magazines, such as *Life* and *Look*. The publishing industry adjusted, putting out magazines for special tastes— everything from those devoted to jogging to those on guns, from wedding outfits to motorcycle gear.

This is a form of narrowcasting. Unlike broadcasting's search for the biggest audience, narrowcasting involves a search for the special audience. Advertisers of Honda motorcycles are unlikely to purchase space in a magazine devoted to needlework, but advertisers would welcome the opportunity to pinpoint their messages to those most likely to purchase their products.

The advent of new programming on cable has prompted traditional broadcasters to examine how they might change their mass-oriented formats. The three big networks have moved to expand their news operations into the wee hours of darkness. Even though audiences are very meager, the networks are betting that the future will see much more informational programming. ABC, CBS, and NBC also began expanding their own early morning news programming to prevent inroads by Ted Turner's Cable

News Network, which has been offered to affiliated and independent TV stations.

Interestingly, the spread of home videotaping has opened up the late night schedule for new fare. ABC wants to develop a market for movies that could be aired in the middle of the night for taping by viewers who would pay for the privilege of watching their own tapes at their convenience. Already, of course, a viewer can program his or her Betamax to record any regular program—including the overnight news—for playback at a more reasonable hour of the day.

It remains to be seen if expanded programming will permit broadcasters to escape an either/or dilemma. Now they either treat an item in a very brief fashion or examine it live, at length, but to the exclusion of other items.

## *Information Processing*

Hope comes from an older technology now undergoing a metamorphosis: the newspaper. Publishers are rushing to provide text services over TV and cable. These systems are often called teletext, although technically that phrase really means text that is carried over the air. Videotext means data that is carried on cable television. The generic term *teletext* will probably come to mean all forms of electronic publishing because for the viewer it makes little difference how the text gets into the set in his or her home.

The form of transmitting does make a difference to the engineers and, of course, to the owners of the various media. When transmitted on the air, text can be inserted by a broadcaster into the vertical blanking interval (that's the line you see when the picture "rolls" on the set). A decoder is needed to switch from regular programming and watch the text. In its simplest form it would display written headlines of the latest news, stock quotations, weather forecasts, sports scores, and the like. The decoder could also be programmed to permit some choice: the viewer could punch a few buttons and see a longer version of a story, for instance.

When it moves on cable, text comes across in much the same way. But the amount of data that can be transmitted increases dramatically. The viewer might have an enormously expanded amount of material from which to choose. One can imagine a person sitting at home in front of a TV set to read the morning newspaper, scanning the headlines on the set, tapping out instructions on a computer keyboard, and reading the day's stories and columns of his or her choice. And, of course, the viewer could tie into the data retrieval services to obtain financial information or facts from accounts that had appeared in the past. Newspapers are ideally situated to provide such services because most now use video display terminals and databanks in their operations to facilitate putting the paper out.

A text service permits viewers to get news on demand, just the items they want, and at greater length if they wish. The new freedom and flexibility offered to viewers means they will not be so dependent upon the friendly news anchor to tell them, "That's the way it is."

The text can also be delivered by hybrid systems where television stations transmit some of the text, but the interactive features are performed over telephone lines. It is the interactive nature of these text services that has newspaper, broadcasting, cable, and telephone company executives excited. Imagine a computerized service that combines want ads, yellow pages, and commercials. Where you can let your fingers do all the walking. Where a choice can be made instantly, a product ordered, and your bank account debited—all through a single device.

The advent of electronic publishing blurs the distinction between broadcasting and common carrier services such as telephone companies, providing "square pegs to fit into the round holes of old regulatory categories."[1]

Aside from the commercial applications and regulatory problems, consider how it would affect the individual viewer. No longer is he or she a passive figure, sitting silently in front of the boob tube. Now the viewer interacts with it, making choices, talking back. Not only will the range of choices be expanded, but the qualitative possibilities are endless.

Information on demand, however, will be limited by economic realities. It is hard to imagine all the new technologies blooming in full force. A viewer might be able to choose between 100 channels of cable, a dozen regular and low-power TV stations, several dozen radio stations, a handful of text services, programming beamed directly from satellites into the home, pay TV transmitted by microwave, and, of course, the nonelectronic offerings of newspapers and magazines. But who is going to pay for all this? Will subscribers foot the bill? Will the advertising dollar be split between so many media that it cannot underwrite quality programming?

Rapid unregulated expansion of new communications outlets may undermine the economic vitality of "free" broadcasting, rendering the new offerings so costly they will be widely available only to the affluent in urban and suburban areas.[2]

Existing communications companies are not standing idly by, awaiting this revolution. In March 1983, networks and local stations won FCC approval to enter the teletext field. But the decision did permit cable companies that relay TV programming to delete the broadcasters' text and substitute words prepared by the local newspaper or cable company itself.

The regulatory future is unclear. Should material appearing in print suddenly be regulated when it appears on television? Some teletext operators plan to delete opinion columns from their services to avoid finding out the answer the hard way.

In addition to having a profound impact on the news profession, these new technologies will have an enormous impact on the economic structure of the media. The big conglomerates, especially the three major networks, are eyeing entry into cable and Direct Broadcast Satellite, and hoping deregulation will reduce the barriers to multiple and cross-ownership of outlets.

## Regulatory Options

It is important to consider what mass media do; they *mediate* by describing and interpreting the world for us. Usually we welcome such mediation of experience. Who, for instance, wants to live through a volcanic eruption? But how many would be fascinated by watching closeup pictures of the eruption on television? Never mind that mediation provides only a partial, reconstructed view of reality. It's still usually more bearable than the real thing.

Interactive systems that rely on computers operate in a somewhat different way. They permit *simulation* of reality.[3] The user of information participates in assembling the information. Although dependent on those who have programmed the system, the user has a much wider choice in selecting and structuring data to meet his or her needs. Of course, simulation isn't the real thing either. And there's always the danger that a glut of information might require greater expenditures of energy just to cope with data overload. This could result in more centralization, specialization—and disharmony.[4]

What *is* certain is that new forms of communicating will create new ways of thinking. Because new technologies destabilize societies, the temptation will be to regulate this unknown, emerging force. There are several ways to cope with these technologies:

*The traditional approach* emphasizes protection of the economic interests of existing communications companies, while requiring that they fulfill requirements designed to serve the public interest. This approach slows development of new technologies, limits new entrants, restricts competition, and maximizes the regulation of the content of material aired by licensees. After all, licensee viability is assured so that it will underwrite public affairs programming and the like. This approach characterized broadcasting until the late 1970s. The "good ole days" of regulation may come to be mourned if explosive technological growth undermines the stability of the industry, bankruptcy becomes rampant, programming quality declines, and broadcasters become even more arrogant toward the public.

*Modest deregulation* seeks to undo the paperwork, content rules, and barriers to innovation that have straightjacketed communications. But it is important to distinguish between different types of regulation: (1) structural rules mandating limits on ownership, and (2) content regulations interferring with choices of format and speech. Lifting both types of regulation could create greater concentration of power in existing media conglomerates. Bigness, per se, is not bad. But it can be harmful when it overwhelms the market and drives out competition. This can be tolerated, or regulated, in some industries. But it poses special threats to democracy when it overwhelms a medium that society insists should assure a vigorous marketplace of ideas. Competition is essential to a marketplace of ideas; monopolies ought not be permitted to corner the market. Here, government policy can play a crucial role by safeguarding market competition, rather than through content regulations. Deregulation can come in many forms; it is important that it encourages diversity, expands opportunity for new entrants into telecommunications, and restricts oligopolistic tendencies.

*The marketplace approach* is a third way of looking at telecommunications reform, and it shares many attributes of deregulation. It would go further, however, in diminishing the role of the FCC as traffic cop over the frequencies. Freely transferable property rights would be accorded to broadcasters and common carriers, frequencies would be allocated by prices, not by government decree, and in many cases consumers would pay for the programming they desired.[5] FCC Chairman Mark Fowler would carry deregulation, as much as possible, toward a marketplace approach.[6] Under his leadership, the FCC voted in 1981 to urge Congress to repeal the Fairness Doctrine and Equal Opportunities Rule. Fowler and his legal aide, Daniel L. Brenner, have suggested lifting the limitations on station ownership, but have recognized the "special problems" posed by concentration of outlets in a local market.[7] Rather than limiting the number of stations any company could own to restrict concentration within communications, they would permit *expanded* group ownership as an alternative to the traditional three-network structure.[8] The Fowler-Brenner proposal suggests charging broadcasters a fee for using the spectrum, and using the revenues to support public broadcasting (which, as they note, would distort the marketplace).

Other proposals go further toward a virtually free market. Milton Mueller has called for a system of private property rights in channels, with the owners having the right to sell the channels freely.[9] Prices would determine the uses of the frequencies, the amount of signal interference would be subject to barter, and, for instance, an unprofitable broadcast property might be sold for use as a land mobile radio service. Frequencies currently set aside for forestry use could be sold for use by taxicab services in urban areas. It would all be determined by the marketplace; the regulatory distinction between broadcasting, common carrier, and private mobile services would evaporate.[10] Mueller asserts that "there is no middle ground" between a pure market and the present system.[11] He recognizes that past FCC policies have fostered monopoly and concentration of power in television, but he provides no safeguards against such domination of the marketplace. It is this aspect that is most troublesome. A free market is attractive. But antitrust provisions must guard against the private squelching of market forces, especially when technology is offering the possibility of many new voices of communication.

Technology is no panacea, but it does offer hope. First, it reduces the scarcity rationale for regulating broadcast content. Second, it could afford citizens many more choices. Third, it could permit interactive communication, and bring healthy feedback into what now is all too passive a system. Fourth, it undercuts the argument that three networks have a pervasive power that must be balanced by government action.

But these advantages of technological change only are maximized in a pluralistic system. If, in the name of deregulation, existing giants in the communications industry are permitted to gobble up new and existing outlets of communication, diversity would be reduced, power would be reconcentrated in the same hands, and the vigorous, wide-ranging debate on public issues could be stifled.

Here are some goals that ought to be kept in mind as society grapples with problems and opportunities posed by technology:[12]

1. *Pluralism.* Diversity in ownership is no guarantee of diversity of ideas and speech, but it is about the best mechanism a market-oriented democracy can devise.

2. *Noncommercial Sources.* The development of public broadcasting, the creation of public channels on cable, and the setting aside of portions of new forms of transmission for public use afford alternative sources of information and opinion.

3. *Voluntarism.* Relying on the goodwill of communications companies provides no guarantee of improvement. But it's worth stressing the need for broadcasters and cablecasters to volunteer time for serious discussion of public issues and afford widespread access for differing spokepersons.

4. *Professionalism.* Irving Kristol has called the news trade an underdeveloped profession. Standards of ethical behavior need to be widely discussed, and transgressions widely publicized.

5.  *Accountability.* Private groups affected by the media—community activists, independent research organizations, and the like—need to scrutinize what the media do. Such nongovernmental scrutiny counterbalances to some extent the power of the press.

## Conclusions

For society, the debate over government regulation of communications comes down to which course carries the greater risk: Does regulation tend to chill vigorous debate and pose the danger of political abuse and manipulation? Or would a broadcasting industry, freed of content regulations, be likely to suppress viewpoints and stifle the public debate?

Here is a summary of the major points developed in this study:

1.  Technological change and emerging methods of communicating have undercut the scarcity rationale for the regulation of broadcast content.

2.  The system of broadcast regulation evolved because of Congress's fear of the political impact of broadcasting.

3.  Politicians seek to maximize their own access to the airwaves, and to neutralize broadcasters' power.

4.  Under the current system, broadcasters seek to maximize profits and placate the powers-that-be.

5.  The Fairness Doctrine, as applied by the FCC, protects broadcasters and affords complainants little chance of success.

6.  The Fairness Doctrine has forced broadcasters to capitulate to demands of interest groups for access to the airwaves.

7.  Complex regulations have been applied inconsistently, leaving the public and broadcasters unsure of which issues must be aired, which issues must be treated "fairly," and what fairness exactly is.

8.  The Fairness Doctrine is largely irrelevant to daily news coverage.

9.  The Fairness Doctrine always has been impotent in curing the real causes of bias in the news.

10.  The Personal Attack Rule has burdened stations with excessive procedures while not affording persons who were attacked on the air an adequate reply remedy.

11.  The Political Editorializing Rule has drastically chilled the expression of opinion by broadcasters.

12.  The regulations on issue advertising have limited expression of views on radio and television.

13.  The Fairness Doctrine has had the unintended impact of thwarting increased access to the airwaves.

14.  Access provisions, while meriting closer study, may share many

of the problems of implementation and adjudication posed under the current system of regulation.

15.   The effect of the Fairness Doctrine, Equal Opportunities Rule, and the Reasonable Access Provision has been the broadcast of conformist, centrist, mainstream opinions.

16.   The rules operate to protect the dominant two political parties from third-party challenges.

17.   Competition among ideas and among broadcasters should be a major goal of public policy. Yet proposals to let market forces prevail in broadcasting must be examined to assure that the market is not dominated by monopolistic giants.

18.   When possible, regulations stressing structural guarantees of diversity in communications are preferable to regulations affecting the content of material which is broadcast.

The picture is not all bad. That's because the regulations usually have not been applied in a heavy-handed way. Broadcasters have wide discretion under the rules and they've often resisted the temptation to play it safe with bland, conformist fare, or strike out on biased, partisan crusades.

## *Options for Reform*

Those considering lifting some—or all—of the content regulations must decide whether they wish to risk that broadcasters will use their licenses to manipulate the public debate for partisan ends, thus suppressing viewpoints with which they disagree while promoting causes and candidates they favor.

The Founding Fathers assumed the risk as regards newspapers, magazines, and other periodicals. Even though licensing of the press was not at issue when the First Amendment was ratified, the danger posed by a vigorous press to the political status quo was well recognized after the Revolutionary War. The Founders were willing to risk it.

I am willing to take a similar risk, even though I am aware of examples of biased and unfair broadcasting. Usually those who are unfair eventually are found out, their credibility suffers, and, one would expect, their influence wanes.

For those willing to risk something, but not everything, there are some intermediate alternatives:

One possibility, already discussed in the previous chapters, is to substitute an access requirement for the Fairness Doctrine. The goal is worthy and one would hope broadcasters would voluntarily increase the amount of access they provide. But a mandatory access plan, while not as burdensome or intrusive as the Fairness Doctrine, suffers from some of the same bureaucratic and adjudicatory shortcomings. If it is a mandatory access scheme, who decides which issues will be programmed? Which spokespersons permitted to air their views? First come, first served? Should kooks be excluded? What about those who want to delve into sexual issues? Secular humanism? Theories of curved space?

If stations are to decide, then aren't all the problems associated with the public trustee notion transferred into the mandatory access arena? Who's to judge if stations have met the requirements in a reasonable, good-faith way? Wouldn't we be heading right back into the intricacies and pitfalls of FCC case-by-case evaluation? Perhaps not, but the danger's there.

A second, partial step at deregulation would be to end case-by-case adjudication under the Fairness Doctrine. Amend the rule to state that a station will be evaluated at license renewal time to see if it has willfully and repeatedly refused to air contrasting viewpoints on major public controversies. This would alleviate some of the problems of Fairness Doctrine application, but many would still remain. The impact of the rule would likely be unchanged.

A third possibility is to combine aspects of a mandatory access rule with the Fairness Doctrine, and require stations to set aside a period each day, perhaps an hour's worth of programming, devoted to discussion of significant public issues. During that time—but that time alone—the Fairness Doctrine would apply. As now, the station would have wide discretion as to what it airs, but it would be subject to the complaint process if it failed to air burning issues or provide contrasting points of view. All other programming would be exempt from Fairness Doctrine application.

A fourth possibility for those unsure of whether to risk letting broadcasters have carte blanche would be to suspend the Fairness Doctrine for a set period to see how licensees behave. If the suspension works, make it an indefinite suspension. If egregious cases arise, the suspension could be revoked, forcing those who abuse the public trust to change their ways.

And what of the big sister of the Fairness Doctrine, the Equal Opportunities Rule, and its younger brother, the Reasonable Access Provision? Those who favor deregulation usually seek their repeal. But it would be possible to keep them intact or alter them to reduce the intrusive nature of the regulations.

One idea would be to apply equal time concepts to advertising, and advertising alone, but extend it beyond candidate ads to include *all* issue advertisements. Thus if Mobil Oil decides to buy time to campaign against windfall profits legislation, supporters of the legislation could buy an equal amount of time, at the same rate. The Cullman Principle, mandating free time to opposing groups that cannot afford to pay for commercial time, would be scrapped. The good aspect of such a change would be that unlike now, everyone would be treated equally. If a station chose to accept advertising on an issue, it could not suppress the other view if an opposing group came along demanding to buy time to refute the first commercial. Some would contend, however, that the bad effect of such a change would be that monied interests would dominate the public debate, selling ideas like soap, denying a voice to the poor.

It could be possible to relax the Equal Opportunities Rule to give stations more discretion over candidate advertisements and appearances. Instead of requiring precisely equal opportunities for opposing candidates, stations could be held to a more general obligation to play fair in permitting political access to the airwaves, with penalties as severe as license revocation for willful and repeated discrimination against candidates. Unfortunately, additional discretion for the broadcaster probably would result in more uncertainty, more complaints, more litigation and—in the long run—more regulation. Perhaps it would be better to continue strict application of the equal time rule to commercial appearances by candidates while exempting all news programs and all free appearances from the rule.

And what of the Reasonable Access Provision? Should candidates for federal office continue to enjoy the privileged position, guaranteed by law, of access to the airwaves in a campaign? The simplest, but riskiest solution is to revoke the rule entirely. It's reasonable to assume that most stations would continue to cover newsworthy candidates and sell advertising time to well-heeled campaigns. Politicians, however, usually are uncomfortable relying totally on broadcasters' goodwill. One possibility would be to accept Henry Geller's suggestion that station compliance with the rule should be judged only at license renewal time, and only those licensees who have willfully and repeatedly refused to provide time to candidates should be punished. That would eliminate intrusive case-by-case adjudication, but it poses risks for a broadcaster who fears that he might lose his license because he cannot get guidance from the FCC when a close case arises.

And what about political editorials? Should candidates who are not endorsed have a right to reply? Our political system does not seem to have suffered from the immunity of newspapers from such a rule. But are not broadcasters likely to have a pervasive, partisan impact? That's hard to predict, but the clear impact of the regulation has been to squelch editorializing by licensees. Even so, one possibility is to retain only the Political Editorializing Rule if society isn't willing to run the risk that broadcasters would cover campaigns thoroughly.

Then there's the Personal Attack Rule. It seems only fair to permit someone who's been attacked to have a chance to respond. Good journalists seek out comments from those who are criticized in news stories; getting "their side of the story" is enshrined in journalism's code of ethics. But should it be enshrined in the law? The convoluted workings of this rule have failed to provide much of a remedy for someone who has been attacked, even if the case falls within the narrow parameters of what the FCC deems a personal attack. Someone who has been libeled, or has had his or her privacy invaded, has a much better recourse to the courts. A person who wins a libel or privacy suit can collect damages, something the FCC cannot provide.

As the Supreme Court has noted, there have been abuses by journalists. But there's growing attention to the activities of the press, and when abuses occur, criticism is likely to follow. Broadcasters depend on the support of their audience and their advertisers. They simply cannot ignore criticism. Despite a tendency to dish it out, many newspersons find it hard to take. That's only human, but it should not obscure the fact that criticism is healthy; criticism improves the accuracy and fairness of the press. The watchdogs in the press corps should welcome watchdogs of their own conduct.

Broadcast fairness must be put in context. The regulations were instituted in radio's infancy. Communications have grown dramatically. It's not off-base to say that there were major growing pains. Many examples of poor performance by stations and networks occurred in broadcasting's adolescence. Journalism is an underdeveloped profession and broadcasting is far from mature. Television news, for example, is younger than I am.

Professional development, self-restraint, open-mindedness, and maturity on the part of broadcasters are the best safeguards against unfairness, partisan bias, and inaccurate, sensational news. But there will never be any guarantees that self-policing by an institution as unwieldy as the media will work.

What is clear is that the regulations have not worked. They have not delivered on their promise to make broadcasting fair. The above examination of the partial steps, the intermediate proposals, and the halfway measures indicates that many of the problems inherent in regulation would persist if the rules were only relaxed.

The real solution is to cut the Gordian knot and end content regulation altogether. That, of course, is not risk-free.

One can only wonder what Madison, Jefferson, Franklin, and other coconspirators against King George would have done. Would they have been willing to run the risk that a free electronic press might abuse its power?

## *References*

1. Richard M. Neustadt, Gregg P. Skall, and Michael Hammer,"The Regulation of Electronic Publishing," 33 *Federal Communications Law Journal* 331, 332 (1981).
2. See Peter J. Kokalis, "Updating the Communications Act: New Electronics, Old Economics, and the Demise of the Public Interest," 3 *COMM/ENT Law Journal* 455.
3. See William Kuhns, "Twice as Natural: Speculations on the Emerging Information Culture," in Howard F. Didsbury, Jr. (Ed.), *Communications and the Future* (Bethesda, Md., World Future Society, 1982), pp. 53–59.
4. See Jeremy Riftkin, *Entropy: A New World View* (New York, Viking, 1980).
5. See Mark S. Fowler and Daniel Brenner, "A Marketplace Approach to Broadcast Regulation," 60 *Texas Law Review* 1, 26 (1982).
6. Id. at 27.
7. Id. at 40.
8. Id.
9. Milton Mueller, "Property Rights in Radio Communication: The Key to Reform of Telecommunications Regulation, Washington, D.C., The Cato Institute, 1982.
10. Id. at 19–22.
11. Id. at 29.
12. The author recognizes that these goals reflect the kind of progressive values common to those in the news media. (See Chapter 6, pp. 125–128.)

# Index